Tick...Tick...

Hear that clock ticking? It's the countdown to the SAT World History Subject Test, which will be here before you know it. Whether you have a year to go or just one day, now is the time to start maximizing your score.

The Test Is Just a Few Months Away!

Don't worry—you're still ahead of the game. However, it is important that you stop delaying and begin preparing now. Follow **The Big Picture: How to Prepare Year-Round** (page 195) to make the most of your time so you'll be ready on test day. (This section gives you strategies to put into place up to a year before you actually take the test.)

Actually, I Only Have a Few Weeks!

Even if you're down to the last few weeks before the test, you still have plenty of time for a full review. To make the best use of your time, turn to **The Main Course: Comprehensive Strategies and Review** (page 39), where you'll find **Strategies for Multiple-Choice Questions** (page 41) to help you ace the questions. **The Diagnosis: How Ready Are You?** (page 51) includes a diagnostic test that allows you to identify areas of weakness so that you can address these. You should also review all of **World History Review** (page 89) for an overview of the big topics usually covered on the SAT World History Subject Test. As you work through this information, keep track of those concepts, facts, and ideas that you need to study. Use the **practice tests** (beginning on pages 205 and 259) to increase your comfort with both the format and the content of the test.

Let's Be Honest. The Test Is Tomorrow and I'm Freaking Out!

No problem! Review the **Introduction** (page ix), focusing on **About the Test** (page x) and **The Essentials: A Last-Minute Study Guide** (page 1), so you know what to expect when you arrive to take the test and have some ideas as to how to approach the test questions. Then, take at least one **practice test** (beginning on pages 205 and 259). Don't worry about your score—just focus on getting familiar with the test. Before you go to bed, review **Quick Test-Taking Tips** (page 7) once more. The tips will walk you through the day ahead.

Finally, relax! Make the most of the tools and resources in this review guide, and you'll be ready to earn a top score.

My Max Score

SAT WORLD HISTORY SUBJECT TEST

Maximize Your Score in Less Time

Northeast Editing, Inc.

Published by Sourcebooks, Inc.
P.O. Box 4410, Naperville, Illinois 60567-4410
(630) 961-3900
Fax: (630) 961-2168
www.sourcebooks.com

Library of Congress Cataloging-in-Publication Data

Northeast Editing, Inc.
   My max score SAT world history subject test : maximize your score in less time / Northeast Editing, Inc.
       p. cm.
   1. World history—Examinations—Study guides. 2. SAT (Educational test)—Study guides. I. Title.
   D21.D44 2013
   907.8—dc23
                                    2012037736

Printed and bound in the United States of America.
VP 10 9 8 7 6 5 4 3 2 1

Also Available in the My Max Score Series

AP Exam Study Aids

AP Biology
AP Calculus AB/BC
AP English Language and Composition
AP English Literature and Composition
AP European History
AP Statistics
AP U.S. Government and Politics
AP U.S. History
AP World History

SAT Subject Test Study Aids

SAT Biology E/M Subject Test
SAT Literature Subject Test
SAT Math 1 and 2 Subject Test
SAT U.S. History Subject Test

ASVAB Study Aids

ASVAB: Armed Services Vocational Aptitude Battery

Contents

Introduction   ix

The Essentials: A Last-Minute Study Guide   1
Quick Test-Taking Tips   7
Big Ideas in World History   13

The Main Course: Comprehensive Strategies and Review   39
Strategies for Multiple-Choice Questions   41
The Diagnosis: How Ready Are You?   51
Diagnostic Test   53
Diagnostic Test Answers and Explanations   72
Using the Diagnostic Test   85
World History Review   89
Review Chapter 1: Prehistory to Early Civilizations   91
Review Chapter 2: The Great Empires   107
Review Chapter 3: The Middle Ages   123
Review Chapter 4: Renaissance, Reformation, and Exploration   139
Review Chapter 5: The Age of Revolutions   151
Review Chapter 6: Industrialization and Imperialism   159
Review Chapter 7: Early Twentieth Century   167
Review Chapter 8: Post–World War II   177
Review Chapter 9: A Globalized World   187

The Big Picture: How to Prepare Year-Round | 195

SAT World History Subject Test Practice Test 1 | 205

Practice Test 1 Answers and Explanations | 235

SAT World History Subject Test Practice Test 2 | 259

Practice Test 2 Answers and Explanations | 290

Glossary | 310

About the Author | 320

Introduction

Everyone comes to the SAT World History Subject Test from a different place. For some, it's the one SAT Subject Test of their high school career; for others, it's just one test of many. Some students have focused on it all year, supplementing their class work with extra study and practice at home. Other students haven't been able to devote the time they would like—perhaps other classes, extra-curricular activities, after-school jobs, or family obligations have gotten in the way. But wherever you're coming from, this book can help! It's been designed to provide maximum assistance no matter where you are on your study path.

You'll find that this book has been divided into three sections: a last-minute study guide to use in the days before the test, a comprehensive review for those with more than a week to prepare, and a long-term study plan for students preparing well in advance.

Think of each section as full of suggestions rather than a rigid prescription. Feel free to pick and choose the pieces from each section you find most helpful. Of course, if you have time, we recommend that you review *everything* and take as many practice tests as you can, as many times as you can.

Whether you have a day to cram or a year to study at leisure, here are some things you should know before diving into the test.

For starters, what is the SAT World History Subject Test, and what does it cover?

About the Test

The SAT World History Subject Test is an examination used nationally to assess student readiness for college-level work in history. Some colleges require potential students to take particular SAT subject tests to qualify either for admission to the school itself or to a particular discipline or major. Some schools may even award college credit if you score highly on the test. Talk to your school guidance counselor about the requirements and possibilities for the schools you're interested in.

The SAT World History Subject Test is designed as a global examination that touches on significant issues and trends in the modern world. More specifically, it

- Tests your knowledge of basic facts and terms as well as your understanding of basic history and geography
- Examines your knowledge of typical cause-and-effect relationships throughout history
- Assesses your ability to interpret artistic materials as well as quotations from speeches, documents, and other published matter
- Analyzes your ability to interpret and apply data from maps, charts, and graphs

The examination takes one hour. During that hour, you'll answer a total of ninety-five multiple-choice questions.

What's Covered

The topics covered on the SAT World History Subject Test break down as follows:

MATERIAL COVERED	ESTIMATED % OF QUESTIONS
Global or comparative	25%
Europe	25%
Africa	10%
Southwest Asia	10%
South and Southeast Asia	10%
East Asia	10%
Americas (excluding the United States)	10%

TIME PERIOD COVERED	ESTIMATED % OF QUESTIONS
Prehistory and civilizations to 500 CE	25%
500 to 1500 CE	25%
1500 to 1900 CE	25%
Post-1900 CE	20%
Cross-chronological	10%

You'll notice the percentages above sum to 105 percent. Just remember that these are estimated percentages, so they'll vary slightly on the actual test.

Note: The SAT World History Subject Test uses BCE (before the Common Era) and CE (Common Era) as chronological designations rather than BC (before Christ) and AD (*anno Domini*), which may be used in certain world history textbooks.

Test Scoring

As you probably already know, SAT subject tests receive a raw score that is converted to a point-based score between 200 and 800.

Here is how the raw score is calculated:

1. For each question you answer correctly, you are awarded one (1) point.

2. For each question you answer incorrectly, you are docked

fractional points. (The amount of fractional points varies depending on the test.) For World History, you lose a quarter of a point (.25) for each question you answer incorrectly.

3. You do not gain or lose points for questions you do not answer.

4. Once your correct answers are totaled and the fractional points deducted, your raw score number is produced. If this number is a fraction, it is rounded up or down accordingly.

5. A complex process called equating is then used to convert the raw score to a scaled score between 200 and 800 (with 800 being the highest score available).

Your score shows college admissions staff how well you performed compared to other students who took the test. For example, the mean or average score for students who took the SAT World History Subject Test in 2011 was 607. What does this mean? Well, if you took the test in 2011 and scored close to a 607, college admissions staff understood that to mean you scored about as well as half the students who took the test nationally.

If you haven't yet taken the test, your goal should be to beat the average score by as high a margin as possible! With this material in hand, you should feel confident about your ability to do just that. Put the material in this book to its intended use so you'll have not only a strong understanding of the key concepts being tested but also ample opportunity to practice tried-and-true testing strategies.

Beyond the material in this book, we make an additional SAT World History Subject Test available to you on our website, mymaxscore.com. That site includes practice tests for other SAT subject tests as well.

Good luck!

THE ESSENTIALS: A LAST-MINUTE STUDY GUIDE

So, it's a night or two before the test and you just don't feel ready. Should you panic? Absolutely not! Now is the time to take a deep breath and finish final preparations. If you've been taking a global history class, studying regularly, and preparing in other ways throughout the year, you should be just about at your goal. All you need to do is calm your nerves by breathing deeply, refresh your mind by reviewing a few key strategies, and get your belongings together for test day. It's not too late to maximize your score!

First, remember that being anxious is just a waste of your energy. You can let your nerves paralyze you, or you can get into a better frame of mind by focusing your thoughts and energies on the things you can do now. That approach is more likely to bring you success than worrying about how nervous you feel. Guide your energy into positive activities that leave you feeling prepared.

Second, if you're testing soon, you don't have a lot of time available, so it's important to make the most of the time you do have. Find a location where you have privacy to study in peace, such as your bedroom (good) or the library (even better, especially if your house is a busy one with a lot of distractions). Tune out the world by turning off your telephone, your computer, and all your other electronic gadgets. Stop texting, quit surfing the Internet, and turn off the music. Ask your family and friends not to disturb you unless it's really important. Close your door (or park yourself in a library cubicle) and get ready.

Getting Ready

Step 1: Review the Test-Taking Tips

Although you're probably already familiar with the format of this test, if it's been a while since you've considered the test setup or if you're just not sure where to start, take a few minutes to review the first section of the book (that means you should also go back to the **Introduction** on page ix before going forward to **Quick Test-Taking Tips** on page 7). If you have only a few days until you test, take time to carefully review **Strategies for Multiple-Choice Questions** (page 41). The strategies are tried and true; they can go far toward giving your score a real boost.

Step 2: Examine the Big Ideas

If you don't have time for a full content review, at least take the time to look over the basics. We've compiled these for you in **Big Ideas in World History** (page 13), which outlines the concepts, themes, and ideas you'll encounter in all parts of this test. If you have time, continue on to the chapter reviews as well.

Step 3: Take a Practice Test

One of the most effective ways to really get to know any test is to take a practice test, preferably one that has been specifically designed to mimic the test in question. In this book, you'll find two complete subject tests for your use (in addition to the diagnostic test). Plus, a third practice test is available to you on the mymaxscore.com website at no extra charge.

When taking practice tests, it's important to pretend that you're really taking the test. That means you should test in a quiet area, avoid looking at any reference material, and time yourself carefully. Use the answer keys provided to see how well you're likely to do if similar questions appear on the actual test. When reviewing your responses, watch for common themes or trends and identify the areas in which you can improve. Once you know where you need the most help, review the appropriate sections in this book, or go back to your class notes and textbook for more detail.

The Night Before: Gather Your Materials

The last thing you want to do the morning of the test is rush around trying to find everything you need. Therefore, we've included a checklist so that you can make sure you've gathered these items together beforehand. Put the checklist items in a backpack or small bag (along with anything else you think you might need). Have your bag ready so that you can grab it and go in the morning:

- Your admissions ticket is critical, so pack this first. Place your ticket in an easy-to-locate side pocket or zippered compartment so you can get your hands on it quickly when entering the test site.

- You will need photographic proof of identity, so bring your photo ID. Acceptable photo identification includes your photo driver's license, state-issued ID, valid passport, or school ID. You can also bring a student ID printed on school stationery; see your guidance counselor if you need this. Store your ID with your admissions ticket.

- Pack several sharpened No. 2 pencils and a no-smudge eraser. Note that this test is graded entirely by computer, so *any* smudging can affect your results. That's why it's important to make sure your erasers won't leave any marks. Also, note that although there *should* be a pencil sharpener available in the testing room, it's probably not a bad idea to pack a portable sharpener, just in case. Ink pens are not acceptable for this test.

- A calculator is not allowed for this test, so don't bring one.

- Plan to wear or bring a watch (a watch, not a phone, as phones aren't allowed in the test room) so that you can keep an eye on the clock as you work. A watch will help you to pace yourself appropriately. Of course, if your watch has alarms, buzzers, or beepers, turn them off!

- Include a small, easy-to-eat snack. Test day will be long, and you may need nourishment. Choose a snack that's high in protein and low in carbohydrates. Avoid messy items like chocolate bars, as these can melt onto your hands and desk. Also avoid nuts, as they can trigger allergies in other testers. Some good choices might be an energy or protein bar or drink, an easy-to-eat piece of fruit such as a banana, or some crackers.

- Pack a bottle of water. You'll want something to drink at some point, and it's best to avoid substances with a lot of sugar or caffeine. Although you may think these will give you a boost of energy, they're more likely to contribute to test jitters—and you'll have enough of those on your own!

- Avoid packing items you can't take into the testing room. For example, phones, pagers, calculators, and other electronic devices are prohibited in the testing room for a variety of reasons.

- Here's one important repeat: pack *only* what you need:

  ○ Admissions ticket

  ○ Photo ID

  ○ Pencils, eraser, and portable sharpener

  ○ Watch and/or timer

  ○ Snack and bottle of water

Test Day: Tips

Here are some other tips for managing test day:

- The night before your test, *don't* stay up all night studying. At that point, you'll be as ready as ever! Instead, concentrate on getting a good night's sleep. It's more important to feel rested and alert than it is to attempt a last-minute cram session.

- Eat a light but satisfying meal in the morning. Protein-rich foods like eggs, nuts, and yogurt are good choices, as they'll fill you up but won't give you a sugar or caffeine crash later. But don't eat too much—you don't want to be sluggish or uncomfortably full. If you must have coffee or another caffeinated beverage, that's fine. Just try not to overdo it.

- Dress in comfortable layers. The testing room might be hot or cold. You can't control the temperature, so you'll need to be able to adjust to it. Also, make sure your clothes are comfortable. Your newest outfit might be fabulous, but the last thing you need during the test is to feel annoyed by pants that are too tight or irritated by fabrics that feel itchy.

- Don't forget your backpack! It has all of your important stuff in it.

- Relax! Once you get to the testing room, take a few deep breaths and try to channel some of your energy into relaxation. Try blowing into your balled-up fists to rid your body of adrenaline. Remind yourself that you know the material, you understand how the test works, and you are ready to go. It's natural to be nervous, but it's better to push that energy into the mental task ahead.

Once the test begins, set everything else in your mind aside and focus on doing your best. You've done all you can to prepare. It's time to make that preparation pay off!

are written in such a way that they intentionally distract you fɪ correct answer. (That's why they're called distracters.) However, review the answer options with a good idea of the answer in mind, ʝ be less confused by other options.

Tip 4: Pay Attention to the Words

As you read the questions and answer choices, pay attention to the wording. Some questions will include words like *not* or *except*. The inclusion of these words radically changes the answer to the question. You're looking for the answer that is *not* true or that does *not* apply. This might seem obvious, but it's actually quite easy to overlook these words when you're reading quickly.

Other questions might include qualifiers. A *qualifier* is a word or group of words that limits or modifies the meaning of another word or group of words. When a qualifier appears in a question, the correct response must appropriately reflect that qualifier. For example, a qualifier might indicate that the correct answer option is the one that is sometimes but not always true. Some commonly used qualifiers include the following:

- *Likely, unlikely*
- *Apt to, may, might*
- *Always, never, often, sometimes*
- *Frequently, probably, usually, seldom*
- *Some, a few, a majority, many, most, much*

In addition, keep an eye out for double negatives, because (just like in math) two negatives make a positive. For example, *not uncommon* actually means "common." So, for example, if a question asks you to identify a trend that was "not uncommon" among a certain population, the question really wants you to find the trend that was common, not the one that was unique.

Answer Options

...etty sure of your answer, make sure you review all ...ions before making your selection. Sometimes more ...r may be correct; however, one choice will always be ...than the others. In addition, the answer you choose should ...address all parts of the question and reflect any qualifier that ...included in the question.

Tip 6: Use Elimination Strategies

The SAT subject tests do penalize you for guessing, but that doesn't mean you should avoid making guesses. What you want to make instead are *educated* guesses; those are guesses you've made after eliminating the answers you know are wrong. Here's how to do this:

- Eliminate any answer you know is wrong. Draw a light line through the answer option in the test booklet.

- Eliminate options that seem unlikely or totally unfamiliar. Circle or underline the parts of the answer that you feel make it a wrong choice.

- Eliminate options that don't seem to fit grammatically with the stem or question. This is a little trickier, but if an option doesn't seem to really fit in with the question, it's likely wrong. Circle or underline the part of the answer that seems sketchy.

- Give each answer option the true-false test. That means you should ask yourself whether the answer option standing alone is true or false. Eliminate those that are false. The true-false test is useful when answer options include specific details; false answers would include misstated facts or faulty reasoning. Circle or underline the part of the answer that you believe is wrong.

- Watch for the inclusion of absolutes such as *all, only, always,* or *never*. These often signify incorrect responses, because an absolute can make an answer that is sometimes right wrong when the absolute is applied. For example, "The moon is never visible during the day" is wrong because although the moon is *usually* invisible during the day, there are times when it is visible. Draw a line through answer options you can eliminate for this reason.

- Look for contradictory paired statements. For example, option A might read, "The sky is green," and option B reads, "The sky is blue." One of the paired answers is frequently the correct answer.

The more answer choices you eliminate, the better your chances are of guessing at the correct answer. If you can eliminate at least two or more of the answer options, you should take a guess.

Once you're ready to commit to an answer, write the letter of your answer choice in the margin of the test booklet next to the question number. Circle it or put a check mark next to it as you did with the questions you answered easily.

Tip 7: Fill Out the Answer Sheet with Care

Make sure you're timing yourself as you work through your examination. When you have about ten minutes left, stop what you're doing and mark your answers in your answer sheet. You will get credit *only* for answers in the answer sheet, so this is a critical step! Make sure you have enough time to transfer the answers from your booklet to your answer sheet.

The SAT subject tests are graded completely by computer, so it's critical that the answer sheet be kept clean and free from any stray markings. Input your answers *carefully*, stopping every few questions to make sure your question and answer numbers correspond before filling in the oval. Also, be sure you have penciled in the answer space completely and haven't left any stray pencil marks in other spaces.

Big Ideas in World History

W orld history is a big topic. As a result, the range of information you'll have to familiarize yourself with in preparation
for the SAT World History Subject Test is quite expan-
sive and can easily become overwhelming. That's why it's important
to know the basics before you get started. To that end, use this section
as a brief guide to some of the major historical topics that frequently
appear on the SAT World History Subject Test. At the very least, be
sure you have a basic understanding of these topics before you attempt
the test.

1. Prehistory to Early Civilizations

According to most scientists, humankind (in its various evolutionary
forms) has been in existence for at least 1.5 million to nearly 2.5 million
years, with *hominids* having existed for as long as 7 million years. The era
of human existence prior to the dawn of *civilization* is known as *prehistory*. Prehistory is typically divided into two eras: the Paleolithic Age and
the Neolithic Age.

The Paleolithic Age stretched from the first appearance of hominids, a humanlike species that was capable of walking upright, to about
8000 BCE. During this period, ancient humans evolved through several

different evolutionary stages that included hominids, *Homo habilis*, *Homo erectus*, and *Homo sapiens*. It is widely believed that *Homo sapiens* emerged only in Africa and later spread to other regions, where it displaced other human species and eventually evolved into *Homo sapiens sapiens*, or modern humans. Early humans depended on hunting and gathering for survival and developed some basic cultural customs, including funerary practices, artwork, and the use of tools.

The Neolithic Age emerged at the end of the last *ice age* (approximately 7000 BCE). As a result of environmental changes wrought by the ice age, humans could no longer rely on hunting and gathering for survival. In response, the formerly *nomadic* people of the Paleolithic Age settled down in permanent villages to work the land. The resulting agricultural revolution led to better health and a larger population. This period also saw the emergence of the first major towns, including Jericho and Çatalhüyük.

Eventually, these communities evolved into the earliest civilizations, or cultures with a written or other form of language, advanced cities and institutions, skilled workers, and technological innovations.

One of the earliest and most notable of these civilizations appeared around 4000 BCE in a region of the Middle East known as Mesopotamia. Located in the valley between the Tigris and Euphrates rivers was an area of particularly fertile soil called the Fertile Crescent. It was here that the ancient civilization of Sumer first developed. Thanks to the annual flooding of the Tigris and Euphrates rivers and the rich layer of silt these floods left behind, Sumer was ideal for agriculture. The community that rose around the area became one of the ancient world's first and most important cultures. The Sumerians used *irrigation* systems, built temples known as ziggurats, invented a form of writing called *cuneiform*, and developed a complex social class system. Around 2300 BCE, Sumer fell under the control of the Akkadians. Over time, the Akkadians were succeeded by a series of other peoples who came to dominate the Mesopotamian region. Perhaps the most notable of these peoples were the Babylonians, whose best-known achievement was the system of laws devised by Hammurabi. The *Code of Hammurabi* established a formal law based on the idea of retaliatory punishment.

The development of civilization was not limited to Mesopotamia. Similar to Sumer's development along the Tigris and Euphrates rivers, the ancient Egyptian civilization developed along the banks of the Nile. Again, thanks to annual flooding and silt deposits, the land around the Nile was exceptionally fertile and easily adaptable for agricultural purposes. By about 3200 BCE, the farming villages that had sprung up along the Nile joined together to form the kingdoms of Lower Egypt in the north and Upper Egypt in the south. Eventually, these two kingdoms were merged by Menes, an Upper Egyptian king who became the first *pharaoh*, or ruler, of the united Egypt. From this point on, the history of ancient Egypt is divided into three eras: the Old Kingdom (3100–2200 BCE), the Middle Kingdom (2100–1650 BCE), and the New Kingdom (1550–750 BCE). It is important to note that there is debate among historians concerning the exact dates of each kingdom, with some estimates varying by as much as two hundred years.

The Egyptians developed a complicated polytheistic religion with many gods of nature. They also created a written language called *hieroglyphics*, which used simple pictures to represent certain ideas or sounds. Like the Sumerians, the Egyptians also had a complex social class system. In addition, the Egyptians created a solar calendar and used a basic type of geometry to complete surveys of their land following the annual floods.

Farther to the east in the region currently known as Pakistan, another civilization formed along the banks of the Indus River. Early in their history, the peoples of the Indus River valley developed complex cities that were precisely designed and even included a simple form of indoor plumbing.

Most of our knowledge about the Indus River valley civilization comes from the period after the *Aryans* invaded the region. These invaders brought many cultural changes to the original Indus society, including, most significantly, a rigid social *caste* system. The influence of the Aryans also led to the emergence of *Hinduism*, which was based on a collection of Aryan chants and hymns called the *Vedas*. The Indus River valley civilization also gave birth to the religion of *Buddhism*.

Another major early civilization was founded in China. Many of the small agricultural towns that had developed along the Yellow River united under the flag of the Xia dynasty (ca. 2070 BCE) and, later, of the *Shang* dynasty (ca. 1600 BCE). This region quickly became the center of Chinese civilization. The people living under the Shang dynasty developed writing, excelled at craftsmanship, and built a thriving society. In the eleventh century, the Shang dynasty was conquered by the Zhou dynasty. Under the Zhou, the ancient Chinese philosophy of *Confucianism* emerged, along with rival philosophies such as *Daoism* and *legalism*. Over time, these philosophies gave rise to the traditional Chinese culture.

Ancient civilizations also formed in the Western Hemisphere. Agricultural societies in Mesoamerica evolved into more complex civilizations, the first of which was that of the *Olmec*. In their time, the Olmec built pyramids, created writing and numerical systems, and established a calendar.

While those civilizations were thriving in the Western Hemisphere, different cultures blossomed in other parts of the world. The Hittites were one of the first cultures to use iron *smelting* to make weapons. The Assyrians became the world's first imperial power and made extensive use of iron weapons and other unique military tactics. The Bantu-speaking people migrated throughout southern and eastern Africa, spreading their language and practicing iron smelting. The Kush of northern Africa established themselves as a powerful iron-trading civilization. Like other African societies, the Nok of western Africa also practiced iron smelting and made terra-cotta sculptures. The Hebrews introduced monotheistic religion and freed themselves from slavery in Egypt. The Phoenicians invented an alphabet that would later influence the languages of Greece and Rome; they also established the colony of Carthage. The Minoans participated in long-distance trade and practiced bronze metallurgy. The Mycenaean people conquered the Minoans and assimilated into their culture.

2. The Great Empires

With the fall of the Mycenaean kingdoms around 1100 BCE, ancient Greece came under the control of the *Dorians*. During the time of the Dorians, the classical Greek political unit, the *polis*, or city-state, emerged. The two most prominent of these city-states were Athens and Sparta. The government of Athens evolved into a direct democracy ruled by the people, whereas Sparta developed into a military state. Both city-states found a common enemy in the Persians of modern-day Iran and joined forces to defend themselves from invasion.

Eventually, Athens's successes in battle against the Persians made it the dominant city-state in all of Greece. This dominance would lead to a destructive battle between Athens and Sparta, called the Peloponnesian War (431–404 BCE), from which Sparta would emerge victorious.

At the height of its influence, Athens made significant intellectual and artistic contributions to world culture. Great thinkers like Socrates, Plato, and Aristotle made important advances in philosophical thought. Greek scientists pioneered new mathematical theories. Athenian artists also developed the concept of drama and wrote great works of both comedy and tragedy. The introduction of the ancient version of the Olympic Games had a significant impact on sports.

Like many other cultures, however, Greece was eventually conquered. In 363 BCE, the Grecian armies fell to Philip of Macedon. Philip's son, who would later be known as Alexander the Great, established a vast empire that spanned across Asia Minor, Mesopotamia, Egypt, and Syria. After Alexander's death in 323 BCE, this empire quickly crumbled.

If any culture could be considered the successor of ancient Greece, it is Rome. The roots of the Roman Empire lie with the Etruscans, who migrated to the Italian Peninsula around 800 BCE. For several hundred years, the Etruscan kings ruled much of Italy, including a small city-state known as Rome. Eventually, Rome's wealthy landowning aristocrats grew frustrated with the Etruscans' monarchical rule and overthrew their king in 509 BCE to establish a republic.

The Romans developed a complex political system that gave the government power. More important, however, they also developed a strong, efficient military force that made conquest simple and effective. By 246 BCE, Rome controlled the entire Mediterranean region. Later, under the command of Julius Caesar, the Roman republic became a dictatorship and, eventually, a vast empire.

During the first century CE, Rome became heavily influenced by *Christianity*. Initially, Roman officials persecuted the Christians, forcing them to fight as gladiators and essentially condemning them to death in the Coliseum. Later, in 313 CE, the Emperor Constantine legalized Christianity and encouraged its spread across the empire.

Over time, centuries of continual resistance from Germanic tribes took its toll on Rome. After the last emperor was deposed in 476 CE, Rome fell into decline.

While Rome ruled in the West, the Han dynasty rose to prominence in the East. This dynasty ruled in China from 206 BCE to 220 CE and became the longest and most influential of all the great Chinese dynasties.

The Han consolidated their power in a strong central government and a complex bureaucracy. They also constructed walls intended to defend their territories from invasion. In addition, they expanded their empire outside of China, conquering and assimilating peoples in both Korea and Vietnam.

The Han dynasty also continued other dynasties' work in building roads for travel and trade. The most significant of these were the Silk Roads, a major trading route connecting China and the East with Europe and the West. The Silk Roads contributed to the spread of Buddhism in the region.

The Han dynasty was weakened by barbarian invasions and epidemics of disease. Civil unrest over these issues and the ever-widening divide between the wealthy and the poor led to revolts and the eventual collapse of the empire in 220 CE.

In India, two major civilizations shaped that region's development. The first, the Mauryan Empire, formed in northwest India around 322 BCE under the leadership of Chandragupta Maurya. The Mauryans established India's first centralized government. Maurya and his successors expanded the empire throughout almost the entire land of India. One of those successors, Ashoka, helped spread Buddhism across India and encouraged a de-emphasis of the caste system.

The Mauryan Empire was later succeeded by the Gupta Empire around 320 CE. The Guptas began a revival of Hinduism and reinstituted the caste system. Under the Guptas, women were subject to strict laws including ritual suicide (sati). Gupta mathematicians made significant contributions to universal knowledge, including the calculation of pi, the development of Arabic numerals, and the concept of zero. Eventually, continuous attack from outside forces led to the decline of the Gupta Empire, which finally collapsed circa 510–530 CE.

In the region of the Arabian Peninsula, the introduction of *Islam* in the early seventh century CE gave rise to more powerful and aggressive empires. After Muhammad established Islam in Mecca, the religion quickly spread among the Arabic people and led to the development of militaristic Muslim empires that spread into other areas by force. By 850 CE, Muslim influence extended throughout the Arabian Peninsula; across much of northern Africa; and even into parts of Europe, most notably Spain.

The first major Islamic dynasty was the Umayyad Caliphate. The Umayyad conquered many peoples and amassed great wealth. Eventually, however, opposition to their harsh rule led to their decline. After their fall, the Umayyad were succeeded by the 'Abbāsid Empire. As opposed to the Umayyad, who simply conquered and ruled by military force, the 'Abbāsid created a resourceful bureaucracy and established themselves as capable administrators of their kingdom. Agricultural success and commercial trade also increased the power and influence of the 'Abbāsid.

3. The Middle Ages

After the fall of the western half of the Roman Empire in 476, the eastern half became the Byzantine Empire. Located on the straits that separated the Black Sea from the Mediterranean, the Byzantine capital of Constantinople was ideally situated to act as a hub for trade routes from across the known world. This contributed significantly to the empire's ability to succeed and flourish for nearly a thousand years.

Also playing a critical role in Byzantium's development as a world power was Justinian, one of its most influential emperors. Justinian sought to improve the Roman laws by which Byzantium was still governed. To that end, he compiled the *Justinian Code*, which established a flexible system of laws designed to protect original Roman law while simultaneously bringing it up to date. Justinian also rebuilt Constantinople, which had been destroyed by rioters, and constructed the famed Hagia Sophia.

In 1054, conflicts over church authority and other practices resulted in the Eastern Orthodox Church splitting from the Roman Catholic Church, forming the Byzantine Church. The influence of the Eastern Orthodox Church later made its way into Russia when Prince Vladimir of Kiev made it the official church of that country. In its final years, attacks from Turkish forces crippled the Byzantium Empire and eventually caused its collapse. Byzantium was severely weakened by the widespread military gains of the Seljuk Turks in Asia Minor in 1071. In 1453, the Ottoman Turks captured Constantinople, bringing the Byzantine Empire to an end.

In Western Europe, the fall of the Roman Empire led to a period of chaos from which various Germanic tribes emerged. These tribes ruled over different parts of the continent. In the region known as Gaul, a line of rulers known as the Carolingians, including such figureheads as Charles Martel and Charlemagne, built an empire that stretched from France to Germany and some areas of Spain.

During this period, the Catholic Church increased its power and influence through close relations with political leaders. Much of Europe also saw an uptick in the number of monasteries and convents across the land.

By the ninth century, Western Europe had become the victim of frequent attacks and violence from both Muslim and Viking invaders. Frightened by these vicious attacks, Europeans were desperate for the kind of protection governments could no longer supply. They found protection in a system of community organization known as feudalism. In the feudal system, peasants could enjoy the protection offered by local lords in return for a pledge of loyalty and faithful service.

In the thirteenth century, China experienced a significant shift in its political state when it was invaded and overtaken by an army of Mongols. Since 1206, Genghis Khan and his successors had been waging a war of conquest that expanded the Mongols' influence into Persia, Russia, and Central Europe. In 1270, under Kublai Khan, the Mongols conquered China and established a tribute empire. After establishing a new capital at Beijing, the Mongols strengthened their power with the help of foreign administrators and ushered in the era called the Mongol Peace, which is also known as the Pax Mongolica. While working to encourage increased trade with Europe along the Silk Roads, the Mongols inadvertently helped to spread the bubonic plague, which also traveled China's trade routes. Weakened by poor leadership and difficult economic conditions, the Mongol Empire collapsed in 1368.

In West Africa, wealth generated from the trans-Saharan gold and salt trade led to the rise of a number of prominent civilizations, including the kingdom of Ghana and the empires of Mali and Songhai. In the east, powerful cities such as Great Zimbabwe emerged thanks to increased trading made possible by their proximity to the Indian Ocean. During this time, both Islam and Christianity grew in popularity among Africans.

Seeking to take back Jerusalem and the rest of the Holy Land from the Seljuk Turks, a group of French and Norman nobles organized the first of what would be a series of *Crusades* against the Muslim Turks. Although none of the Crusades was ultimately successful, they did have a profound impact. The Crusades encouraged Western European economic growth, increased the power of monarchs across Europe and the political power of the Catholic Church, revitalized trade, and more.

The revival of trade, in particular, had a major impact on Western Europe. It increased the need for manufacturing and banking. Importantly, it also encouraged the growth of cities and towns where merchants could live, work, and store their goods. As the number of merchants in cities and towns increased, a new middle class began to appear. Known as the *bourgeoisie* in France, the burghers in Germany, and the burgesses in England, the emerging middle class would go on to play an important role in the development of modern societies.

The increase in medieval cities and towns also led to the rise of centralized national governments. In England, King John was forced to sign the *Magna Carta*, which placed limits on his power and guaranteed the rights of the nobles and eventually the rights of all English citizens. In France, regional monarchies arose from the feudal system and were slowly integrated into a national government. Later, with the establishment of the Third Estate in the Estates-General, the common people of France gained the ability to participate directly in government.

This period was not without strife, however. Between 1346 and 1361, the bubonic plague, also known as the black death, swept across Europe, leaving thousands (probably millions) dead in its wake. About one-third of the European population died out as a result of this plague.

Across the Atlantic Ocean, a number of largely isolated civilizations developed in the Americas. At their height from 250 to 900, the Maya flourished in a region of Mesoamerica that spanned Mexico's Yucatan Peninsula and parts of modern-day Belize and Guatemala. The Maya created a solar calendar; compiled the most advanced system of writing in the Americas; and, like the Gupta Empire in India, introduced the concept of zero.

The Maya were succeeded by the Toltec, a warlike people from southwest Mexico. The Toltec built their empire through violent conquest and made human sacrifices in honor of the war god. Their empire collapsed around 1200, only three hundred years after it first gained prominence in 900.

With the fall of the Toltec came the rise of the Aztec. The Aztec, originally a nomadic people from northern Mexico, established a permanent *settlement* at Tenochtitlán and formed an empire through alliances with neighboring peoples. Like the Toltec, the Aztec were regular practitioners of human sacrifice. Violent tendencies and internal discord weakened the Aztec Empire and made it ripe for conquest by the Spanish in 1519.

The *Inca* gained prominence shortly after the Aztec and built a vast empire in South America. Theirs was the largest such empire anywhere in the Americas. Although they never developed written language as did their Mesoamerican neighbors to the north, the Inca developed a device called a quipu, which was used to manage government records. Among their most significant accomplishments was the construction of a network of roads to facilitate long-distance trade. By the 1520s, civil wars had weakened the Inca Empire, to the extent that it was easily conquered by foreign invaders.

4. Renaissance, Reformation, and Exploration

In the fourteenth century, a wave of renewed interest in the arts, sciences, and intellectualism swept across Europe. This era of rebirth is commonly referred to as the *Renaissance*. The cornerstones of the Renaissance were a strong belief in reason and humanity. Of particular interest during this period was the concept of *humanism*, which emphasized reason; reflected an admiration of the classical Greco-Roman civilizations; and dealt with the common, day-to-day problems that typical people faced. The Renaissance was also a time of great devotion to the revival of the arts and literature.

The Renaissance began in the city-states of northern Italy, which were more urbanized than many other European cities and quite wealthy from the increase in trade spurred on by the Crusades. This sort of wealthy urban environment was the perfect catalyst for an intellectual revolution. Among the major figures of the Italian Renaissance were authors like Niccolò Machiavelli and Dante Alighieri and artists such as Leonardo da Vinci, Michelangelo, Raphael, and Donatello.

Eventually, the ideas of the Renaissance spread northward. The Northern Renaissance meshed the characteristic humanism and realism of the Italian Renaissance with a more profound devotion to religion. Some of the key personalities of the Northern Renaissance are the authors Thomas More, William Shakespeare, and Desiderius Erasmus, as well as artists like Rembrandt and Albrecht Dürer.

The religious element of the Northern Renaissance would prove particularly influential throughout Europe. The philosophies of the Renaissance encouraged people to question the authority of the Catholic Church. This, in turn, led to a radical change in religious thought that eventually resulted in the Protestant Reformation of the early sixteenth century. Angered by what many viewed as the church's abusive use of its powers, religious people across Europe began turning away from Catholicism in favor of Protestantism and other forms of Christianity. This movement was led by reformers such as Martin Luther, who, in response to the Catholic Church's sale of *indulgences*, nailed his *Ninety-Five Theses*, or complaints against the church, onto the door of a cathedral in Germany.

As a result of the Protestant Reformation, the Catholic Church lost much of its political power and was forced to undergo its own internal reformation. This internal reformation, which is known as the Counter-Reformation, led to, among other things, the establishment of Jesuit colleges across Europe, a ban on the sale of indulgences, and the formation of a church court known as the Inquisition.

As the Renaissance and the Protestant Reformation were unfolding in Europe, the Ottoman Empire was rising to power in the East. After the Mongols defeated the Seljuk Turks, the Ottoman Turks seized the region of western Asia known as Anatolia, which had once been controlled by Byzantium. Many of the Ottomans considered themselves Islamic warriors, known as *ghazi*, and were intent on conquering nonbelievers and spreading Islam. Under the leadership of a *ghazi* named Osman Bey, as well as his successors, the Ottomans expanded their empire to include Constantinople, Egypt, Syria, Iraq, and North Africa. They even managed to claim some territory in Eastern Europe. Although the size of their empire and the scope would change significantly over time, the Ottoman Empire would continue to exist in some form until 1923.

In the fifteenth century, during the Renaissance, Europeans also began to exhibit an increased interest in lands beyond their own. With the availability of improved technology and a strong desire for economic profit, the emerging nations of Europe began to turn their attention to exploring previously unknown parts of the world and establishing colonies and trading posts. Portugal and Spain were particularly aggressive in these ventures. Portugal was determined to find a sea route to India, finally doing so in 1498 thanks to Vasco da Gama, who arrived at India by sailing around the southern tip of Africa.

Spain, which had just expelled its Muslim occupiers in 1492, used its newfound wealth and power to fund a westward expedition helmed by Christopher Columbus that resulted in the "discovery" of the Americas, which Europeans referred to as the New World.

These explorative discoveries further increased trade and led to European dominance of the seas. Eventually, disputes about commercial maritime activities between the nations resulted in the Seven Years' War (1756–63). With global dominance on the line, Great Britain fought against France for control of the Indian Ocean and against both the French and the Spanish for control of the Americas. British victories on both battlefronts allowed them to become the dominant maritime power for more than a century.

During this period, the colonization of the Americas proceeded quickly. While Britain and France settled much of the eastern portion of North America, the Spanish set their sights on southern and middle America. Spanish conquistadors overthrew many of the native civilizations of this region, including the Aztec and the Inca.

As nation-states developed in Europe many of them came to be ruled by a monarchical government. Absolute monarchs ruled nations such as France, Spain, and Russia. Constitutional monarchies ruled other nations, such as Great Britain and the Netherlands.

Simply put, absolute monarchs ruled absolutely. They held supreme power over the state and in many cases claimed this by divine right; this meant they believed that God granted power directly to them and that they were answerable only to God. They were personally entitled to run the state however they saw fit, and they could lay claim to the sovereign property of the empire.

Constitutional monarchies worked a little differently. Although they were also headed by monarchs, constitutional monarchies were framed by laws that limited the monarch's power to varying degrees.

Some of the major monarchies that ruled Europe between the sixteenth and eighteenth centuries were those of Philip II of Spain, the Bourbons of France, the Hapsburgs of Austria, the Hohenzollerns of Prussia, and Ivan the Terrible and other notable czars of Russia.

As these monarchs solidified political power, Europe was again swept up in a revolution: in this case, the *Scientific Revolution*. New ideas in scientific thought emerged throughout Europe. Scientific researchers such as Copernicus, Johannes Kepler, Galileo, Isaac Newton, René Descartes, and Francis Bacon all made significant contributions to various scientific fields and helped further strengthen Europe's dominant position.

This revolution also extended to philosophy and other disciplines in the intellectual movement known as the *Enlightenment*. Most Enlightenment philosophies centered on the idea that human beings were essentially good and could be improved through proper education. These philosophies also encouraged the value of reason over faith. The Enlightenment played an important role in the development of the modern Western world, ultimately encouraging social progress, inspiring a shift toward a more secular society, and elevating the importance of the individual over the larger society.

5. The Age of Revolution

From the end of the seventeenth century through the twentieth century, Europe and its colonies experienced a long series of revolutions that changed the face of the world. These revolutions demonstrated the growing desire for self-rule and independence from oppressive governments or colonial dominance.

The age of revolutions began with the bloodless English Revolution of the seventeenth century. Following the death of Queen Elizabeth I in 1603 and the difficult reigns of both King James I and King Charles I, England was plunged into a violent civil war between Puritans (and other non-Anglicans) and the English Parliament. This led to the dictatorial rule of Oliver Cromwell. When Cromwell died in 1658, the English throne passed to Charles II, whose reign involved the passing of important social legislation, such as the Habeas Corpus Act in 1679. Charles II was succeeded by James II, who was later replaced in a bloodless coup transferring power to William of Orange and Mary, the sister of James II. This exchange of power, which came to be known as the English Revolution, led to the English Bill of Rights, signed by William and Mary in 1689. The bill further limited monarchical power by disallowing the English monarch to veto parliamentary laws, enact taxes without parliamentary approval, obstruct freedom of speech in Parliament, or infringe on citizens' right to petition grievances.

The people of France also grew increasingly dissatisfied with conditions at this time. In particular, the inequities of the Estates-General, in which the Third Estate, or the bourgeoisie middle class, was underrepresented and heavily burdened by the clergy and aristocrats of the First and Second Estates, outraged many commoners. Eventually, this dissent turned into a violent revolution that resulted in the end of the French monarchy and led to the formation of a new republican government led by the Jacobin Club. This arrangement was short-lived, however.

Following the execution of the deposed King Louis XVI, France experienced the horrific Reign of Terror, during which the republican government viciously executed anyone considered an enemy. When the leader of the republic, Maximilien de Robespierre, was himself executed, the republic was dissolved and a new government, called *The Directory*, was formed. Within three years, The Directory was overthrown by French general Napoléon Bonaparte, who installed himself as dictator in 1796.

For nearly twenty years, Napoléon waged a bitter war across Europe in an attempt to build a French empire. At the height of his power, Napoléon extended French territory to include most of the European continent, but key political and military mistakes led to his downfall and eventual defeat at the Battle of Waterloo in 1815.

Other revolutions also occurred outside of Europe. At this time in the colonies of North America, the American Revolution ended British dominance of the continent and led to the establishment of a new country, the United States of America. In 1791, the enslaved African people of the French colony of Saint-Domingue in the Caribbean began a revolt. They succeeded in ousting the French and declared their independence as the new nation of Haiti. The Haitian Revolution marked the first time African slaves were able to free themselves from European colonial rule.

Various revolutions also took place in the Spanish-controlled colonies of the Americas. In the 1810s and 1820s, revolutionaries in South America rebelled against the Spaniards and won independence for the countries of Venezuela, Ecuador, Argentina, and Chile, as well as others. Brazil gained its independence from Portugal after the Portuguese monarch fled in 1822.

Around the same time that Spain lost control of its holdings in South America and Middle America, it also lost its control over Mexico. After gaining its independence in 1821, Mexico was governed by a series of rulers, including Antonio Lopéz de Santa Anna, Benito Juárez, and Porfirio Díaz, who ultimately failed to strengthen the country or significantly improve conditions. This led to the Mexican Revolution, in which revolutionary leaders Emiliano Zapata and Francisco "Pancho" Villa fought to bring democratic reforms to the country. The successful end of the revolution in 1919 brought a new constitution and a promise of land reforms, an increase in rights of women and workers, and improvements in education.

6. Industrialization and Imperialism

In the mid-eighteenth century, another revolution was beginning in Europe: the *Industrial Revolution*. This revolution had its roots in England, where agricultural advances made it possible to feed the population with less farm labor. Many farmers were displaced and migrated to the urban areas that were ideal for industrial operations. With government support and the influence of England's place in the global trade market, industrialization quickly spread throughout the country.

Eventually, industrialization also spread outside the country. Over time, other European countries, notably Belgium and Germany, also became industrialized. This phenomenon was mostly limited to Europe, however. Muḥammad 'Alī, an Ottoman ruler, helped industrialize the nation of Egypt. In the East, the governments of Russia and Japan also began to institute programs and policies that encouraged industrialization.

The Industrial Revolution brought many significant changes. It caused a noticeable upsurge in the rate of urbanization and helped further enlarge the already-growing middle class. Unfortunately, it also led to deplorable social conditions, including dangerous working conditions in factories, an increase in child labor, unreasonably low wages, long working hours, and poor housing conditions. On a global scale, the Industrial Revolution served to widen the divide between industrialized and nonindustrialized countries, it increased trade, and it renewed interest in the colonization of lands that could serve as sources of raw materials. This interest in raw materials, along with prominent European beliefs about racial superiority, fueled the spread of *imperialism* in the nineteenth and early twentieth centuries. Many countries, particularly Great Britain, France, and the Netherlands, became major imperialist powers, establishing colonies in Africa, Southeast Asia, the Pacific islands, and elsewhere.

Imperialism often had severe consequences for native populations. In many cases, the natives were forced to work on plantations that grew cash crops to be traded or sold abroad, or to work in mines that produced valuable natural resources for the imperialist nations that controlled them. This prevented the natives from growing the crops they needed to support themselves and their families. In addition, native markets were often flooded with cheap goods imported from the controlling nation, thus preventing growth in the local economy.

In East Asia, both China and Japan took steps (albeit very different ones) to avoid falling under imperialist control. China, which was increasingly influenced by Western imperialist nations such as Great Britain, responded with rebellions and other forms of resistance. Japan, in contrast, responded to foreign imperialist threats by industrializing and becoming an imperialist nation itself.

Many of the colonies established by the imperialist nations of Europe would remain under their control well into the twentieth century.

7. Early Twentieth Century

The rise of imperialism increased tensions between the imperialist nations of Europe and, in the early twentieth century, led to a precarious and volatile scenario. Disputes over territorial control, a rising sense of nationalism, and increasing militarization all set the stage for major European conflicts. Issues among Germany, Austria-Hungary, France, Britain, and Russia had Europe teetering on the brink of war.

At the same time, the final remnants of the declining Ottoman Empire in the East led to new independent nations with differing agendas and political viewpoints. In the Balkans, Austria-Hungary and Serbia were in a heated confrontation over Austria-Hungary's annexation of Bosnia. On June 28, 1914, Archduke Franz Ferdinand, the heir to the throne of Austria-Hungary, was assassinated while on an official visit to the Bosnian capital of Sarajevo. Just a month later, after diplomatic relations broke down, World War I was under way.

At the outset of the war, the central powers of Germany, Austria-Hungary, Bulgaria, and the Ottoman Empire fought against the Allied nations of Great Britain, France, and Russia. Later in the conflict, Russia would switch sides, and both the United States and Japan would join the Allies.

The war itself was particularly deadly. New battlefield techniques, such as trench warfare, and advanced weaponry, such as machine guns and poison gas, made the front lines of the war particularly dangerous places. Approximately 15 million people were killed and about 20 million more were injured.

In March 1917, with his country severely weakened by its war effort, the Russian leader Czar Nicolas II stepped down and left his nation in the hands of a provisional government. Although faced with massive human loss and internal civil unrest, the provisional government was determined to remain in the war. In November of that year, the Bolshevik Party, a communist regime led by Vladimir Lenin, seized control of the government and, within a few months, pulled Russia out of the war. While Russia's withdrawal from the war seemed to pave the way for a German victory, American forces joined Europe and turned the tide of the battle. By November 1918, the Germans were forced to concede defeat and sign an armistice officially ending the war (November 11).

The following year, a peace conference was held at the palace of Versailles in France to work out the final terms. With little influence on the proceedings, Germany was forced to agree to the Treaty of Versailles, which required it to return French territory, give up its African and Pacific colonies, adhere to stringent military restrictions, accept responsibility for the war, and pay upward of $30 billion in reparations over a thirty-year period. These harsh terms would cause great resentment and economic difficulties in Germany and would fuel the forces that eventually led to World War II.

World War I also had serious repercussions for Russia. Lenin's takeover of the Russian government did not go smoothly. From 1918 to 1920 he and the Bolshevik Red Army fought a bloody civil war against the White Army. In the end, the Bolsheviks were victorious and Lenin rose to national power. In 1922, Lenin reorganized Russia into a group of self-governing republics united under a central government. He renamed Russia the Union of Soviet Socialist Republics (USSR, or Soviet Union). When Lenin died in 1924, control of the Soviet Union fell to Joseph Stalin, who quickly founded a violent totalitarian state.

While Russia morphed into the Soviet Union, much of Europe lay in ruins. World War I had taken a heavy toll, especially on those nations on the losing end of the affair. The Treaty of Versailles left Germany a broken nation and other countries, such as Italy, in perilously unstable conditions. These factors led to the rise of ultranationalist, authoritarian governments. In Italy, the Fascist dictator Benito Mussolini rose to power in 1922. In Germany, the National Socialist Party, also known as the Nazi Party, eventually assumed control under the dictatorial leadership of Adolf Hitler. Hitler quickly transformed Germany into a totalitarian state. He instituted public programs designed to help revive the decimated nation. He also began to systematically deprive Jewish and other "non-pure" citizens of their individual rights, believing them to be responsible for Germany's problems.

In Asia, Japan, which had been economically struggling as a result of the Great Depression, abandoned its democratic government in favor of a militaristic one. It also chose to resolve economic issues via territorial expansion. Japan invaded Manchuria (1931) and China (1937). With these attacks, Japan ignited the Pacific phase of what was about to become World War II.

In the mid-1930s, Hitler, in clear defiance of the Treaty of Versailles, began to rebuild the Germany military. In 1936, he, Mussolini, and Japanese leaders signed an agreement uniting the three countries as the Axis powers. The stage for World War II was set. This conflict officially began on September 1, 1939, when Hitler's forces launched an air attack against Poland known as the *blitzkrieg*. Caught by surprise, Poland was easily conquered, and Hitler annexed the western half of the country. On September 3, France and England declared war.

In the early portion of the war, the Axis powers seized a significant amount of European territory, including France (1940). In 1941, Germany and Japan made pivotal decisions that would drastically change the outlook of the war. Germany, which had previously agreed to remain on peaceful terms with the Soviets, invaded Russia and forced the Soviets to the Allied side. On December 7, Japan attacked the American naval base at Pearl Harbor, Hawaii, bringing the United States into the conflict.

Another significant event in 1941 was the implementation of Hitler's program of genocide, the Final Solution, designed to eliminate the Jewish population. As part of this program, Hitler eventually transported Germany's Jews to concentration camps, where they were either pressed into labor or executed. Hitler dealt this fate to other minority groups as well. By the end of the war, the Holocaust had claimed approximately 6 million lives.

On the European battlefront, Allied forces entered France at the Battle of Normandy in 1944 and eventually liberated France from the Germans. Within a year, the Allies forced the Germans to retreat to Berlin, where they surrendered on May 7, 1945, shortly after Hitler's suicide.

In the Pacific, several bloody U.S. victories in the Pacific islands pushed Japan back to its mainland. Hoping to avoid a costly land campaign, the United States attempted to convince Japan to surrender, but efforts were not successful. Believing they had no other options, in early August, the Americans dropped two atomic bombs on Japan: one on Hiroshima and one on Nagasaki. Japan surrendered soon thereafter. World War II was over.

8. Post–World War II

Following World War II, Germany was initially divided among the victorious Allied nations, with Great Britain, France, and the United States controlling the western half of the country and the Soviets controlling the east. The Soviets installed communist governments in Eastern-bloc countries as a means of preventing further military attacks from the West. With the establishment of these satellite nations, the "*Iron Curtain*," as Winston Churchill called it, fell across Europe and the Cold War began.

Anxious to prevent the spread of *communism*, the United States established the Truman doctrine, which aimed to contain communism by helping to protect susceptible nations. This sort of diplomatic warfare was the means by which countries on both sides of the Iron Curtain waged the Cold War. Both the Soviet Union and the United States, however, prepared for the possibility of a real war and, in addition to stockpiling other arms, built arsenals of nuclear weapons.

In 1949, Mao Zedong seized power in China. The following year, Mao's government agreed to an alliance with the Soviet Union that increased global concerns about the spread of communism. Just over ten years later, however, the two nations became divided over the leadership and direction of the Communist Party and ended their agreement.

The first real military conflict of the Cold War came in 1950, when communist North Korea crossed the 38th parallel and invaded South Korea. This action sparked the Korean War, in which American and United Nations troops pushed the North Koreans back over the South Korean border and into their own territory before Chinese forces entered the fray and pushed the U.S. and UN armies back to the former border at the 38th parallel. A cease-fire agreement established a permanent border there that would be surrounded by a demilitarized zone. The two Koreas would remain divided.

A similar conflict over the spread of communism erupted in Southeast Asia in the 1960s via the Vietnam War. Since the nineteenth century, Vietnam had been under French control. During World War II, the Japanese drove out the French. When the Vietnamese eventually expelled the Japanese, the French attempted to regain control of their former colony. This led to conflict that ultimately ended with a divided Vietnam ruled by the communist government of Ho Chi Minh with the *Vietcong* in the north and the democratic government of Ngo Dinh Diem in the south. Over time, the region became increasingly unstable, and in 1965, a total communist takeover seemed imminent. Seeking to prevent any further communist gains, the United States launched an attack against the North Vietnamese. The war effort proved unsuccessful, however, and, in the face of growing antiwar sentiment, by the end of 1973 the United States pulled its troops, allowing the North Vietnamese to take over the country.

Like Vietnam, in the years following World War II, other countries previously under imperialist control gained independence. In 1947, India broke from Great Britain and became the world's largest democracy. The split also resulted in the formation of the Islamic country of Pakistan. In later years, other Southeast Asia countries, such as Burma (later Myanmar), Indonesia, the Philippines, and others were also freed from imperialist control. In Africa, the countries of Ghana, Nigeria, and Kenya all gained independence from Great Britain. The Belgian Congo (today the Democratic Republic of the Congo) freed itself from Belgian rule in 1960. The French colony of Algeria and the Portuguese colony of Angola also gained independence.

Another important event that would help shape the world after World War II was the formation of the Jewish state of Israel in 1948. For some time, displaced Jewish peoples had been immigrating to Palestine. Their growing numbers became a concern for Arabs living in the region. In the wake of the war, the United Nations created Israel, giving the Jewish inhabitants of the area 55 percent of Palestine. This immediately caused hostilities between the Israelis and their Arabic neighbors. Although Israel won the initial skirmish, the conflict has continuously persisted.

Throughout the latter half of the twentieth century, many of the satellite nations established by the Soviet Union gradually turned away from communism. By 1989, the Soviets lost control of East Germany. These losses significantly weakened the once-powerful Soviet Empire. In 1991, following the election of Boris Yeltsin as president, the communist regime of the Soviet Union began to collapse. When the defeated President Mikhail Gorbachev resigned on Christmas Day 1991, communist control over the Soviet Union came to an end.

9. A Globalized World

In the years since World War II, the world has become increasingly glo-balized. Far-reaching forms of media, such as radio, television, and the Internet, have created a global, interconnected culture.

Another key factor in the emergence of a globalized world has been the development of world trade. Trade agreements such as the North America Free Trade Agreement (NAFTA), the Latin American Free Trade Agreement (LAFTA), and the Association of Southeast Asian Nations (ASEAN) have all encouraged free trade among nations around the world.

Globalization has also made us more aware of some of the major issues we face as a world community. In many ways, our dependence on energy sources has increased significantly. In particular, our dependence on oil has played a major role in shaping the modern world. In 1960, many of the Middle Eastern countries responsible for most of the world's oil sup-ply joined together to form the Organization of the Petroleum Exporting Countries (OPEC). Although OPEC's policies initially had a significant impact on the world economy, its influence was later diminished as the result of both overproduction and internal discord surrounding the Iran-Iraq War and the Gulf War.

Some environmental issues, most notably *global warming*, have also become concerns. Scientists have learned that air pollution generated by fossil fuels has damaged Earth's atmosphere and led to what is known as the greenhouse effect, which causes global temperatures to rise. Although there have been many attempts to address this issue, climate change persists and continues to cause global problems, including strong storms and flooding.

Among the few positive results of the Cold War were technologi-cal achievements. Most important, the space race between the United States and the Soviet Union significantly increased space exploration. In the latter half of the twentieth century and into the twenty-first cen-tury, space programs have led to walking on the moon, the building of space stations, and the launching of space probes that significantly increased our knowledge of outlying planets. The Cold War also gave us our earliest communications satellites. Since that time, communications technologies, particularly the Internet, have revolutionized the way we live and connect with one another every day.

Unfortunately, the rise of the global era has not been without some serious challenges. In recent years, global terrorism has become a major concern. Especially since the September 11, 2001, terrorist attacks in the United States, global awareness of terrorist activities has grown significantly. The war on terror continues to be a major concern for countries around the world.

In spite of the challenges, the modern era has produced many positive changes. In many places, civil rights have been secured through the efforts of reformers and human rights organizations. In the United States, Dr. Martin Luther King Jr. led African Americans in their struggle for equal rights in the 1950s and 1960s. As the twentieth century drew to a close, human rights had become one of the most important topics in the global political arena.

Civil rights pertaining specifically to women have also been an issue of particular interest around the world. In the Western world, new laws protect women as they enter the professional world and take on larger roles in politics. Although the women's rights movement has not been as successful outside the Western world, progress continues to be made.

As the world has become increasingly globalized, a global culture has emerged in which both capital and technological ability are of key importance. One of the most dominant aspects of this global culture is the spirit of consumerism, which has been fueled by industrialization and continually rising standards of living. Although the globalized world has faced many challenges, it has continued to adapt and thrive.

THE MAIN COURSE: COMPREHENSIVE STRATEGIES AND REVIEW

Take a deep breath and try to relax. You still have a few weeks before the test, so you have plenty of time to study before the big day. Follow this plan so you feel more prepared.

- Read the comprehensive **Strategies for Multiple-Choice Questions** on pages 41–50.

- Take the **Diagnostic Test** that begins on page 53. The Diagnostic Test will help you in two ways. First, it will give you a stronger understanding of the level of information you need to know to be successful on this test. Second, you will get some experience answering the kinds of questions asked on this test. As you go through the answers, you can pinpoint areas in which you may need to focus your studies. For example, you might need to spend more time studying certain eras, or you might need to focus on particular question types.

- Review key topics in world history by working through the Chapter Review portion of this book, which begins on page 89. Pay special attention to topics covered earlier in the school year, as well as any weak areas you identified via the Diagnostic Test.

- Take at least one more practice test before test day. You can also find a third practice test on our website at mymaxscore.com.

- The night before the test, review **The Essentials: A Last-Minute Study Guide** on pages 1–37, including **Quick Test-Taking Tips** and **Big Ideas in World History**.

- Pack your materials for the next day, get a good night's sleep, and you'll be ready to maximize your score.

Strategies for Multiple-Choice Questions

About the Test

The questions on the SAT World History Subject Test are all multiple choice. Each test includes ninety-five questions, and you'll have sixty minutes to complete the test. That means you'll have about half a minute to answer each question. For each question, you'll select the best answer from a group of five possible choices.

When taking the SAT World History Subject Test, you'll encounter a variety of question types, each of which requires a different strategy or approach. The information on these pages is meant to introduce you to the different types of questions on the test and provide you with helpful strategies for tackling each one. Use these strategies to improve your test-taking skills and maximize your score.

How It's Scored

The questions on the SAT World History Subject Test are scored by computer, so it's important that you work neatly and avoid smudging on your answer sheet. For each question you answer correctly, you earn one (1) raw point. You do not earn any points for questions you skip, so you aren't penalized for failing to answer questions. However, for any question you answer incorrectly, you lose a quarter of a point (.25).

Strategies for Answering Questions

Although all the questions on this test are of the multiple-choice variety, several different types of multiple-choice questions exist. It's important to take the time to become more familiar with the specific types of questions on the test. This section is specially designed to help you prepare for the different kinds of questions you may find on the test. First, however, we'll look at some general testing strategies.

Basic Question-Answering Strategies

As highlighted in **Quick Test-Taking Tips** on page 7, there are some important general strategies that you should keep in mind when answering questions on the SAT World History Subject Test. Using these basic strategies on test day will help you answer questions as efficiently and accurately as possible.

1. SKIM THE QUESTIONS

It is important to remember that the SAT World History Subject Test is a closely timed sixty-minute test. As such, it is critical to spend a minimal amount of time on each individual question. One way you can cut down on the time you need is to start by skimming through the test questions and answering the easiest ones first. Since you receive one raw point for every correct answer, skimming through the test and answering the questions you are sure of ensures that you will get credit for these. You can also save time by recording your answers to these questions on the test next to the number of the question or on a separate sheet of paper. This will save you the time it would take to find and fill in these answers on your answer sheet. Then you can go back and fill in the answers later—but make sure you leave yourself enough time to do so! You will not get *any* credit if you don't mark your answers on the answer sheet.

2. ANSWER QUESTIONS MENTALLY

Read each question and try to answer it in your head before you review the answer choices. Often, answer choices are designed to distract you from the correct answer and may confuse you. Answering the question mentally will help you arrive at the correct answer by avoiding confusion from misleading choices.

3. CONSIDER ALL ANSWER CHOICES

Even if you have read the question and answered it in your head, you should still read all the answer options before making your final selection. Keep in mind that there may be more than one correct answer; in such cases, you have to choose the *best* or the *most correct* choice. That means that it's important to review all your options before making your final selection.

4. READ CAREFULLY

When you are reading questions and answer choices, pay careful attention to the wording. Some questions may include negative words such as *not* or *except*. These have a significant impact on the meaning of the question and can lead to completely avoidable mistakes. Some questions may also include modifiers, which are words or phrases that limit or modify the meaning of another word or phrase. Common modifiers include *always*, *only*, *frequently*, *occasionally*, and so on. In some cases, a modifier may be used to direct you to seek an answer choice that is correct under certain circumstances but that is not always true otherwise.

In addition, watch out for double negatives, which are two negative words used together to create a phrase with a positive meaning. Examples include *not uncommon*, which actually means "common," and *not infrequently*, which means "frequently."

5. USE ELIMINATION STRATEGIES

A key point to remember with SAT subject tests is that they penalize you for guessing—you lose one-quarter of a point (.25) for every wrong answer. Of course, that doesn't mean that you shouldn't take a guess at some answers, but it does mean that you should make only educated guesses.

Start by first eliminating the choices you know are wrong. In many cases, you can also eliminate those choices that seem unlikely or that appear totally unfamiliar. For questions for which the answer choice completes the question stem, you should also eliminate any answer choices that don't make grammatical sense.

Another way to eliminate incorrect answer choices is to use the true-false test. This involves reading each answer choice and considering whether that choice is true or false when it stands on its own. If a particular answer choice is false on its own, you can assume that it can't be the right answer.

You can also often eliminate answer choices that use absolutes, such as *all*, *always*, *only*, and *never*, since an absolute can invalidate an answer that might otherwise be sometimes correct. For example, "The Romans were always at war with their neighbors" is wrong; although the Romans were *sometimes* at war with their neighbors, there were also many times when they coexisted peacefully with the people who lived near their borders.

Finally, when reading through the answer choices, look for contradictory paired statements. One of these is usually the correct answer. At the very least, you can eliminate the option that's incorrect. For example, if a set of answer choices includes "Russia was politically stable in 1917," and a second answer reads "Russia was politically volatile in 1917," you can usually assume that one of these is likely the correct answer and that you can eliminate the other.

Types of Questions

This section provides a brief overview of the different types of questions you will encounter on the SAT World History Subject Test.

Straightforward Questions

The straightforward question is the type of multiple-choice question that you normally encounter on a wide variety of tests. These questions usually appear in the form of a question to answer or a statement to complete. For example, "Which Roman ruler was responsible for initiating the Pax Romana?" or "Martin Luther wrote the *Ninety-Five Theses* mainly as a response to…"

Keep two important strategies in mind when answering straightforward questions.

MAKE SURE YOU KNOW WHAT IS BEING ASKED

Before answering a question, make sure you fully understand it. Read the question more than once, especially if it is long or includes complex wording. Once you have identified exactly what you are looking for, read through the answer choices. Knowing exactly what to look for before reading the answer choices can help you to get an idea of what the correct answer might be and which incorrect answers you can eliminate.

READ EACH ANSWER CHOICE CAREFULLY

In many cases, more than one answer choice may sound like it could be correct at first. Remember to read through all choices and select the one you think would be the *best* answer.

Quotation Questions

Some questions on the SAT World History Subject Test are based on quotations. These usually come from famous historical speeches or important works of literature. You may be asked to identify the author, speaker, or work; to discern the deeper meaning or philosophical basis of the quote; to determine another famous person who held similar or opposite views; or some other such question.

The following is an example of a typical quotation-based question:

> "In depicting the most general phases of the development of the proletariat, we traced the more or less veiled civil war, raging within existing society, up to the point where that war breaks out into open revolution, and where the violent overthrow of the bourgeoisie lays the foundation for the sway of the proletariat."

The quotation is taken from

A.   *The Protestant Ethic and the Spirit of Capitalism* by Max Weber
B.   *Utopia* by Sir Thomas More
C.   *The Wealth of Nations* by Adam Smith
D.   *The Communist Manifesto* by Karl Marx and Friedrich Engels
E.   *Reason in History* by Georg Wilhelm Friedrich Hegel

Keep two important strategies in mind when answering quotation questions:

READ THE QUOTATION CAREFULLY

To determine the correct answer to a quotation-based question, you must understand the quotation's meaning. Read the quotation carefully, and read it more than one time if necessary. The better you understand the quote, the better your chances of answering the question correctly.

MAKE SURE YOU KNOW WHAT IS BEING ASKED

As with other question types, you should always make sure you understand the question before reviewing the answer choices. Is the question asking you to identify the author or another famous person with a similar philosophy? Are you being asked to identify an opposing party, philosophy, or work?

Negative Questions

Negative questions are unique to the SAT World History Subject Test because they require you to select the "wrong" answer. Negative questions are easy to identify because they usually contain the word *except* or *not*. In context, a negative question might look like this: "Which factor did NOT contribute to the rise of National Socialism in Germany after World War I?" or "All of these were results of the French Revolution EXCEPT..."

Keep two important strategies in mind when answering negative questions.

REMEMBER THAT YOU ARE LOOKING FOR THE "WRONG" ANSWER

With negative questions, you are looking for the wrong choice among a field of right choices. Also, keep in mind that if any part of an answer choice is incorrect, the entire statement is incorrect.

CHECK YOUR ANSWER BY USING IT TO COMPLETE THE STATEMENT

When you are answering a negative question that requires you to complete a statement, you can check your answer by inserting it into the statement to determine whether it makes sense. If it doesn't, it's probably wrong.

Image Questions

Some questions on the SAT World History Subject Test include an image. Both the subject of the image and the related question can vary widely. Some questions include images of a work of art and ask you to identify the art style (for example, impressionism). Other images may be of famous structures and ask you to identify the originating culture. Still other questions may offer a political cartoon and ask you to translate its meaning.

Keep two important strategies in mind when answering image questions.

USE CONTEXT CLUES TO FIND THE CORRECT ANSWER

Sometimes, the images used for these questions may contain context clues that can guide you toward the correct answer. For example, suppose you are shown an image of the Coliseum and asked to identify the culture it represents. Even if you are unable to immediately identify the building itself, you may be able to infer that it is representative of ancient Rome just by paying attention to the style of architecture.

EXAMINE POLITICAL CARTOONS CAREFULLY

Questions that require you to interpret political cartoons can be tricky. In many cases, the intended meaning of a political cartoon may not be readily apparent. Some political cartoons may also contain small, easy-to-overlook details that are crucial to meaning. Before you try to answer these questions, make sure that you have examined the image carefully and are confident that you understand the message.

Map, Chart, and Graph Questions

Finally, some questions on the SAT World History Subject Test require you to use a map, chart, or graph to arrive at the correct answer. Before you attempt any of these questions, you should feel confident in your ability to accurately interpret the visual information.

On most tests, you are likely to encounter a few map-based questions. These questions usually ask you to simply use a given map to determine the correct answer. In many cases, the exact type of map used for these questions varies. Along with basic geographical maps, you may also find maps that illustrate military campaigns, trade routes, historical trends, or other information. To do well on these questions, you need to make sure that you are capable of reading and interpreting a wide variety of maps.

You will also likely encounter a few questions that require you to interpret a chart or graph. To answer these questions correctly, you need to know how to read a chart or graph and understand the information it contains. Most commonly, these questions require you to be familiar with pie charts, bar graphs, line graphs, and tables.

There are usually two types of chart and graph questions: trend identification and detail and/or comparison. Trend questions ask you to analyze a graph or chart to identify the trend that it represents. Detail and/or comparison questions ask you to pick out or compare certain details from the graph or chart.

The following table is an example of a type of graph common to the SAT World History Subject Test.

IMPERIAL COLONIZATION OF SOUTHEAST ASIA, CA. 1850s

COLONY	CONTROLLING IMPERIAL POWER
Borneo	Netherlands
Burma	Great Britain
French Indochina (Vietnam)	France
India	Great Britain
Malaysia	Netherlands
Malay States	Great Britain
New Guinea	Netherlands
North Borneo	Great Britain
Philippine Islands	United States

A trend-identification question might ask you to choose the imperial power that exercised the most control over Southeast Asia in the 1850s, on the basis of the chart. A detail and/or comparison question, in contrast, might ask you to determine the imperial power that was in control of Malaysia at the time.

Keep three important strategies in mind when answering map, chart, or graph questions.

STUDY THE MAP, CHART, OR GRAPH FIRST

It's always a good idea to carefully examine the map, chart, or graph before you read the question. Suppose you find yourself faced with a chart-based question. Take a moment to look at the chart and try to determine its overall meaning before you look at the question. Since you can refer back to the chart at any time, you don't need to remember specific details. Spending a little time getting familiar with the chart will help you to better understand the question, which may be difficult to interpret correctly if you have skipped right to the question.

WHEN STUMPED BY THIS TYPE OF QUESTION, SKIP IT AND COME BACK IF YOU HAVE TIME

Some maps, charts, or graphs may be difficult to interpret. If you are having a hard time with a map, chart, or graph, it may be in your best interest to just move on. These questions often consume more time than other types of questions. Since your test time is limited, it may be best to skip questions such as this.

PAY ATTENTION TO LABELS

Most maps, charts, and graphs have labels that provide information about the contents. Take these into consideration when reviewing.

The Diagnosis:
How Ready Are You?

Diagnostic Test

This chapter includes a diagnostic test, which covers a combination of topics that may appear on the SAT World History Subject Test. It has been designed to help you practice for the SAT World History Subject Test and identify areas of weakness, ultimately helping you improve your score. After taking the diagnostic test, you might recognize that you are spending too much time with each question or that you are not reading the questions closely enough. You might discover that you consistently struggle with certain types of questions or with questions that address specific topics or ideas. All of these issues are resolvable. However, to identify them, it is essential that you complete the diagnostic test in an environment that closely mimics the actual testing environment.

Therefore, you should follow these guidelines:

- Block out one hour for the diagnostic test. Stay within this time frame. Stop testing when you reach the end of the allotted time.
- Select an environment that is quiet, with a minimal amount of distraction, such as a quiet room in your home, at your school, or in the local library.
- Turn off your cell phone and your computer. Ask family and friends to avoid disturbing you during the testing period.

- While taking the multiple-choice section, have *only* the examination and information sheet open. Don't use any other resource materials! You're only cheating yourself.
- Again, don't cheat! Even though you may be tempted, looking up the answers will only hinder your progress.
- As you take the test, have a highlighter available. Use it to quickly mark any term or concept that seems unfamiliar. Later, you can use this information to direct your studies.
- Finally, make sure you follow any instructions provided.

Once you have completed the examination, assess your score by checking your answers against the key provided at the end of this section. More information about assessing your performance is provided in that section.

Good luck!

Diagnostic Test

SAT Subject Test in World History
Time—60 minutes
95 questions

Directions: Each of the questions or incomplete statements is followed by five answer choices. Choose the answer choice that best answers the question or best completes the incomplete statement.

Note: This test uses the chronological designations BCE (before the Common Era) and CE (Common Era). These designations correspond to BC (before Christ) and AD (*anno Domini*), which are used in some history texts.

1. The Petition of Right, which was drafted in 1628, attempted to restrict Charles I from doing any of the following EXCEPT

    A. requiring citizens to quarter soldiers in their homes
    B. declaring martial law during peacetime
    C. enacting taxes without parliamentary approval
    D. suspending a law passed by Parliament
    E. imprisoning people without regard to due cause

2. The concept of a state ruled by philosophers and built on a structure of class divisions determined by intelligence was most strongly supported by

    A. Aristotle
    B. Euclid
    C. Plato
    D. Pythagoras
    E. Socrates

3. Which of the following is the most important aspect of the samurai code of conduct, known as the bushido?

    A. Loyalty to the feudal lord
    B. Preservation of personal honor
    C. Protection of the emperor
    D. Defense of territory
    E. Acceptance of death

"It has been thought a considerable advance towards establishing the principles of Freedom to say that Government is a compact between those who govern and those who are governed; but this cannot be true, because it is putting the effect before the cause; for as man must have existed before governments existed, there necessarily was a time when governments did not exist, and consequently there could originally exist no governors to form such a compact with. The fact, therefore, must be that the individuals, themselves, each, in his own personal and sovereign right, entered into a compact with each other to produce a government: and this is the only mode in which governments have a right to arise, and the only principle on which they have a right to exist."

4. The text above was part of a pamphlet written in support of which of the following?

   A. Russian Revolution
   B. Velvet Revolution
   C. Haitian Revolution
   D. Glorious Revolution
   E. French Revolution

5. Chinese trade during the Song dynasty was most strongly influenced by the

   A. restoration of centralized governance
   B. invention of the magnetic compass
   C. enactment of the Confucian civil service system
   D. building of the Grand Canal
   E. diffusion of Buddhism across China

6. The political theories of communism and fascism share all of the following tenets EXCEPT

    A. adherence to single-party rule
    B. loyalty to the state
    C. opposition to social democracy
    D. dissolution of social classes
    E. support of dictatorial leadership

7. Which of the following is the most direct cause of World War I?

    A. Invasion of Poland
    B. Formation of the Triple Alliance
    C. Annexation of Bosnia
    D. Onset of the Russian Revolution
    E. Assassination of Franz Ferdinand

8. Which of the following was made clearer to modern scholars after the discovery of the Rosetta stone in 1798?

    A. Laws of ancient Mesopotamia
    B. Origins of Hinduism
    C. Written language of ancient Egyptians
    D. Trading practices of Sumerian society
    E. Agricultural methods of ancient China

9. The civilization depicted in the photograph above

   A. placed little emphasis on education
   B. conquered much of Europe
   C. introduced the concept of drama
   D. practiced Zoroastrianism
   E. depended on the Nile River

"We shall not flag or fail. We shall go on to the end. We shall fight in France, we shall fight on the seas and oceans, we shall fight with growing confidence and growing strength in the air, we shall defend our island, whatever the cost may be. We shall fight on the beaches, we shall fight on the landing grounds, we shall fight in the fields and in the streets, we shall fight in the hills; we shall never surrender."

10. The quotation above referenced the hard fighting in which of the following wars?

   A. World War I
   B. World War II
   C. Korean War
   D. First Balkan War
   E. Six-Day War

11. All of the following are true about the people of ancient Mali
    EXCEPT

    A. they built their wealth through gold and trade
    B. they established Timbuktu as a major city
    C. they were sometimes ruled by Muslim leaders
    D. they organized villages on the basis of kinship
    E. they relied on a strong governmental system

12. The creation story contained in the *Popol Vuh* was written by the

    A. Aztec
    B. Inca
    C. Maya
    D. Olmec
    E. Toltec

13. British imperialism in India resulted in all of the following EXCEPT

    A. enactment of restrictive trading policies
    B. increased productivity in native industries
    C. improved medical care and sanitation
    D. increased exportation of raw materials
    E. expansion of the transportation system

14. The Mongolian occupation of China, which occurred during the
    thirteenth and fourteenth centuries, improved China's economic
    stability by

    A. decreasing taxes on imported goods
    B. leading to an extension of the Grand Canal
    C. decentralizing the Chinese government
    D. encouraging Chinese industrialization
    E. making travel on trading routes safer

15. Which factor played an important role in the escalations of both the French and Russian revolutions?

   A.   Rise of industrialization
   B.   Oppressive monarchical rule
   C.   Previously failed uprisings
   D.   Influence of communism
   E.   Demand for women's rights

16. Which of the following answers lists the wars in the correct chronological order?

   A.   Thirty Years' War, Crimean War, Boer War, Hundred Years' War
   B.   Crimean War, Hundred Years' War, Boer War, Thirty Years' War
   C.   Hundred Years' War, Thirty Years' War, Crimean War, Boer War
   D.   Boer War, Crimean War, Hundred Years' War, Thirty Years' War
   E.   Hundred Years' War, Boer War, Thirty Years' War, Crimean War

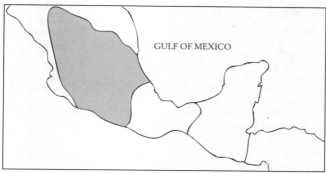

Peoples of Mesoamerica, 300–1519 CE

17. Around 1400 CE, the shaded region on the map above was inhabited by the

   A.   Aztec
   B.   Inca
   C.   Maya
   D.   Olmec
   E.   Toltec

18. Which of the following would a believer in legalism LEAST LIKELY support?

    A.   Strong family values
    B.   Loyalty to rulers
    C.   Equal access to education
    D.   Submission to state policy
    E.   Censorship of media

"What the bourgeoisie, therefore, produces, above all, is its own grave-diggers. Its fall and the victory of the proletariat are equally inevitable."

19. The statement above MOST clearly reflects a major tenet of which political philosophy?

    A.   Communism
    B.   Democracy
    C.   Fascism
    D.   Theocracy
    E.   Totalitarianism

"However well educated and clever a native might be, and however brave he may prove himself, I believe that no rank we can bestow on him would cause him to be considered an equal of the British officer."

—Lord Kitchener, British military commander in India

20. This statement supports which of the following generalizations about colonial powers and the native populations they govern?

A. Colonial powers usually controlled native populations primarily through military force.

B. Colonial powers often viewed themselves as racially superior to native populations.

C. Colonial powers tended to use native populations to bolster their military strength.

D. Colonial powers were needed to help govern less capable native populations.

E. Colonial powers encouraged native populations to improve their individual statuses.

21. The United Nations deployed an international military force in South Korea in 1950 primarily because

A. North Korea threatened to launch a nuclear attack against South Korea

B. North Korean and Chinese ships attacked South Korean ships in the Yellow Sea

C. North Korean troops had crossed the 38th parallel into South Korean territory

D. North Korea acquired nuclear weapons from the Soviet Union

E. North Korea was on the verge of overthrowing the South Korean government

22. According to the traditional Hindu caste system, an unskilled worker would be considered part of which class?

    A. Brahmans

    B. Harijans

    C. Kshatriya

    D. Shudra

    E. Vaishya

23. Ho Chi Minh returned to Vietnam in 1941 and founded the Vietminh in response to a crisis primarily concerning

    A. increasing communist influence in Vietnam

    B. American militarization of South Vietnam

    C. the dictatorial leadership of Ngo Dinh Diem

    D. French colonial control over Vietnam

    E. the geopolitical division of North and South Vietnam

24. The main purpose of the World War I era cartoon above was to

    A. encourage American involvement in the war effort

    B. demonstrate the might of German naval forces

    C. discourage international trade during the war

    D. imply German barbarism and disregard for human life

    E. illustrate the weakness of Allied military forces

25. Which of the following occurred during the New Kingdom period of ancient Egyptian history?

   A. Reign of the pharaoh Khafra
   B. Carving of the Rosetta stone
   C. Building of the pyramids
   D. Expulsion of the Hyksos
   E. Construction of the Sphinx

26. Which of the following was true of both the Kush and the Bantu-speaking people of ancient Africa?

   A. Both modeled their forms of leadership after the ancient Egyptians.
   B. Both developed ironworking to make iron-tipped weapons and tools.
   C. Both began as migratory cultures that eventually settled in a single region.
   D. Both spread their languages throughout Africa through cultural intermarriage.
   E. Both were chiefly agrarian and relied on farming and raising animals.

27. The Battle of Trafalgar was a key naval victory for the British in their war against

   A. Austria-Hungary
   B. France
   C. Germany
   D. Portugal
   E. Spain

28. All of the following are true about the Inca civilization EXCEPT

    A. they used a system of parallel descent in which daughters inherited from their mothers and sons from their fathers
    B. they demanded that neighboring communities pay them tributes as a means of funding their imperial expansion
    C. they believed that their ruler was a god that descended from the sun and that his main wife represented the moon
    D. they allowed conquered communities to retain their individual culture and local leaders in return for allegiance to the empire
    E. they performed most of their sacrifices using animals like llamas or guinea pigs instead of humans

29. The Taj Mahal in Agra, India, was originally built to serve as a

    A. fortress
    B. monastery
    C. mosque
    D. palace
    E. tomb

30. During the Punic Wars, Rome fought in three separate campaigns against the

    A. Carthaginians
    B. Gauls
    C. Illyrians
    D. Macedonians
    E. Samnites

SCHOOL LIFE EXPECTANCY IN YEARS		
COUNTRY	MEN	WOMEN
El Salvador	12	12
Somalia	3	2
Cambodia	10	9
Spain	16	17
Ethiopia	9	8
Honduras	11	12

Source: CIA World Factbook

31. Which of the following statements is best supported by the information in the table above?

   A. Both men and women in technologically advanced countries have greater access to secondary education than do their counterparts in developing nations.
   B. Politically stable nations are more likely than unstable ones to have equal access to education for both men and women.
   C. Women in developing nations have less access to education at any level than men do.
   D. Women have relatively equal access to education as their male counterparts in most developing nations.
   E. Access to quality education at any level depends on the overall poverty level of the nation.

32. Which country did Britain establish in Asia before India earned its independence in 1947?

   A. Afghanistan
   B. Bangladesh
   C. Pakistan
   D. Nepal
   E. Turkmenistan

33. All of the following were factors in the decline of both the Roman Empire and the Han dynasty EXCEPT

   A.   difficulty with governmental administration due to their large size
   B.   violence from political resistance groups within their borders
   C.   poor agricultural yield, famine, and rapidly spreading epidemics
   D.   barbarian invasions along their borders that negatively affected trading
   E.   division by generals who attempted to seize power and proclaim themselves emperor

34. In the nineteenth century, which region of colonial Southeast Asia was an independent nation that served as a "buffer zone" between other imperially governed states?

   A.   Burma
   B.   Singapore
   C.   Borneo
   D.   Sumatra
   E.   Siam

35. The city of Great Zimbabwe rose to prominence during the thirteenth century primarily as a result of its

   A.   possession of working gold mines
   B.   strong agricultural economy
   C.   widespread military conquests
   D.   control of a key trading route
   E.   political ties to the Roman Empire

"It is mere human talk to preach that the soul flies out [of purgatory] immediately [when] the money clinks in the collection box."

36. Which of the following religious leaders most likely made the statement above?

    A. John Calvin
    B. Ignatius of Loyola
    C. Martin Luther
    D. John Knox
    E. Ulrich Zwingli

37. The Neolithic Revolution was a fundamental shift in the human way of life during the prehistoric era that was primarily marked by the

    A. emergence of early governments
    B. development of agricultural techniques
    C. formation of organized religions
    D. beginning of systematic trade
    E. construction of early tools and machines

38. Which Mesoamerican culture used chinampas to increase the amount of agricultural land available for use in its capital city?

    A. Inca
    B. Olmec
    C. Maya
    D. Aztec
    E. Toltec

39. An interest in natural resources and commodities such as oil, tin, and rubber led the Dutch to colonize which region of Southeast Asia starting in the seventeenth century?

    A.   Indonesia

    B.   Malaysia

    C.   Burma

    D.   Siam

    E.   Philippines

40. Which of the following modern countries is NOT matched with the imperial power that once controlled it?

    A.   Bosnia   Austrian-Hungarian Empire

    B.   Cambodia   Mongol Empire

    C.   Yemen   Umayyad Empire

    D.   Turkey   Ottoman Empire

    E.   Guyana   British Empire

41. In his 1776 book *The Wealth of Nations*, economist Adam Smith advocated the laissez-faire economic philosophy and specifically condemned

    A.   communism

    B.   feudalism

    C.   imperialism

    D.   mercantilism

    E.   capitalism

42. Which of the following Chinese dynasties instituted the first civil service examination?

    A. Tang
    B. Zhou
    C. Sui
    D. Qin
    E. Han

43. The Four Noble Truths form the basis of which major Eastern religion?

    A. Hinduism
    B. Sikhism
    C. Daoism
    D. Buddhism
    E. Shintoism

44. Which of these answers best describes how Germany and Japan were similar in the lead-up to World War II?

    A. Both nations wanted to isolate themselves from foreign influence.
    B. Both nations were convinced of their ethnic superiority.
    C. Both nations were interested in territorial expansion for economic gain.
    D. Both nations were suffering because of heavy losses incurred in World War I.
    E. Both nations supported the ethnic and racial cleansing of minority groups.

45. The Spanish settlers who governed colonies in Mesoamerica imported Africans as a source of labor instead of enslaving Native Americans primarily because

    A.   Africans were more obedient to Europeans than Native Americans
    B.   Africans were more resistant to disease than Native Americans
    C.   Africans were a cheaper source of labor than Native Americans
    D.   Africans were more skilled at manual labor than Native Americans
    E.   Africans were easier to communicate with than Native Americans

"At this point one may note that men must be either pampered or annihilated. They avenge light offenses; they cannot avenge severe ones; hence, the harm one does to a man must be such as to obviate any fear of revenge."

46. The quotation above is taken from which of the following?

    A.   *The Communist Manifesto*, Karl Marx and Friedrich Engels
    B.   *In Praise of Folly*, Desiderius Erasmus
    C.   *Utopia*, Sir Thomas More
    D.   *The Prince*, Niccolò Machiavelli
    E.   *Two Treatises of Government*, John Locke

47. Aside from gold, the most valuable and highly traded commodity in the West African kingdom of Ghana was

    A.   salt
    B.   ivory
    C.   slaves
    D.   grain
    E.   rice

48. All of the following are examples of trading agreements EXCEPT

   A. NAFTA
   B. OPEC
   C. LAFTA
   D. GATT
   E. ASEAN

49. The Chinese ruled over Vietnam between roughly the first and tenth centuries CE. During this period, the Chinese encountered the most resistance from the Vietnamese when they attempted to

   A. implement their civil service and bureaucratic systems
   B. introduce the Vietnamese to the Confucian ideology
   C. de-emphasize the role of women in Vietnamese society
   D. employ traditional Chinese agricultural methods
   E. convert the Vietnamese to the Buddhist religion

50. The rise of feudalism in Western Europe was primarily the result of

   A. political unrest caused by severe famine
   B. fear of attack from foreign invaders
   C. the collapse of the Carolingian dynasty
   D. disputes about church authority over state matters
   E. an increase in trading with overseas countries

END OF DIAGNOSTIC TEST

Diagnostic Test Answers and Explanations

Answer Key

1. D	26. B
2. C	27. B
3. A	28. B
4. E	29. E
5. B	30. A
6. D	31. D
7. E	32. C
8. C	33. B
9. C	34. E
10. B	35. D
11. D	36. C
12. C	37. B
13. B	38. D
14. E	39. A
15. B	40. B
16. C	41. D
17. A	42. E
18. C	43. D
19. A	44. C
20. B	45. B
21. C	46. D
22. D	47. A
23. D	48. B
24. A	49. C
25. D	50. B

Answer Explanations

1. **D.** The Petition of Right, which Parliament asked Charles I to sign in return for money he desperately needed to fund his war efforts against both France and Spain, was intended to place several new restrictions on the power of the monarchy. Under the terms of the agreement, the king would no longer have the authority to require citizens to quarter soldiers in their homes, to declare martial law during peacetime, to enact taxes without prior approval of Parliament, or to imprison people without regard to due cause. The king's ability to suspend a law passed by Parliament, which was later restricted with the signing of the Bill of Rights in 1689, was not part of the Petition of Right.

Difficulty Level: Medium

2. **C.** In his most famous work, *The Republic*, Plato outlined his vision of the ideal state. According to Plato, the ideal state was an intellectual aristocracy in which the most intelligent members of society held power while those of lesser intelligence would be strictly confined to various forms of labor according to their individual abilities. He went on to claim that if members of each part of the society fulfilled the obligations of their specific roles, society would function harmoniously.

Difficulty Level: Medium

3. **A.** While all of the responsibilities listed were part of the bushido, the central theme and most defining aspect of this code of conduct was absolute loyalty to the feudal lord. As the primary code of conduct for both men and women in the samurai class, the bushido was designed to protect Japanese feudal communities from dangerous bandits who wandered throughout the countryside.

Difficulty Level: Hard

4. **E.** The quotation, taken from Thomas Paine's *Rights of Man*, was written in reference to and in support of the ongoing French Revolution in 1791. In this excerpt, Paine denounces the idea of hereditary government and instead argues that governments are created by the people

they serve, adding that this is the only lawful way a government can be created.

Difficulty Level: Hard

5.   **B.** The invention of the magnetic compass had the most significant impact on Chinese trade during the Song dynasty. The magnetic compass allowed the Chinese to expand their trading routes further into the Indian Ocean and the Persian Gulf than had ever been possible before. In addition, the invention of the magnetic compass allowed the Chinese to open a direct trading route to the eastern African coast.

Difficulty Level: Medium

6.   **D.** Although communism and fascism both include similar viewpoints on many political issues, their individual philosophies on social classes differ sharply. Fascism favors the existence of a system of social classes, but communism calls for the total dissolution of class delineations.

Difficulty Level: Medium

7.   **E.** Although World War I was precipitated by a series of related events, the single most significant event was the assassination of Archduke Franz Ferdinand on June 28, 1914. His death at the hands of Gavrilo Princip, who was in favor of Bosnian self-rule, led Austria-Hungary to declare war on Serbia, which eventually led to the outbreak of World War I.

Difficulty Level: Easy

8.   **C.** The Rosetta stone—which was discovered by French soldiers who were serving in Egypt under the command of Napoléon Bonaparte—contained inscriptions, each written in Greek, Demotic, and hieroglyphics. This discovery marked the first time that linguists were able to translate the meaning of hieroglyphics, the written language of the ancient Egyptians.

Difficulty Level: Easy

9.   **C.** The photograph depicts the Parthenon, one of the best-known architectural ruins of the ancient Greek civilization. Along with their great contributions to science, mathematics, philosophy, and literature,

the ancient Greeks are also remembered for creating the art of drama. Greek drama was divided into two categories: tragedy (which often focused on a strong central character with a flaw) and comedy (which contained humorous and satirical scenes).
Difficulty Level: Easy

10. **B.** The quote in question, which was spoken by British Prime Minister Winston Churchill on June 4, 1940, was made in reference to England's ongoing military efforts in the early portion of World War II.
Difficulty Level: Easy

11. **D.** The Mali Empire of West Africa, which flourished between approximately 1235 and 1403 CE, was a strongly governed imperial state that owed much of its wealth and power to its considerable gold holdings and trading practices. Their success was also due to strong leadership, especially that of the Muslim ruler Mansa Mūsā. The Mali also established Timbuktu as one of the major African cities of the period. Unlike the Bantu civilization, however, they did not organize their villages on the basis of kinship.
Difficulty Level: Hard

12. **C.** The *Popol Vuh* was one of the sacred books of the Maya and contains the Mayan interpretation of the creation story. Believed to have been written between 1554 and 1558 CE, the *Popol Vuh* offers a historical chronology of the Quiché Maya and contains a time line of royal succession from their founding to 1550 CE.
Difficulty Level: Medium

13. **B.** One of the most disastrous effects of British imperial rule in India was the impact it had on that country's native industries, particularly the textile industry. Looking for a cheaper alternative to the relatively expensive handmade textile produced by the native Indian textile industry, the British opted to import more affordable textiles from their own factories in Great Britain. As a result, the Indian textile industry all but collapsed.
Difficulty Level: Medium

14. **E.** The Mongolian occupation of China led to an era of peace known as the Pax Mongolica. The peaceful atmosphere of this era made traveling on the major trade routes around China much safer, which increased trade between Asia and Europe.

Difficulty Level: Hard

15. **B.** The French and Russian revolutions were both motivated by oppressive monarchs. The extravagant spending and abusive behavior of King Louis XVI incited the French Revolution. Similarly, the oppressive policies of czars Alexander II, Alexander III, and Nicholas II sparked the Russian Revolution.

Difficulty Level: Medium

16. **C.** The correct chronological order is Hundred Years' War, Thirty Years' War, Crimean War, and Boer War. The Hundred Years' War was a long-term battle between Britain and France that took place intermittently between the fourteenth and fifteenth centuries. The Thirty Years' War unfolded across much of Europe and lasted from 1618 to 1648. The Crimean War, fought primarily between Russia and the Ottoman Empire, took place in the mid-1850s. Finally, the Boer War, which pitted the Dutch settlers of South Africa against the British, broke out in 1899.

Difficulty Level: Medium

17. **A.** The land in the shaded region of the map was inhabited by the Aztec circa 1400 CE. The Aztec, originally a nomadic people from northern Mexico, first entered the Valley of Mexico in approximately 1200 CE. About 125 years later, they established a permanent settlement on an island at the center of Lake Texcoco, which became their capital city of Tenochtitlán. The Aztec Empire continued to flourish until Hernán Cortés conquered it in 1521.

Difficulty Level: Easy

18. **C.** The philosophy of legalism is based on the belief that personal freedoms lead to disorder. As such, concepts such as censorship and submission to the government are critical components of legalism. Equal

access to education, in contrast, would be in stark contrast with the tenets of legalism. Instead, supporters of legalism advocated for a strictly controlled education system divided by class.

Difficulty Level: Medium

19. **A.** The quote reflects one of the major tenets of communism. Taken from *The Communist Manifesto* by Karl Marx and Friedrich Engels, the quote describes the Marxist belief that the fundamental inequality in most economies would lead to a revolt of the proletariat workers against the middle-class bourgeoisie. The ultimate goal of such revolt, they believed, would be the establishment of a communist state.

Difficulty Level: Hard

20. **B.** Lord Kitchener's statement supports the generalization that colonial powers often viewed themselves as racially superior to native populations. Kitchener and other British military leaders believed that they were superior to the people they ruled.

Difficulty Level: Medium

21. **C.** The Korean War was ignited when North Korean troops crossed over the 38th parallel and into South Korean territory. In response to this aggression, the United Nations sent an international military force to defend South Korea and push the North Korean invasion force back across the 38th parallel. A ceasefire agreement eventually established a border between North and South Korea near the 38th parallel with a demilitarized zone on either side.

Difficulty Level: Medium

22. **D.** In the traditional Hindu caste system, unskilled workers are considered part of the class known as Shudra. The highest level of the caste system, which was reserved exclusively for priests, is the Brahmans caste. The Kshatriya caste consisted of rulers and warriors. The Vaishya caste includes skilled workers, traders, merchants, and some minor officials. The Harijans caste, also referred to as the pariah, is made up of members of Hindu society often known as the untouchables.

Difficulty Level: Hard

23. **D.** Ho Chi Minh's return to Vietnam in 1941 and his establishment of the Vietminh, which was also known as the League for the Independence of Vietnam, was a result of ongoing French colonial control. Independence movements in Vietnam and other parts of French Indochina began to appear in the 1930s. Ho Chi Minh emerged as a major figure in these movements and was condemned to death by the French government. Minh was forced to flee, but he returned in 1941 and founded the Vietminh.

Difficulty Level: Hard

24. **A.** This cartoon is meant to condemn German military actions and encourage American involvement in World War I. The cartoon depicts the sinking of the *Laconia*, a British ocean liner that was torpedoed by a German U-boat. The American flags in the illustration show that several Americans were on board when the ship was sunk.

Difficulty Level: Medium

25. **D.** During the New Kingdom period, between 1550 and 700 BCE, the Hyksos were expelled from Egypt. The Hyksos crossed the Sinai Peninsula and invaded Egypt around 1650 BCE. They ruled over the Egyptians for about a century before they were finally expelled around 1550 BCE.

Difficulty Level: Medium

26. **B.** The Kush and the Bantu-speaking people both developed methods of ironworking that allowed them to make iron-tipped weapons and tools. Although it remains unclear whether they invented or borrowed the process, the Bantu-speaking people were among the first to practice ironworking, using the process mainly to create iron-tipped weapons. The Kush also used ironworking to make weapons and tools, but they traded most of their iron creations with other cultures in return for other goods.

Difficulty Level: Hard

27. **B.** The Battle of Trafalgar was a major victory for the British in 1805 in their struggle against France during the Napoleonic Wars. In need of

naval support for his ground troops fighting in southern Italy, Napoléon ordered Admiral Pierre de Villeneuve to bring his fleet of thirty-three ships through the Strait of Gibraltar. British Admiral Horatio Nelson met Villeneuve near Cape Trafalgar and engaged him with a fleet of twenty-seven ships. Nelson's historic victory cemented the British position as the dominant European naval force for more than one hundred years.

Difficulty Level: Easy

28. **B.** Unlike the Aztec and other Mesoamerican civilizations, the Inca did not force neighboring communities to pay tributes. Instead, the Inca required these communities to offer their assistance in various ways, including helping with public building projects, working in their mines, or performing agricultural duties.

Difficulty Level: Hard

29. **E.** The Taj Mahal was originally built to serve as a tomb. The Mughal emperor Shah Jahān ordered the construction of the Taj Mahal in 1631 as a memorial to his late wife, Mumtāz Maḥal. Maḥal, who had also served Jahan as a trusted political adviser, died as a result of complications during childbirth.

Difficulty Level: Easy

30. **A.** Rome fought against the Carthaginians in the Punic Wars. The first Punic War (264–241 BCE) was between Rome and Carthage over control of the islands of Sicily and Corsica. The Roman navy eventually gained control of the sea-lanes in the region, forcing Carthage to surrender. The Second Punic War (218–201 BCE) began when the Carthaginian general Hannibal crossed the Alps and invaded Italy. After a bloody campaign in Italy, Hannibal was forced to retreat because of an invasion in Carthage. Shortly after his return, the Carthaginians were defeated. The Third Punic War (149–146 BCE) was ignited when Carthage refused to move its city further inland. This final conflict ended with the total destruction of Carthage.

Difficulty Level: Medium

31. **D.** On the basis of the information included in the table, the statement

that women have relatively equal access to education as their male counterparts in most developing nations is most accurate. According to the table, there is no more than one year's difference between the school life expectancy of men and that of women in the developing nations listed. (School Life Expectancy is the number of years of education citizens in a country receive during their lives.) Given this, it is possible to draw the conclusion that access to education in these countries is roughly equal for both men and women.

Difficulty Level: Medium

32. **C.** Great Britain divided the Indian subcontinent into the separate nations of India and Pakistan. Great Britain established Pakistan after Islamic leaders raised concerns about the power that India, a mostly Hindu culture, would have in the region once it gained independence.

Difficulty Level: Medium

33. **B.** While both the Roman Empire and the Han dynasty fell into decline as a result of many of the same factors, the influence of violent political resistance groups was a unique problem for the Han dynasty. During the course of its reign, the Han dynasty faced violent internal struggles brought about by resistance groups like the Red Eyebrows and the Yellow Turbans. These groups formed in response to what they perceived as ineffective governance and poor living conditions.

Difficulty Level: Hard

34. **E.** Siam, which remained free of imperial governance, served as a "buffer zone" between the British-controlled colony of Burma and French Indochina. Siam, known today as Thailand, achieved its unique status as a result of territorial disputes between the French and British. Unable to come to terms on any plan for mutually colonizing Siam, the French and British simply agreed to allow it to serve as an independent neutral area.

Difficulty Level: Hard

35. **D.** Great Zimbabwe became one of the most prominent African cities in the thirteenth century because it controlled a key trading route. In

the 1200s, Great Zimbabwe took control of a critical trading route that connected the central African gold fields with the trading port of Sofala. After assuming control of the route, the city grew wealthy and powerful.

Difficulty Level: Hard

36. **C.** The above statement was taken from the *Ninety-Five Theses*, a major work of the Protestant Reformation written by German priest Martin Luther. In October 1517, Luther nailed the *Ninety-Five Theses* to the door of a cathedral in Wittenberg, Germany, as a means of sparking public debate about the Catholic Church's practice of selling indulgences, which were simple slips of paper said to guarantee forgiveness of the buyer's sins. In reality, the sale of these indulgences was a method of raising funds for the rebuilding of St. Peter's Basilica.

Difficulty Level: Medium

37. **B.** The Neolithic Revolution, which is also commonly known as the Agricultural Revolution, was a major shift of the human way of life that was primarily caused by the emergence of agricultural techniques. This revolution began after a series of ice ages left Neolithic humans unable to rely solely on the hunting and gathering techniques they had used to acquire sustenance in the past. Faced with an insufficient supply of resources for their survival, humans were forced to turn to agriculture and establish permanent settlements.

Difficulty Level: Hard

38. **D.** The Aztec pioneered the practice of using man-made plots of land called chinampas to increase the agricultural land available for use. Since the Aztec capital of Tenochtitlán was built on an island in the middle of Lake Texcoco, the amount of agricultural land was limited. The Aztec augmented their existing land with additional floating plots of land made from rafts. These rafts were made of reeds that were woven together and topped with fertile soil.

Difficulty Level: Hard

39. **A.** Driven by an interest in the region's oil reserves and the availability of commodities like tin and rubber, the Dutch began actively

colonizing the region of Southeast Asia known as Indonesia in the seventeenth century. Colonists organized plantations and opened numerous trading posts. By the turn of the eighteenth century, the Dutch had come to dominate Indonesia, renaming it the Dutch East Indies.

Difficulty Level: Medium

40. **B.** The present-day country known as Cambodia was not controlled by the Mongol Empire. Before being colonized by the French in the nineteenth century, modern Cambodia was ruled by the Khmer Empire, which reached the height of its power around the turn of the thirteenth century. The Khmer Empire, perhaps best known for constructing the Hindu temple structure of Angkor Wat, amassed control over a vast swath of Southeast Asia thanks to a strong economy based largely on the cultivation of rice.

Difficulty Level: Hard

41. **D.** In *The Wealth of Nations* economist Adam Smith argued that governments should take a "hands-off" approach to economics; he condemned mercantilism. He argued that the common mercantilist policy of using protective tariffs to safeguard home industries was counterintuitive to free trade. Smith also argued that labor, not land, was the source of a nation's true wealth. He also stated that governments should not be involved in a nation's economic affairs.

Difficulty Level: Hard

42. **E.** The implementation of the first civil service examination in Chinese history occurred during the reign of the Han dynasty. As the Chinese civil service developed during the Han dynasty, the need for a recruitment system that would ensure that civil service agencies were staffed by competent, honest men increased exponentially. The Han system of civil service training and examination was designed to address this issue and improve governmental efficiency.

Difficulty Level: Medium

43. **D.** Founded by and based on the teachings of Siddhartha Gautama (later known as Buddha), Buddhism was built on the principles known

as the Four Noble Truths. These truths state the following: all human life is filled with sorrow and suffering; suffering is caused by desire; through rejection of desire, people passing through a series of reincarnations can reach nirvana; and nirvana is reached by strict adherence to the Eightfold Path.

Difficulty Level: Medium

44. **C.** Germany and Japan had similar interests at the beginning of World War II in that they both wanted to expand their territories and economics. However, the countries also had very different motivations in other ways. For example, Germany was interested in gaining power in Europe, while Japan was interested in gaining power in Asia.

Difficulty Level: Hard

45. **B.** The Spanish settlers of Mesoamerica favored using imported Africans as a source of labor over the Native Americans already present in the regions because Africans were more resistant to disease. As a result of their previous isolation from Europeans and other foreign cultures, the Native Americans of Mesoamerica were highly susceptible to European diseases, such as smallpox, and were quickly debilitated. Africans were much more resistant to both European and tropical diseases.

Difficulty Level: Medium

46. **D.** The above quotation is taken from *The Prince*. One of the premier works of political literature of the early Renaissance, *The Prince* was written by Niccolò Machiavelli in 1513 and was first formally published in 1532. In this renowned work, Machiavelli provided for current rulers and future rulers a guide to acquiring power, establishing a state, and maintaining it by any means necessary.

Difficulty Level: Medium

47. **A.** Second only to gold in worth, salt was a vitally important and extremely valuable commodity in the kingdom of Ghana. The unusually high value of salt in West Africa was largely because the region had no natural sources of the mineral, which was vital to human life. To ensure the viability of their community, the people of Ghana relied on a

lucrative trade route that brought a steady supply of salt into their king-dom from the Sahara desert in the east.

Difficulty Level: Medium

48. **B.** The North American Free Trade Agreement (NAFTA), the Latin American Free Trade Agreement (LAFTA), the General Agreement on Tariffs and Trade (GATT), and the Association of Southeast Asian Nations (ASEAN) all are examples of trading agreements. The Organization of Petroleum Exporting Countries (OPEC) is a multina-tional organization designed to aid in the coordination of the petroleum policies of its member nations. First established in September 1960, OPEC is currently composed of twelve member countries including Saudi Arabia, Iran, Iraq, Kuwait, and Venezuela.

Difficulty Level: Easy

49. **C.** While the Vietnamese readily accepted the implementation of Chinese practices in regard to civil service, Confucianism, Buddhism, and agriculture, some of the cultural differences between the two societies ultimately sparked resistance. The de-emphasis of the role of women in the Vietnamese society, for example, led to increased tensions between the Vietnamese and the Chinese. Eventually, this cultural con-flict led to resistance efforts that ultimately ended with the restoration of Vietnamese independence in 939 CE.

Difficulty Level: Hard

50. **B.** The political system of feudalism came to dominate Western Europe primarily because of the European peoples' fear of attack from foreign invaders. After the Germanic invasions that led to the fall of the Roman Empire in the fifth century and the numerous Viking intru-sions of the ninth century, Europeans were left terrified and desperate for some form of protection from further violence. The feudal system offered the otherwise defenseless inhabitants of Europe with a sense of protection and safety.

Difficulty Level: Hard

Using the Diagnostic Test

Calculating Your Score

Calculating your raw score for the SAT Subject Test in World History isn't difficult. Follow the steps below to approximate your raw score.

1. Count the items you answered correctly. Write that number here:

_____

2. Count the items you answered incorrectly. Write that number here, then perform the calculation:

_____ × .250 = _____

3. Subtract the results of #2 from the total in #1:

_____ – _____ = _____

4. Take the results of #3 and round up or down as necessary to obtain a whole number: _____

This is your raw score. The College Board goes one step further and translates your raw score into a scaled score. It isn't necessary to take that extra step to determine how well you'll perform. If you obtained a high raw score (maximum: 80), that would translate to a high scaled score (800). Congratulations! You're definitely ready to ace this exam. If, on the other hand, you obtained a low raw score (say, 20 or under), that would translate to a low scaled score, roughly 450. Remember, you want to hit *at least* the average national score (for 2011, this was 607 for the SAT Subject Test in World History). Although the exact number you must achieve will vary from year to year, you should try to get a minimum raw score of around 50 to hit the average.

Improving Your Score

How do you feel about your performance? Remember, the diagnostic examination in this book is meant to help you identify your weak areas and show you where you may need to improve in terms of either the content you are studying *or* your actual test-taking habits. Don't underestimate the importance of good test-taking habits; for standardized examinations such as this one, your approach is every bit as important as the knowledge you bring to the table.

Assess your performance *honestly*. Go back through the test and review the questions you answered correctly, those you answered incorrectly, and those you skipped. Can you identify patterns or trends in your incorrect or missed answers? Did you make dumb mistakes by failing to read all of the answer options or by misreading the questions? Did you miss many core concepts? Also review the vocabulary terms you highlighted. Are these similar in nature or related to particular concepts or ideas? If you have time, make an effort to follow up on this material. Close the gaps in your knowledge so they aren't a problem when you get to your actual test.

Finally, how did you do with time? Did you run out of time? Were you rushing to finish within the allotted time period? Did you spend too much time on each individual question? Or did you fail to spend *enough* time? Remember, successful test-taking is as much about managing your time as it about understanding the content.

A Final Word about the Diagnostic Test

Finally, don't feel too bad if you didn't do well on this diagnostic test the first time through. After all, the entire point of this book is to give you the opportunity to identify areas for improvement and to give you the materials for practice. Use this book to test and retest, until you feel thoroughly comfortable with both the setup and the content of the examination.

Before moving on, head back to **The Main Course** and review the test-taking strategies discussed there. Now that you've had an opportunity to test, some of the test-taking strategies will make a whole lot more sense to you. As you move forward, you'll be able to see more specifically how you can apply these strategies to your advantage.

World History Review

As the test date of your SAT World History Subject Test approaches, you will need to take some time to prepare for the test. Here are some things you might want to do before the big day arrives:

- Get started by taking the **Diagnostic Test** on page 53. The diagnostic test will help you become familiar with the format of the test and the types of questions you will encounter on it. Once you have finished the test, check your answers and look for any subject areas or question types you had difficulty with. Watch for trends in specific time periods, subject matter, or type of question. You may need to spend a little extra time brushing up on any (or all!) of these.

- Review all the test's key topics by reading through all of the sections in this review chapter. Again, pay close attention to any areas you struggled with on the diagnostic test.

- Read through the question strategies on pages 41–50. Take some time to familiarize yourself with the different types of questions that you will encounter on the SAT World History Subject Test. We've provided lots of helpful hints for tackling them.

- Take the practice tests! You will find two full-length practice tests in this book. Taking both of them will help to improve your understanding of the material as well as your ability to work through the test accurately and efficiently. If you would like even more practice, you can find an additional practice test on our website: mymaxscore.com.

- On the night before you take the test, take another look at **The Essentials: A Last-Minute Study Guide** (page 1) and reread that material to make sure that you are fully prepared on test day.

- Pack up everything you need for the test, and get some sleep! By the time you arrive for your test, you will be ready to maximize your score!

Review Chapter 1: Prehistory to Early Civilizations

The earliest stages of humankind's existence on Earth are traditionally referred to as *prehistory*. This period, which is generally accepted to span from the emergence of the earliest humanlike species to the dawn of early civilizations, is divided into two distinct eras: the Paleolithic ("ancient stone") Age and the Neolithic ("new stone") Age.

The Paleolithic Age

It is widely believed that the first humanlike species appeared in Africa somewhere between 3 million and 6 million years ago. These early relatives of modern humans, known as *hominids*, were known for their ability to walk upright. The earliest preserved example of a hominid is "Ardi," a female who belonged to a hominid species known as *Ardipithecus ramidus*. Previously, this honor belonged to "Lucy," a member of the *Australopithecines* hominid species, who was discovered in Ethiopia by Donald Johanson in 1974. *Australopithecines* were the first species of hominid to produce and use simple tools made of stone.

Around 2.5 million years ago, *Homo habilis* (literally "handy man") appeared. These were the first hominids to be classified in the same species as modern humans. *Homo habilis*, like *Australopithecines*, also used basic stone tools.

The following major evolutionary step for humankind came with the emergence of *Homo erectus* about 1.4 million years ago. Well-known examples of *Homo erectus* include Java Man and Peking Man. *Homo erectus* made tools that were larger and more varied than those of their predecessors.

One of the most important stages of human development came when *Homo sapiens* ("wise humans") first appeared between approximately 500,000 and 195,000 years ago. For a time, two separate *Homo sapiens* species coexisted: *Neanderthals* and early modern humans, *Homo sapiens sapiens*. Both species made tools, used fire, and developed funerary rituals. Eventually, the Neanderthals went extinct between 35,000 and 28,000 years ago.

Scientists tend to disagree over exactly how *Homo sapiens* evolved and spread across the globe. The most widely accepted theory states that the evolution of *Homo erectus* into *Homo sapiens* occurred in Africa and that the species spread as *Homo sapiens* began to move out of Africa. The other theory holds that *Homo erectus* had already begun to migrate out of Africa when the shift toward *Homo sapiens* began, which means that *Homo sapiens* would have evolved in other regions of the world (e.g., Asia) at roughly the same time.

Although early humans evolved a great deal throughout the course of the Paleolithic Age, there are a number of key cultural attributes that define the period. Most notably, all Paleolithic human species were hunter-gatherers, meaning that their survival depended on their ability to hunt wild animals and gather whatever edible plant life they could find. As a result, most early humans were *nomadic*, moving from place to place to find new sources of food.

Over time, the early humans developed tools; learned how to use fire for cooking and heating; and near the end of the Paleolithic era, began to create art in the form of cave drawings. It was also during this time that the first spoken languages began to develop.

The Neolithic Age

The end of the Paleolithic Age was marked by a series of ice ages that had a profound impact on how early humans lived. By about 7000 BCE, the ice ages had significantly changed the landscape of Earth. Traditional practices of hunting and gathering no longer provided humans with sufficient food for survival. As a result, humans were forced to turn to agricultural pursuits to meet their need for sustenance. This Agricultural Revolution (or Neolithic Revolution) marked the beginning of the Neolithic Age.

One of the first and most significant changes spurred on by the rise of agriculture in the Neolithic Age was a shift from nomadism to the establishment of permanent settlements. Because people had to depend on the land for survival, they were forced to set up settlements where they could work the soil and grow crops.

The emergence of agriculture also affected the size of the human population. The nutritional benefits provided by crops grown in permanent settlements were significantly greater than the benefits provided by the food humans procured through hunting and gathering. As a result, this shift toward agriculture helped improve human health and led to an increase in the overall population.

Agriculture also had an important impact on the role of women in early societies. Initially, agriculture gave women an important social status, most likely because they were often responsible for carrying out the duties of farming. Later, however, as farming became a job that required the use of heavy equipment, agriculture became a male-dominated field. Although women no longer enjoyed the high social standing that came with being responsible for carrying out agricultural duties, their social status was bolstered as they took on other duties, such as raising children, preserving food, and managing household affairs.

Finally, the Agricultural Revolution also led to the development of the first small towns. As populations grew, it became increasingly apparent that not everyone needed to be a farmer. This resulted in the specialization of labor and development of other businesses and services, as well as early forms of trade. Eventually, this encouraged the growth of small towns, such as Jericho and Çatalhüyük. In time, as these small towns grew into cities and early civilizations began to emerge, the Neolithic Era gradually came to a close.

Emergence of Civilization

As cities and towns began to appear in the ancient world, the cultures that developed around them began to grow into civilizations. A civilization is a complex society in which a large number of people share a broad range of characteristics. Most civilizations include elements such as an urban center of development, a clear religious structure, organized political and military systems, an economic social-class structure, a written language, and participation in artistic and intellectual endeavors.

Many of the earliest civilizations were formed in river valleys. These valleys offered the type of rich, fertile soil that was ideal for agricultural pursuits. One of the earliest and most important of those civilizations was located in a region of the Middle East known as the Fertile Crescent, which stretches in an arc from the Persian Gulf to follow the Tigris and Euphrates rivers northwest into Turkey and southwest to the Mediterranean Sea.

Mesopotamia and Sumer

In the Middle Eastern region that today is Iraq, the fertile valley between the Tigris and Euphrates rivers was settled by the Sumerians sometime between 4500 and 3500 BCE. This area would later be called Mesopotamia ("land between the rivers") by the Greeks. The valley was uniquely suitable for agricultural development. Every year, the Tigris and Euphrates would flood their banks and leave behind a layer of enriching silt. Although these violent floods often caused damage, the silt deposits left behind made the land perfect for farming. As a result, Sumer quickly flourished into one the most advanced and historically significant civilizations of its time.

Another reason for the success of the Sumerian civilization was the development of an advanced irrigation system that further increased the agricultural viability of the land. This resulted in food surpluses that led to increases in population and served as the foundation of the civilization.

Aside from agriculture, the Sumerians also made important contributions in many other areas. One of their most significant accomplishments was their written form of language, known as *cuneiform*. Cuneiform writing was made by pressing a stylus into moist clay. The language itself was composed of pictographs that represented various ideas and sounds.

As the civilization developed, the Sumerians became increasingly interested in trading with other cultures. Eventually, they developed trading relationships with other communities both near and far, often exchanging agricultural products, glass, and pottery for other goods. At its height, the Sumerian trading business extended over a significant portion of the ancient world.

In terms of religion, Sumer was a polytheistic society, which meant that the Sumerians believed in a system of many gods. Specifically, they believed that their gods controlled nature, and because nature and weather were so vital to their way of life, the Sumerians generally viewed their deities with fear and trepidation. The best surviving record of the Sumerian religion is the *Epic of Gilgamesh*, the world's first epic poem. *The Epic of Gilgamesh* offers a detailed description of the Sumerians' relationship with their deities and includes the Sumerian version of the creation story, as well as a flood story quite similar to Noah in the Judeo-Christian Scriptures.

Like most other great civilizations, Sumer had a distinct, three-tiered social-class system. The Sumerian upper class was composed of kings, priests, members of the nobility, and government officials. The middle class was composed of traders, farmers, and artisans. The third and lowest class was reserved for slaves.

Because of the fertility of the land, Sumer was a prime target for invasion and, despite its thriving economy, was eventually conquered. The first major invasion of Sumer came around 2300 BCE, when the Semitic warrior Sargon the Great seized control in the name of the Akkadian Empire. Although the Akkadian Empire would eventually decline, Sumer and the rest of Mesopotamia would fall under the control of various other cultures. Most notable among these were the Babylonians, who are best known for the penal code created by the emperor Hammurabi (ca. 1750 BCE). The *Code of Hammurabi*, like other legal systems from the Mesopotamian region, was based on a system of retaliatory punishment (for example, "an eye for an eye").

Over time, Mesopotamia's prominence on the world stage fell into decline. In the sixth century BCE, the Persians took over the region, and likely as a result of overuse, the once-rich land of the Fertile Crescent slowly became unable to support what remained of the once-great land of Sumer.

Ancient Egypt

While Sumer was developing along the banks of the Tigris and Euphrates rivers, another civilization was developing in a similar fashion farther to the west. The Nile River in Egypt also flooded its banks each year, making the soil in the surrounding area ideal for agriculture. The Egyptians built farming villages along the Nile, the earliest of which may have appeared around 4400 BCE. As did the Sumerians, the Egyptians augmented their supply of water through artificial means. They built special reservoirs from which they could transport water into their fields through a system of ditches.

One of the key differences between Egypt and Sumer was in their vulnerability to attack from outside invaders. Whereas Sumer was relatively exposed and susceptible to invasion, Egypt was more protected by natural barriers. The rapidly flowing water of the Nile River; the vastness of the Mediterranean Sea; and the massive, inhospitable deserts that surrounded Egypt all served to isolate the region and protect it from invaders.

As Egyptian civilization developed, the farming villages that sprang up along the Nile eventually united with one another to form two separate kingdoms. Around 3200 BCE, the villages in the north became Lower Egypt, and those in the south became Upper Egypt. This arrangement lasted only about one hundred to two hundred years, however, before the two kingdoms were united into a single Egypt by a king named Menes. As a result of the unification, Menes became the first *pharaoh*, or ruler of the entirety of Egypt.

Egypt's history from this point on is divided into three main periods: the Old Kingdom (3100–2200 BCE), the Middle Kingdom (2100–1650 BCE), and the New Kingdom (1550–700 BCE). In addition, the Middle Kingdom was both preceded and followed by brief intermediate periods.

The Old Kingdom era, which began with the unification of the Egyptian kingdoms, was marked by the construction of a large number of extravagant tombs, monuments, and other buildings. Most notably, the pharaoh Khufu (2589–2566 BCE) ordered the building of the Great Pyramid of Giza, while his son, Khafra, oversaw the creation of the *Sphinx*, a large stone carving of his head on the body of a lion.

During the time between the Old Kingdom and the Middle Kingdom, Egypt experienced a period of chaos when the central power of the pharaohs diminished and the kingdoms became divided again. Thanks to the powerful leadership of the pharaohs of the Middle Kingdom, Egypt was eventually reunited. The great achievements of this era included the construction of the pharaoh Mentuhotep's great mortuary complex and a renewed interest in literature and the visual arts.

Following the Middle Kingdom era, Egypt was overrun by foreign invaders known as the Hyksos, who would control the region for about a century. The New Kingdom era began with the expulsion of the Hyksos from Egypt. Among the notable events of the New Kingdom was the beginning of the construction of tombs in the Valley of the Kings under Thutmose I, as well as the brief reign of famed pharaoh Tutankhamen ("King Tut").

Throughout most of history, the Egyptians, like the Sumerians, were polytheistic, which means they worshipped a variety of gods. They developed complex funerary rituals that included *mummification* and the use of ornate burial chambers. For a brief time between 1349 and 1336 BCE, the pharaoh Akhenaton attempted to convert the Egyptians to the monotheistic worship of a single sun god. However, the priests refused to accept this new religion, and it ultimately failed.

Another similarity between the Egyptians and the Sumerians was the nature of their social structures. Egypt, like Sumer, had a rigid, three-tiered social class system with priests and nobles at the top, common peasantry in the middle, and slaves at the bottom.

One of ancient Egypt's greatest achievements was its written language, known as *hieroglyphics*. This unique language used pictures to represent a wide range of ideas and sounds. Our ability to translate hieroglyphics is, in large part, due to the discovery of the *Rosetta stone*, a carving with identical inscriptions in hieroglyphics, Greek, and Demotic (a variation on basic hieroglyphics). First located by Napoléon Bonaparte's forces during his Egyptian campaign in 1798, the Rosetta stone allowed linguists to decipher hieroglyphics.

In the waning years of its power, Egypt fell under the control of the Greeks and, later, the Romans. When it eventually became a province of Rome, ancient Egypt's history as an independent civilization came to a close.

Indus River Valley Civilization

The development of civilization was not limited to Sumer and Egypt. In the region known today as Pakistan, another civilization formed in the Indus River valley. Although we know relatively little about the original Indus River civilization, its subsequent incarnation would have a substantial impact on the development and culture of the Indian subcontinent.

Most of what is known today about this civilization comes from the ruins of two major cities, Harappā and Mohenjo-daro. Both cities provide evidence for the sophistication of the early Indus River society. Most notably, Harappā and Mohenjo-daro had nearly identical layouts, with meticulously designed street plans, similarly constructed buildings, and a simple form of indoor plumbing. It is believed that the Indus River civilization flourished before it fell into decline around 1900 BCE.

Around 1500 BCE, the Indus River valley was invaded by a race of Indo-Europeans known as the Aryans. The Aryans, who came from parts of today's Iran and Afghanistan, a warrior people that rode horses, ate meat, and hunted with bow and arrow, marched onto the Indian subcontinent through the Khyber Pass and immediately assumed control over the native Indus Valley people. One of the most significant changes the Aryans made to the traditional Indus way of life came with the introduction of a new system of social stratification. Because the Aryans were of a lighter skin tone than the native Indus people, the class system was based on skin color. Believing themselves to be superior, the lighter-skinned Aryans reserved the three uppermost classes for themselves. The highest-ranking class (Brahman) was occupied by priests (known as *Brahmins*). Warriors and rulers belonged in the second class (Kshatriya) and farmers, traders, artisans, and freemen in the third (Vaishya). The lowest class (Shudra) included unskilled workers, peasants, and bonded serfs. A separate category of social outcasts also existed; they were known as *pariahs*, or untouchables. Eventually, the classes established by the Aryans became fixed social castes determined solely by birth.

The primary historical record of the Aryan-era Indus River valley civilization is the *Vedas*, a four-volume collection of hymns, prayers, magical texts, mantras, chants, and a priestly textbook for conducting rituals. In addition to their role as a form of historical documentation, the Vedas eventually became one of the main spiritual texts of the religion that would soon come to dominate the Indian subcontinent: *Hinduism*.

The most influential result of the Aryan invasion of the Indus River valley was the emergence of the Hindu religion. Based on the Vedas, as well as other works such as the *Upanishads*, the *Mahabharata*, and the *Ramayana*, Hinduism would eventually become a major world religion.

Hindus typically believe that life as we see it is no more than an illusion and that all people are reincarnated after death on the basis of their *karma,* or their deeds in life. People find themselves in a higher or lower caste in the next life depending on whether their karma is good or bad.

THE PRIMARY DEITIES OF HINDUISM			
NAME	**TITLE**	**ASPECT**	**VEHICLE**
Brahma	The Creator	Male	Swan
Vishnu	The Preserver	Male	Garuda (bird)
Shiva	The Destroyer	Male	Bull
Saraswati	Goddess of Knowledge, Music, and Arts	Female	Swan
Lakshmi	Goddess of Wealth and Prosperity	Female	Owl
Parvati	The Divine Mother	Female	Lion

Hinduism was not the only major world religion to be established on the Indian subcontinent. Around 500 CE, questions about the meaningfulness of Hinduism led to the birth of Buddhism. This spiritual system was the brainchild of a young philosopher named Siddhartha Gautama. After taking a long, unsuccessful journey in the hopes of finding an explanation for suffering in the world, Gautama came to the conclusion that suffering was the result of humankind's desires. Renaming himself *Buddha* ("The Enlightened One"), for the remainder of his life, Gautama continued to teach his followers, who subsequently spread Buddhism throughout India and the world.

TENETS OF BUDDHISM
THE FOUR NOBLE TRUTHS

1. Human life is filled with sorrow and suffering.
2. Suffering is caused by desire.
3. By rejecting or removing desire, suffering is ended.
4. Nirvana is attained by following the Eightfold Path.

TENETS OF BUDDHISM

THE EIGHTFOLD PATH

1. Right view
2. Right intention
3. Right speech
4. Right action
5. Right living
6. Right effort
7. Right mindfulness
8. Right meditation

Ancient China

Like the Tigris and Euphrates rivers in Mesopotamia, the Nile River in Egypt, and the Indus River on the Indian subcontinent, the Huang He (Yellow River) in China also gave birth to one of the great early civilizations. The Huang He was named for its high concentration of *loess* (yellow silt) and was the birthplace of Chinese civilization. Despite regular devastating floods, a string of agricultural villages sprang up along the river's banks and produced key crops like wheat and millet.

Sometime around 1600 BCE, the agricultural villages along the Huang He were united under the banner of a nomadic people known as the *Shang*. As the Shang spread their customs and ideas among the people of the Huang He valley, they laid much of the groundwork for the way of life that would flourish in China for thousands of years to come. Among the most significant contributions of the Shang was the establishment of a new system of social stratification. In Shang society, the highest level of the social strata was reserved for kings, whereas warriors, artisans, traders, and peasants occupied the other levels.

The Shang also made scientific and technological contributions to Chinese society, such as introducing bronze as a material for producing weapons and other goods. During the Shang dynasty the Chinese began to cultivate silkworms and produce silk, which would later become one of China's most valuable trading commodities.

Perhaps the most important contribution of the Shang, however, was the introduction of a system of writing. The written language of the Shang used *ideographs* (characters) to represent various ideas. Most surviving examples of the Shang language were written on oracle bones. These were animal bones on which people inscribed questions for the deities. The bones would be taken to a spiritual guide known as an *oracle*; the oracle would heat the bones and find the answer to the question on the basis of the cracks that formed in the bone.

After a reign of about six hundred years, the Shang dynasty weakened. Around 1046 BCE, the Shang were overthrown by the Zhou dynasty. The Zhou based their claim to the Shang throne on what they termed the *mandate of heaven*, which they believed granted them the divine right to rule China. In the years following the rule of the Zhou, many of the succeeding dynasties would seize power using this same pretense.

Many historians agree that the most significant development during the Zhou dynasty was the emergence of a philosophy known as *Confucianism*. The creation of Confucius (Kung-fu-tzu), this philosophy espoused reverence of elders and ancestors, sound government, and the value of education. Confucius taught that social harmony could be achieved only if educated men controlled the government. The rise of Confucianism also led to the emergence of two alternative schools of philosophical thought: Daoism and legalism, founded by Lao Tzu and Shang Yang, respectively. *Daoism* revolved around the ideas of living closely with nature and following Dao ("the Way"), advocating a minimal government. *Legalism*, conversely, promoted the idea of a strong government with the power to prevent disorder.

Ancient Civilizations in Africa and the Americas

While these civilizations developed in the East, other civilizations emerged in other regions of the world. In Africa one such civilization was that of the migratory, Bantu-speaking people. The early Bantu lived near the rain forests of present-day Nigeria before they began migrating southward and eastward around 2000 BCE. In the course of their travels, the Bantu encountered and assimilated many of the hunter-gatherer societies found in sub-Saharan Africa at the time. With the skills they acquired from these people and the discovery of a reliable source of sustenance in the form of crops such as bananas and yams, which were first brought to the island of Madagascar by sailors from Southeast Asia and subsequently spread westward through mainland Africa, the Bantu-speaking people expanded their territory to include a significant portion of the continent.

The Bantu migration had two key effects on cultures throughout sub-Saharan Africa. First, the spread of the Bantu language into Arabic regions led to the development of a new language called *Swahili*, a blend of Bantu and Arabic languages. Second, the Bantu speakers eventually developed the process of iron smelting. As with their language, they spread their iron-smelting techniques to other cultures as they traveled.

By around 1000 CE, the migration of the Bantu-speaking people established permanent settlements; however, they continued to migrate throughout the first millennium. Initially, Bantu society was based on a system of individual kinship groups, each led by a single family in charge of an entire family or group. Social expectations in Bantu society were often determined by the *age grade*, or a group in which people were divided by age. All those who fell into a specific age group were expected to carry out the responsibilities deemed appropriate for that age.

In time, a number of powerful kingdoms would emerge from the Bantu society, including the central African kingdom of Kongo, which eventually became the centralized state of the Bantu and, thanks to a thriving economy and viable currency, maintained a strong place among African cities until the sixteenth century.

As the number of permanent settlements grew, the kingdom of Kush in Eastern Africa also rose. Located in an area south of Egypt and rich with natural iron deposits, the Kush used their smelting techniques to turn their primary city, Meroe, into a major hub in the iron trade. As a result of this trade dominance, Meroe remained a major power until around 150 CE, when Kush fell under the control of the kingdom of Aksum.

The Nok, a West African culture from the region known today as Nigeria, was yet another African community that pioneered iron smelting. Primarily existing between 900 BCE and 200 CE, the Nok used their supply of iron and smelting skills to produce tools that could be used for agriculture and hunting. The Nok were also known for their terra-cotta sculptures.

Although it was largely isolated from the rest of the world, the Western Hemisphere also had a number of early civilizations. By around 7000 BCE, numerous small agricultural societies began to appear in parts of both North and South America. Historians theorize that these populations migrated to the Americas via land bridges, which appeared as a result of a variety of natural processes such as the rising and falling of sea levels and the movement of plate tectonics.

Around 1200 BCE, the Olmec became the first major civilization to emerge in the Americas. The Olmec constructed pyramids, compiled a basic system of written language, and invented both a numbering system and a sophisticated ritual calendar. Evidence also suggests that the Olmec may have been actively involved in trade with other cultures. Eventually, the Olmec would be succeeded by a number of other civilizations that would dominate the Americas until the arrival of Europeans.

Review Questions

1. Sumer and Egypt were similar in all of the following ways EXCEPT

   A. agricultural dependence on the silt left behind by flooding
   B. belief in a polytheistic religion centered on deities of nature
   C. enjoyment of protection from invasion by natural barriers
   D. development of distinct systems of written language
   E. engagement in trade with other nearby cultures

2. A follower of the Chinese philosophy of Daoism would MOST agree with which statement?

   A. Government intrusiveness should be kept to a minimum.
   B. Government works best when run by well-educated men.
   C. Government should be focused on strengthening the state.
   D. Governments that allow too much freedom are doomed to fail.
   E. Governments have an obligation to suppress independent thought.

3. Which of these was NOT a characteristic of early humans in the Paleolithic Age?

   A. Ability to make and use simple tools
   B. Tendency to live in permanent settlements
   C. Reliance on hunting and gathering techniques
   D. Propensity for creating artistic cave drawings
   E. Mastery of fire for cooking and heating purposes

4. Buddhism was founded in part as a response to questions about which faith?

   A. Islam
   B. Daoism
   C. Judaism
   D. Hinduism
   E. Christianity

5.   The Kush city of Meroe rose to prominence mainly because of its natural supply of

    A.   salt
    B.   iron
    C.   gold
    D.   grain
    E.   silver

Answer Explanations

1. **C.** Although Sumer and Egypt had many similarities, the degree to which the natural surroundings safeguarded each from invasion was quite different. Whereas Egypt was relatively insulated from outside attacks by dangerous waterfalls, impassible deserts, and the vast Mediterranean Sea, Sumer was more exposed and was, in fact, subject to invasion on numerous occasions.

2. **A.** The teachings of Daoism state that since people are generally incapable of self-governance, the least government is the best government. As a result, followers of Daoism would be most likely to agree with the statement "Government intrusiveness should be kept to a minimum."

3. **B.** The early humans of the Paleolithic Age did not usually live in permanent settlements. Because these humans were primarily hunter-gatherers, they were forced to move from place to place to find food. They were mostly nomadic. Humans would not begin to establish permanent settlements until the agricultural revolution of the Neolithic Age.

4. **D.** In its early stages, Buddhism arose in part because some followers questioned Hinduism.

5. **B.** Meroe became a major trading power mainly because of its natural iron deposits. With such vast amounts of readily available iron at their disposal, the Kush, having developed their own smelting techniques, managed to produce a variety of iron goods that they could use for trading with other cultures. The iron trade eventually made Meroe one of Africa's principal trading cities.

Review Chapter 2:
The Great Empires

Ancient Greece

As civilizations developed around the world, one particularly important civilization emerged in the Aegean Sea region: Greece. At its height, ancient Greece would become one of the most influential cultures in history, leaving behind a legacy that is still felt today.

The Roots of Ancient Greece

The first civilization to appear in the Aegean region was that of the Minoans, who settled on Crete, an island located south of the Greek mainland, and thrived between 2600 and 1450 BCE. The Minoans were commercially active, establishing trading relations with many other civilizations. The remains of the palace at Knossos, an extravagant royal dwelling, is evidence of their vast wealth.

Around 1450 BCE, the Minoan culture fell into an abrupt decline. Although the exact cause of the decline is unknown, the prevailing theory is that it resulted from an invasion by the Mycenaeans, who lived on the Greek mainland. The warlike Mycenaeans assumed control of Crete between 1700 and 1100 BCE and started their own trading network. For a time, the Mycenaean civilization prospered and conquered other Aegean islands. Before long, however, Mycenaean cities on the

Greek mainland began to destabilize as different invaders overran them. Wracked by internal struggles, the Mycenaean civilization finally collapsed around 1100 BCE.

The end of the Mycenaean civilization marked the beginning of a difficult time in Greek history, known as the Dark Age. Although a number of peoples lived in Greece at the time, a group called the *Dorians* largely dominated the region. During the Dorian period, a significant number of Greeks migrated to Asia Minor. This led to a sharp decline in food production, and Greece plunged into a state of disarray. Perhaps the main reason Greece survived the Dark Age was the emergence of a new political unit called the *polis* (city-state). Each city-state, which was composed of a major city and the land surrounding it, was independently governed. Isolated from one another by Greece's mountainous landscape, the city-states flourished, and Greece slowly emerged from the Dark Age.

Another important element in Greece's revitalization was the introduction of new written language. The original written languages of the Greeks, which had been created by the Minoans and the Mycenaeans, were lost in the Dark Age. The Greeks constructed a new language based on a modified version of the Phoenician alphabet. Once this language was in place, the earliest examples of Greek literature began to appear. Most notable among them were the works of the famed poet Homer. Around the ninth century BCE, Homer wrote the *Iliad* and the *Odyssey*, a pair of epic poems telling the story of the Trojan War. These serve as two of the earliest written records of Greek culture and mythology.

The Rise of Sparta and Athens

As classical Greece developed, two of its city-states emerged as the dominant cultural epicenters of the civilization: Sparta and Athens. Although the two were quite dissimilar, they would each play crucial roles in Grecian history.

SPARTA

Sparta was an agricultural military state located on the Peloponnesian Peninsula. Its population was composed of a relatively small percentage of actual Spartans and a large majority of agricultural laborers known as *helots*, who were people whom the Spartans had conquered in Laconia and Messina. The Spartan government, though it had a ceremonial dual monarchy and a freely elected assembly, was, in fact, governed largely by a group of five elected officials known as *ephors*.

The all-encompassing goal of the Spartans was to increase the strength of the state through military force. The entire Spartan society was built around its military. All Spartan men were required to serve in the military, and all Spartan women were expected to produce healthy children, particularly boys, since they were a vital resource for the military. When male children reached the age of seven, they were removed from their homes and placed in military barracks. Although they were free to leave the barracks once they turned thirty, military service continued until they reached the age of sixty.

The Spartan commitment to the military state was so strong that the population lived under strict laws that severely limited personal freedoms. As a result of their single-minded devotion to their military, the Spartans, in stark contrast to the Athenians, made few contributions to the arts or sciences.

ATHENS

Early in its history, Athens, which was located on the peninsula of Attica, was ruled first by a monarchy and, later by wealthy landowners. This system of government proved ineffective and led to severe economic turmoil. Eventually, Athens evolved into a direct democracy governed by an assembly in which all official citizens of society had a say in legislative matters. However, official citizenship was limited to male Athenians over the age of twenty-two who had served in the military.

As opposed to the extreme military focus of Sparta, Athens was a highly cultured society. The Athenians placed great value on arts and sciences and made significant contributions to both fields. One scientific field in which the Athenian Greeks particularly excelled was philosophy. Athens produced many of the world's earliest and most influential philosophers, and they made significant contributions to the fields of astronomy, chemistry, physics, mathematics, and others.

KEY GREEK PHILOSOPHERS		
PHILOSOPHER	LIVED	NOTABLE ACCOMPLISHMENTS
Socrates	470–399 BCE	Introduced the "Socratic method" of teaching that encouraged students to question everything.
Plato	c.428–348/347 BCE	Wrote *The Republic*, in which he outlined his idea of a perfect state as one ruled by philosophers.
Aristotle	384–322 BCE	Student of Plato; theorized about government and argued that a constitutional government would be the best form of governance for most peoples.

Although the Athenians produced many valuable examples of literature, architecture, sculpture, and other forms of art, their greatest artistic contribution was to the field of drama. The plays written by Greek dramatists were classified as one of two forms: tragedy or comedy. Tragedies were serious dramas that often focused on a strong main character who possessed many great qualities and one fatal flaw. Some of the most notable tragedies included *Oedipus Rex* and *Antigone* (both written by Sophocles) and *Medea* (written by Euripides). Comedies were lighter dramas that included humor and satire. Among the best-known Greek comedies was *Lysistrata*, written by Aristophanes.

Like other Greeks, the Athenians adhered to a polytheistic religion centered on humanlike gods. Greek deities included Zeus, the chief god; Hera, his mate; Athena, the goddess of wisdom; Apollo, the god of the sun; Aphrodite, the goddess of love; Poseidon, the god of the sea; and Hades, the god of the underworld, among many others.

Persia

In the fifth century, Athens and Sparta faced a mutual enemy from the east: Persia. Hailing from present-day Iran, the Persians built a vast empire through military force. As early as 546 BCE, the Persians had turned their attention toward Greece, conquering several of the Greek city-states located in Asia Minor. Later, after some of these city-states attempted to revolt with the help of the Athenian navy, the Persians sought to take revenge on Athens and establish a presence on the Greek mainland.

The animosity between the Greeks and Persians culminated in the Persian Wars, which lasted from 490 to 449 BCE. At the Battle of Marathon, the first of the two major battles of the conflict, the Athenians defeated the Persians. Determined to attack Athens directly, the Persians devised a battle plan that required them to first take on the Spartans at Thermopylae. Although the three-hundred-man Spartan army was vastly outnumbered and largely powerless to stop the Persian advance, they fought to the very end to slow the Persians as much as possible. Eventually, the Persians reached and sacked Athens. Later the Athenian navy defeated them. The Athenians then joined forces with a number of other Greek city-states to expel the Persians from Greece completely.

The Athenian victory secured Athens's place as the leading Greek city-state. As Athens became increasingly powerful, its relationships with some of the other city-states grew strained. In particular, the relationship with Sparta became tense. When Sparta chose to defend the Corinthians against Athenian advances, the Spartans and Athenians declared war on each other. Known as the Peloponnesian War, this conflict led to Athenian defeat and the end of classical Greek culture.

Alexander the Great

The squabble between Athens and Sparta continued even after the Spartan victory. Philip II of Macedon, the monarch of the Macedon kingdom to the north of Greece, seized the opportunity to attack his southerly neighbors. By 336 BCE, his forces had taken full control of Greece. A short time after, Phillip II was assassinated; his son Alexander succeeded him. Alexander the Great, as he came to be known, had once been a student of Aristotle. He would go on to build one of the world's first great empires.

Alexander's army defeated the Persians in 333 BCE. Over the following two years, he conquered Egypt, Mesopotamia, Asia Minor, and Syria, all with the goal of uniting the territory under his imperial control. Alexander's efforts took him as far east as India, where he intended to complete his mission of conquest. By the time he got there, however, his troops, who had been fighting constantly for years, refused to move into the Indian subcontinent and subsequently dispersed. Not long after, Alexander died of a fever at the age of thirty-two.

Alexander's conquests gave rise to Alexander's vision of the *Hellenistic* culture, or one that combined many elements of East and West. Alexander also spread the Greek culture throughout the ancient world. After Alexander's passing, Athens and Sparta resumed their place as the dominant Greek city-states. Their power was greatly diminished, however, and they were highly vulnerable to invasion. As a result of their collective weakness, in 146 BCE, they fell under the control of the newest power emerging in the Mediterranean region: Rome.

Rome

With Alexander's defeat of the Persians and the decline of the Greeks, the civilization of Rome on the Italian Peninsula was positioned to become the leading culture of its time. Eventually, Rome would become one of the most widespread and dominant empires in history.

Early Rome

According to legend, Rome itself was founded in 753 BCE by Romulus, who, along with his twin brother Remus, was said to have been abandoned as a young child along the banks of the Tiber River by his father

Aeneas. According to the story, a she-wolf rescued Romulus and Remus, and Romulus later founded Rome and proclaimed himself its first king.

In reality, Rome can be traced back to around 800 BCE, when a group known as the Etruscans entered and settled in the Italian Peninsula. The Etruscans established a monarchical government and a strong military force. Etruscan culture would have a significant impact on that of their Roman successors.

The Roman Republic

In 509 BCE, the landowning aristocracy of Rome dethroned the Etruscan king. In his place, they established the Roman Republic. The Republic divided citizens into two classes: *patricians* and *plebeians*. The patricians accounted for the upper class of Roman society and exercised the most political control. They were responsible for electing both the *consuls*, the "executive branch" of the Roman government, and the members of the Senate, Rome's major legislative body.

Initially, the plebeians, who comprised the majority of Rome's population, held very little political power beyond the right to vote. In time, members of the plebeian class would be allowed to hold seats in the Senate. They also operated their own assembly, the *Tribal Assembly*, through which they could elect *tribunes*, or representatives who supported their interests.

One of the most important accomplishments of the early Roman government was the writing of the *Twelve Tables* in 451 BCE. The Twelve Tables set forth the fundamental tenets of Roman law, guaranteeing that all Roman citizens had a right to be protected by law. Although they were modified over time, the Twelve Tables remained an integral part of the structure of Roman society.

In time, Rome began to expand beyond its original borders. By 265 BCE, Rome had assumed control of almost all of Italy. Rome's ability to conquer neighbors was due, in large part, to a large and skilled army. The army was divided into a series of *legions*, each of which was composed of about five thousand to six thousand well-trained men. In addition, a cavalry division complemented each legion. Enrollment in the Roman army was mandatory. Landowning citizens were expected to serve and supply their own weapons and other equipment.

Rome's success in expanding its territory was also attributable to its policies toward the natives that were conquered. Those geographically closest to Rome were allowed to become legal Roman citizens. More distant peoples were granted all the privileges of citizenship, save for the right to vote. Others were permitted to maintain their own governments and were simply considered allies. This uniquely tolerant approach to conquest strengthened Rome's power and tightened its grip over its territories.

The first major test of Rome's military might came in a series of battles with the North African people of Carthage, known as the Punic Wars. As two of the leading powers in the western Mediterranean region, Rome and Carthage frequently found themselves in territorial disputes.

The First Punic War erupted in 264 BCE, and was fought for control of Sicily, an island with vital grain resources. Rome eventually emerged victorious. The Second Punic War (218 BCE) began when the Carthaginian general Hannibal marched his troops across the Alps and into Italy with the intention of taking Rome itself. Although his campaign was initially successful and resulted in massive losses for the Romans, he was eventually forced to retreat back to Carthage to defend the homeland against an invasion led by the Roman general Scipio. Once back in Carthage, Hannibal and the remnants of his forced were defeated.

The Third Punic War (149 BCE) marked Rome's final triumph over Carthage. Although any notion of Carthage being an actual threat to the Roman Republic had long since passed, the Romans were still anxious to avenge the heavy losses they endured at the hands of Hannibal. To that end, they launched a vicious attack on Carthage that destroyed the city. To ensure total victory, the Romans went so far as to salt the soil and either kill or enslave all surviving Carthaginians.

The Republic Becomes an Empire

The end of the Punic Wars marked the beginning of a difficult time for Rome. Managing Rome's vast territory was a formidable challenge. Of particular concern was the ever-increasing economic gap between the wealthy and the poor. In many Roman-conquered lands, large estates called *latifundia* appeared shortly after fighting had ceased. The owners of these estates were able to create an agricultural workforce by enslaving the former inhabitants of the land. Smaller landowners soon found themselves unable to compete and quickly becoming impoverished.

Rome's increasingly unstable economic situation led to a period of unrest and civil war. During this time, a number of military leaders came into power and attempted to alleviate the turmoil, though none of them were successful. The chaos continued until 49 BCE, when Julius Caesar took control of Rome.

Caesar began his ascent when he joined General Pompey and an aristocrat named Crassus to form the first *triumvirate*. The following year, he became consul and worked to gain the people's favor. He then spent the following ten years as proconsul of Gaul and used his military expertise to secure the entirety of Gaul in the name of Rome. In 49 BCE, following the death of Crassus, Caesar returned to Rome with the goal of seizing power from Pompey. For a time, he fled to Egypt, where he gained an important political supporter in Cleopatra, whom he installed as queen there. Before long, he returned to Rome, displaced Pompey, and accepted the title of "dictator for life."

As dictator, Caesar continued his public policies of appeasement by awarding citizenship to the people living in Roman provinces and by giving public land to military veterans and the poor. As popular as he was among the common people of Rome, he was distrusted and despised by many of the senators whose power he had greatly reduced. Convinced that he was trying to turn the Republic into a monarchy, the senators decided to take matters into their own hands, and Caesar was stabbed to death on the floor of the Senate on March 15, 44 BCE.

With Caesar's death, Rome entered another period of civil war to determine who would succeed Caesar as leader of the Republic. Initially, control of Rome fell into the hands of another triumvirate, this time composed of Marc Antony (a close military ally of Julius Caesar's), Lepidus, and Octavian (Caesar's nephew and adopted son). This arrangement lasted only a short while, as Lepidus was forced out and Octavian and Antony became bitter rivals. While commanding his military forces abroad, Antony met and fell in love with Cleopatra. Retreating to Egypt with Cleopatra, Antony assumed control of the eastern half of the empire and left the western half to Octavian. The two soon went to war with one another and Octavian emerged victorious. Antony and Cleopatra, unwilling to submit to Octavian's authority, took their own lives. Octavian then assumed total control of Rome and took on the title of *Augustus* (27 BCE), meaning "exalted one." With this, the Roman Empire was born.

For the following 207 years, Rome enjoyed a period of peace known as the *Pax Romana*. During this time, the ailing empire was revitalized and expanded to its greatest extent. Rome was at its height.

Rome and Christianity

As most other cultures of its time, the Romans practiced a polytheistic religion. Roman religion borrowed heavily from the spiritual heritage of the classical Greeks. It was the religion of Christianity, however, that would eventually come to dominate the Roman Empire.

In 63 BCE, the Romans took control of a region of Palestine inhabited by the Hebrews. They named this region Judea. It was here, around 4 BCE, that Jesus Christ, a figure who some believed was the Messiah promised to the Hebrew people in their sacred Scriptures, was born. Upon turning thirty years old, Jesus took up a public ministry with the help of his twelve apostles, spreading his teachings about *monotheism*, the relationship between God and man, and the promise of eternal life. Within just a few years, Hebrew and Roman officials alike began to view Jesus as a potential threat to authority. He was put to death. However, his message was spread by his followers across the Mediterranean and, eventually, into Rome itself.

Early Roman Christians took serious risks to practice their newfound faith. Abandoning traditional Roman religion and refusing to acknowledge the divinity of the emperor, the early Roman Christians were violently persecuted. Despite the hardships it faced, the Christian community of Rome grew quickly. In time, the influence of Christianity became so great that by the fourth century Emperor Constantine legalized its practice, and in 380 CE, Theodosius made it the official religion of the empire.

Once Christianity became a formally recognized religion, it developed its own organizational structure. The church as a whole was led by the bishop of Rome (the *pope*), while separate *dioceses* were controlled by *bishops*, who, in turn, led the priests who operated local parishes.

The Fall of Rome

While Christianity flourished, Rome crumbled. For some time, the Germanic tribes living in areas just outside Rome's borders had been undertaking periodic incursions into Roman territory. In the 400s, many of these tribes, threatened by the approach of Attila the Hun, began pushing deeper into Roman territory in the hopes of finding safety there. In addition, civil war caused a sharp decline in trade. These and other factors led to another economic crisis that significantly weakened the empire.

Desperate to repair the failing empire, the emperor Diocletian chose to split it in half between two emperors, in the hopes that this arrangement would make it easier to govern. The once-massive Roman Empire was divided into smaller eastern and western empires. While Rome itself remained the western capital, Constantine named Constantinople the capital of the east.

In the meantime, the Germanic tribes continued to press inward into Roman territory to escape the Huns. One of the tribes, the Visigoths, sacked the city of Rome in 410 CE. Later, the Romans would be forced to ally themselves with the Visigoths as a defense against the Huns. Although they won the battle, the Roman army was left in shambles and was unable to defend Rome further. In 476 CE, the last western Roman emperor, Romulus Augustus, was overthrown. Although Constantinople would continue on for nearly a thousand more years, the Roman Empire was at an end.

The Han Dynasty

As Rome reigned in the west, another power rose to dominance in the east. Between 206 BCE and 220 CE, the Han dynasty ruled over China during one of the most important and influential periods in its history.

The Han dynasty first rose with the fall of the Qin dynasty in 206 BCE. Upon defeating the Qin, rebel leaders Gaozu (also known as Liu Bang) and Xiang Yu assumed control of their territories and established separate kingdoms. Eventually, the two turned on each other in a bid for power. In the end, Gaozu emerged victorious and founded the Han dynasty.

As emperor, Gaozu quickly moved to establish a strong central government to control and secure the entire empire. In part, the operation of this government was made possible by a complex bureaucracy that was funded through the implementation of a tax system. Rather than making monetary contributions, peasants fulfilled their tax obligations by handing over part of their yearly agricultural harvest to the government. They were also required to complete a month of government labor or military service on a yearly basis. The Han government used this system of enforced labor to complete a variety of projects that helped improve the Chinese way of life.

The Han dynasty also used taxes to fund its educational system. In addition to maintaining an imperial university, the Han government established the first Chinese civil service test. This commitment to education was mainly due to adherence to Confucian philosophy.

In time, the Han dynasty moved beyond its original borders and evolved into an empire, conquering both Korea and Vietnam. The Han culture was also spread through migration to various parts of Southeast Asia.

The Silk Roads

Perhaps the single most important factor in the success of the Han dynasty, however, was the development of the Silk Roads, which were a series of trade routes that connected China to the west. The trading network built by the Chinese along the Silk Roads was a significant source of financial prosperity and helped to establish China on the world stage. Composed of both land and sea routes, the Silk Roads allowed China to conduct trade with the Roman Empire, Africa, other parts of Asia, and beyond.

As the name implies, the most important product traded along the Silk Roads was silk. As a particularly valuable commodity, silk was traded extensively, and the methods for its production quickly spread across China. Other trade goods included iron, spices, jewels, olive oil, and grain, among others.

The influence of the Silk Roads went beyond trade. The Silk Roads contributed to the spread of various religions between the cultures it connected. Early in their history, the Silk Roads helped facilitate the spread of Buddhism throughout the Eastern world. Later, the Silk Roads would also be an important conduit for the spread of Christianity into the Mediterranean region.

Unfortunately, the Silk Roads also helped encourage the spread of disease. Epidemics of disease in both Rome and China spread via the Silk Roads and caused significant declines in population. The reduced population, in turn, led to a decline in trade along the Silk Roads and diminished their importance.

The Fall of the Han Dynasty

As with Rome, the great success of the Han dynasty led to the circumstances that would eventually threaten the empire. Unequal distribution of land increased economic disparity between the rich and poor. In addition, the Han faced the challenges of simultaneously defending their borders from neighboring peoples while trying to expand territory. This inhibited the ability to do either and ultimately weakened their empire. The empire was further destabilized by ineffective government rule and peasant revolts.

In 9 CE, the turmoil in China led to the overthrow of the Han dynasty by Wang Mang, who installed himself as leader. By 23 CE, subsequent revolts forced Wang Mang to abdicate. After this brief interruption, the Han dynasty returned to power. Conditions failed to improve, however, and with the addition of epidemic disease and invasion by the neighboring Hsiung-nu, the empire continued in its decline. When the Han dynasty finally collapsed in 220 CE, hordes of barbarians flooded across its borders. As a result, China was plunged into a four-hundred-year period of turmoil and disorder.

Review Questions

1. During the first Punic War, the Romans were MOST interested in acquiring Sicily because it

   A. offered an array of natural resources
   B. could serve as a strategic military base
   C. would allow Rome to avenge civilian losses
   D. would increase Rome's ability to trade with the East
   E. could serve as a key location in a Carthaginian invasion of Italy

2. The Battle of Thermopylae was key to Athenian victory in the Persian War because it

   A. prevented the Persians from reaching and sacking Athens itself
   B. wiped out a large portion of the Persian army before it reached Athens
   C. delayed the Persians' approach and gave the Athenians time to prepare
   D. eliminated the Persian navy and forced them to rely on a land attack
   E. weakened Persian morale and left the soldiers unwilling to fight

3. Who split the Roman Empire into two halves?

    A. Augustus
    B. Diocletian
    C. Julius Caesar
    D. Constantine
    E. Marc Antony

4. Usage of the Silk Roads for trade declined near the end of the Han dynasty primarily due to

    A. economic conditions that made long-distance trade too expensive
    B. constant warfare that made roads unsafe for travel
    C. a decrease in the demand for silk goods in the Mediterranean
    D. a devastating shortage of Chinese silk
    E. epidemic disease that traveled along the roads and decimated the population

5. During the Dorian period, Greece experienced food shortages as the result of a

    A. period of unusually warm and dry weather conditions
    B. decrease in trade with other Mediterranean cultures
    C. long-term agricultural blight that damaged crops
    D. trend of immigration out of the Greek mainland
    E. war with Persia that used significant resources

Answer Explanations

1. **A.** Rome was primarily interested in taking control of Sicily during the first Punic War because of the valuable natural resources it provided. As a major grain-producing territory, Sicily could provide some strategic advantages to Rome, which was dependent on outside sources of grain for survival.

2. **C.** The Battle of Thermopylae played an important role in Athens's

success in the Persian Wars because it delayed the Persian army's approach and allowed the Athenians time to prepare for battle. At Thermopylae, the Persians had to first annihilate a three-hundred-man Spartan army to pass through the mountains and reach Athens. Although they were vastly outnumbered, the Spartans prevented the Persians from proceeding to Athens long enough to give the Athenians time to prepare. Although Athens was initially sacked, the Athenian navy eventually defeated the Persians.

3. **B.** The Roman Empire was formally divided into two halves by Diocletian. By 286 CE, the Roman Empire, which was in the midst of an economic crisis, had grown too large to be effectively governed in a single location by a single leader. To remedy this situation, Diocletian divided the empire in two.

4. **E.** The decline in trade along the Silk Roads near the end of the Han dynasty was primarily the result of a significant reduction in the population caused by epidemic disease that traveled the road. Because the Silk Roads connected so many different regions of the world, it was an ideal conduit for the transmission of disease. By the end of the Han dynasty, various diseases had taken a heavy toll on the population in China and elsewhere. As a result of the diminished population, trading decreased.

5. **D.** The food shortages that occurred in Greece during the Dorian period were the result of a trend of immigration out of the Greek mainland. During the Dorian period, also known as the Dark Age, many Greeks who had been living on the mainland immigrated over the Aegean Sea to Asia Minor. This trend caused a decline in food production on the mainland that left the remaining population to endure severe food shortages.

Review Chapter 3:
The Middle Ages

The Byzantine Empire

After the fall of the Western Roman Empire, the Eastern Roman Empire, Byzantium, continued to flourish for nearly a millennium. Byzantium thrived for many years as a result of its geographical location adjacent to an important strait, the Bosporus, which connected several seas and placed Byzantium at the center of several key trading routes. Because a massive amount of wealth was regularly exchanged along these trading routes, Byzantium prospered, but it was also a prime target for invaders.

The Rise of Byzantium

Following its emergence as the sole remnant of the Roman Empire in 395 CE, Byzantium began to develop as a major power in the Mediterranean world. In 527 CE, Justinian, one of the most influential emperors in Byzantine history, came to power. During the course of his reign, Justinian achieved several important accomplishments.

Justinian made it his goal to reclaim as much territory as possible of the former Western Roman Empire, which had been lost to Germanic tribes. Over time, Justinian's forces successfully regained control of the majority of Italy and some parts of Spain. By the end of his reign, he had also extended his empire into North Africa, Asia Minor, Syria, and Palestine.

More significant than his territorial conquests, however, were Justinian's attempts to codify Roman law. Byzantium had inherited a wealth of materials related to Roman law. Faced with the prospect of having to interpret the law through a confusing hodgepodge of Roman and Byzantine legal treatises, judicial commentaries, and so on, Justinian decided that the best course of action was to simplify the law using a system of codification. The Justinian Code was the end result of this effort. This code organized and simplified Roman law into a format that would be used for the remainder of Byzantium's existence.

Finally, Justinian rebuilt the capital city of Constantinople, which had been destroyed during a series of riots over taxes. The crown jewel of Justinian's new Constantinople was the famed Hagia Sophia. A high-domed church built in the typical Byzantine style of architecture, the Hagia Sophia would later be converted into a mosque by the Turks.

The Fall of Byzantium

The decline of the Byzantine Empire began with the death of Justinian in 565 CE. In addition, an outbreak of the plague lasted until around 700 CE, which significantly reduced the population. A weakened Byzantium was attacked by several enemies. The most notable invasion came from the Seljuk Turks, who eventually assumed control of much of the east, reducing Byzantium's food supply and its ability to collect taxes from the region.

Byzantium was also weakened by a major split in the Catholic Church. Theological differences, particularly over the use of icons, led to a bitter division among church leaders. In 1054, the church experienced a schism that led to the development of two separate groups of Catholics: the Roman Catholic Church in the West and the Eastern Orthodox Church in the East.

As Byzantium struggled to right itself, the Seljuk Turks began to experience difficulties of their own. When Seljuk leader Malik-Shāh died in 1092, the Seljuk Empire began to collapse. Leaders of Western Europe saw this as an opportunity to challenge the Seljuks for control of the "Holy Land" in a series of battles known as the *Crusades*. Although the Seljuks ultimately emerged victorious in the thirteenth century, they were still weak. Eventually, they were overthrown by another group of Islamic Turks known as the Ottomans. With very little land left under its control and few resources, Byzantium fell to the Ottomans in 1453.

Post-Roman Europe

After the fall of Rome, much of Western Europe came under the control of different Germanic groups, many of which were united by their conversion to Christianity. Eventually, one of these kingdoms, located in what was once the Roman province of Gaul, emerged as the most powerful. The success of the Franks was due in no small part to the support they received from the Roman Catholic Church, which increased both the power of the Franks and the political authority of the church itself.

The Franks reigned in Gaul until the eighth century, at which time the Carolingians came to power. In *Carolingian Gaul*, governmental power was held by a figure known as the *majordomo* (mayor of the palace) instead of a king. The first significant majordomo was Charles Martel, who increased the size of the Frankish territory and prevented the Turks from entering Western Europe. Martel was later succeeded by his son, Pippin the Short (also known as Pippin III), whose son Charlemagne would later become the most influential ruler in the entire Carolingian line.

Upon taking the throne, Charlemagne began to construct a vast European empire that extended to Rome and encompassed all of France, parts of Spain, as well as the Saxony region of Germany. His power was so great that in 800 CE, Pope Leo III crowned him Holy Roman Emperor, a move that placed him in control of a large portion of Western and Central Europe and increased the political authority of the pope. As a ruler, Charlemagne chose to travel around his kingdom solidifying control while leaving the governance of local regions to his counts.

Following Charlemagne's death in 814 CE, his crown passed to his son, Louis the Pious. However, neither Louis nor any Carolingian successor was able to maintain Charlemagne's empire. Eventually, the power of the Carolingians diminished and political solidarity dissolved.

Feudalism in Europe

The fragile situation in Europe was further exacerbated by a new threat: the Scandinavian Vikings. As a result of severe food shortages in their homeland, the Vikings traveled to other lands in search of food and new homes. The violence of their invasions left most Europeans terrified. A desperate need for protection from invasions of this sort led to the rise of the feudal system across Western Europe. In the feudal system, individuals (*vassals*) pledged their loyalty to a local lord. The lord ensured their safety in return for help with military service or agricultural work. As part of this agreement, vassals would receive *benefices*, or special privileges, usually in the form of a land grant known as a *fief*.

The feudal system also gave rise to *serfdom*, a central component of the economic system that evolved around feudalism. Most European communities were based around individual manors, or self-sufficient estates owned by nobles. The majority of the peasants that lived on the manor were considered *serfs*, who were permanently bound to the land. Even in cases when a noble sold his manor to another noble, the serfs remained with the manor and were given protection in exchange for agricultural and other duties.

Feudalism in Japan

As this system spread across Europe, a different form of feudalism developed in Japan. By this time, Japan had adopted the Chinese system of centralized government; however, the Japanese favored militarism over the bloated bureaucracy of the Chinese system. The era of centralized government in Japan culminated with the reign of the Heian court (794–1185). The rise of estates in Japan led to the development of a feudal system in which landowners called the *daimyo* ran the estate with help of warriors called *samurai*. The daimyo ensured the safety of the peasants, who were loyal to the lord in return. Like the serfs in Europe, the samurai were tied to the land.

The Mongols in China

The Mongols originated from a region just northwest of China. Starting in 1206, the Mongols launched a period of conquest that would eventually net them a massive empire to include a large portion of Asia, Persia, Russia, and much of Europe to the east of Vienna.

The domination of the Mongols began with early conquests in Asia. Led by Temujin, better known as Genghis Khan, the Mongols used military expertise and siege warfare technology to overpower the natives. The Mongol Empire expanded so rapidly that by Genghis Khan's death in 1227, it was necessary to divide the empire into four separate regions to maintain control. Each region was called a *khanate* and was ruled by a descendant of Genghis Khan. The four khanates were located in Persia, Russia, Central Asia, and China.

The Persian khanate began in 1231, when the Mongols invaded Persia and massacred a large portion of the population. After nearly thirty years, the Mongols finally overthrew the region. Rather than assuming direct control, however, the Mongols permitted the Persians to run their own government in exchange for regular tributes and peaceful relations.

The Russian khanate, also known as the Khanate of the Golden Horde, began with a Mongol invasion in 1237. During their occupation of Russia, the Mongols kept the Russians isolated from Western influences. The Mongol occupation led to the emergence of Moscow as a prominent Russian city, thanks to Prince Alexander Nevsky, who cooperated with the Mongols and conquered Russian cities that refused to pay tribute. The Mongols remained in Russia until Ivan III forced them out in 1480.

The Mongols also invaded Eastern Europe. In the 1240s, they seized control of various parts of the Polish, Hungarian, and German regions of

Europe. Although they attempted to push further eastward, they were eventually stopped at Vienna and forced to retreat.

By far the largest and most important region of Mongol dominance was China. In 1270, the Mongols established a Chinese tribute empire under the command of Kublai Khan, the grandson of Genghis Khan. Calling their empire the Yuan dynasty, the Mongols adopted the Chinese form of centralized government but instituted a number of changes. For example, the Mongols eliminated the civil service examination, allowed greater religious freedom, and put an end to Confucian education. The Mongols refused to assimilate into Chinese culture, and preferred to live separately. Although the Yuan dynasty later attempted to extend its reach into Japan and part of Southeast Asia, these excursions ultimately proved unsuccessful.

Between the 1250s and the 1350s, the Mongol-dominated Eurasian region enjoyed an era of extended peace called the Mongol Peace. During this period, the Mongol presence ensured that travel along the Silk Roads was safe, which helped to increase trade and prosperity. The Mongols also used diplomacy and established peaceful relationships with peoples from regions they did not control.

The increase in trade brought on by the Mongol Peace had unforeseen consequences. Although it was well known that disease traveled easily along the Silk Roads, the world was unprepared for the spread of the bubonic plague (known as the black death). Having been brought into China by the Mongols themselves, the plague spread outward along Eurasian trade routes and into Europe and Africa. In Europe, nearly a third of the population was wiped out by the plague.

In the fourteenth century, the Mongol Empire went into decline as the result of inept government and economic problems. Unable to control their spending, the Mongols printed more and more money, which in turn severely depressed its value. After losing the Persian khanate in 1335, the Mongols faced revolts from the Chinese. Already weakened by the bubonic plague, the Mongol Empire could no longer support itself. It collapsed in the face of Chinese resistance in 1368.

The Rise of Cities and Nation-States

During the latter half of the Middle Ages, the increase in trade led to urbanization. Many of the trading hubs of the medieval world grew into major cities that generated significant wealth. In many areas of Europe, urbanization helped lay the foundation for the return of centralized government and the end of feudalism.

Africa

Trade was a major factor in the emergence of several prominent African cultures and urban centers during this period. In West Africa, the kingdom of Ghana became an empire thanks to its ability to control the gold and salt trades. In some parts of Africa, salt was extremely scarce, and as a result of the crucial role it played in sustaining human life, its value in the region rivaled that of gold. Ghana continued to thrive until it was conquered by Muslims in 1076.

The gold and salt trades also contributed to the rise of Mali in West Africa. One of the larger Mali cities, Timbuktu, eventually became a major trading hub. The Mali trading empire flourished until 1403, by which time the sub-Saharan gold fields had shifted further east and out of Mali control. As the Mali fell into decline, the Songhai quickly took their place. Seizing control of the new gold fields, the Songhai rose to and remained in power until they were defeated by Moroccan invaders in 1591.

In southeast Africa, Zimbabwe also flourished thanks to the gold trade. Although Zimbabwe did not directly control any gold fields, the city of Great Zimbabwe was located near one of the key trading routes between the central African gold fields and the African coast. This helped the city become prosperous.

Europe

The Viking threat began to subside in the tenth century, allowing trade to reemerge. Trade, a growing population, and improved agricultural abilities helped restore economic stability in Western Europe and encourage the growth of cities.

One of the key factors in the return of trade in Europe was the Crusades. Although the Crusades ultimately failed in their primary objective, they did have a direct impact on trade. For the duration of the Crusades, the ships that transported troops to the Holy Land also returned various luxury goods to Italy. These goods traveled along various trade routes across the European mainland. Many of the cities through which these routes passed quickly grew into major urban centers.

In addition to reestablishing trade, the Crusades helped to foster economic growth, the exchange of ideas, and the shift of political power away from nobles and toward more powerful monarchs. They also contributed to the increasing political power of the Catholic Church and the pope.

Urbanization in Western Europe led to advancements in manufacturing and banking. As urban centers expanded, workers were needed. Many serfs left the feudal manors to reside in urban areas. As urban centers grew, the first trade organizations, known as guilds, were founded. Guilds helped establish uniformity in pricing and ensure that trade was conducted honestly. A new middle class arose among the city dwellers who took part in manufacturing, craftsmanship, banking, and other forms of commerce.

The transition away from the feudal system was hastened by the arrival of the bubonic plague in 1346. By 1351, the population of Europe was decimated. The serf population was particularly devastated by the plague, and a severely depleted workforce virtually crippled the feudal system. Technological advances and a second agricultural revolution further weakened feudalism.

EMERGENCE OF CENTRALIZED GOVERNMENTS

The roots of centralized government in Western Europe can be traced back to England and France. In England in the ninth century, Alfred the Great forced out the Viking invaders and united all of England under his rule. This unification was later strengthened following the Norman invasion of 1066. The Normans were led by William, Duke of Normandy.

William successfully invaded England and took the throne. As king, William declared all of England his property and doled out land to the Norman lords that were loyal to him. This unique form of feudalism marked the beginning of centralized government in England.

The evolution of centralized government in England took another major step forward in 1215 during the reign of King John. The nobility were frustrated by high levels of taxation and forced the king to sign a document guaranteeing basic political rights. Known as the *Magna Carta*, this document placed limitations on the power of the monarch and strengthened the rights of the nobility. Later, the Magna Carta would be adopted as a representation of the rights of all English people, not just the nobility.

In 1295 the first parliament was formed. Based on an earlier English legislative body called the Great Council, the first parliament, often referred to as the *Model Parliament*, had two houses: the *House of Commons*, composed of burgesses and knights, and the *House of Lords*, composed of bishops and nobles. This basic parliamentary model proved so successful that it continues to thrive today.

Centralized government in France also began with the unification of feudal communities. In 987, a group of feudal lords in a small region of France united under the leadership of Hugh Capet. Although the Capetian kingdom was initially small, it grew significantly over time with a series of successful rulers. The Capetian kingdom eventually encompassed all of modern-day France.

THE HUNDRED YEARS' WAR

Feudalism in Western Europe was ultimately brought to an end by the Hundred Years' War, which France and England fought for control of the French throne. The war began in 1337 when the last Capetian king died without a legitimate heir, and England's King Edward III declared himself ruler of France. After more than a century of fighting, France emerged victorious. By the war's end in 1453, the French monarchy had been strengthened and the sense of nationalism in both countries had grown significantly.

Mesoamerican Cultures

While medieval Europe was experiencing Viking invasions, feudalism, the plague, and the rise of nation-states, important civilizations were emerging in Mesoamerica. Starting around 250 CE, a number of Native American cultures appeared and came to dominate the regions of Middle and South America. Among these cultures were the Maya, the Toltec, the Aztec, and the Inca.

Maya

While the Olmec civilization was still in existence, another civilization, the Maya, emerged and incorporated many aspects of Olmec tradition into their own. Situated on the Yucatán Peninsula and in parts of modern-day Belize and Guatemala, the Maya were an agricultural civilization centered on the cultivation of crops such as maize and beans. They constructed complex urban cities, including the capital Tikal and Chichén Itzá. They also constructed truncated pyramids in honor of their gods, such as the deity Quetzalcóatl.

The Maya are noted for their scientific advancements, including intricate solar and lunar calendars; the introduction of the mathematical concept of zero; and an advanced, glyph-based written language. The Maya practiced *polytheism* and believed the creation story told in the sacred Mayan book called *Popol Vuh*. They also occasionally made human sacrifices, which was common among many Mesoamerican cultures.

Like many other cultures at the time, the Maya developed a tiered social system with the nobility at the top, merchants and artisans in the middle, and peasants at the bottom. The Mayan government was a monarchy headed by a king who was considered both a political and spiritual leader.

The Maya thrived into the ninth century, at which point their urban centers were mysteriously abandoned. Although the exact reason for their disappearance is unknown, it is believed to have been precipitated by war or soil depletion. Within a century, the entire Mayan civilization was reduced to a few city-states.

Toltec

Following the collapse of the Mayan culture, their territory came to be occupied by a number of nomadic peoples. Around 900 CE, the Toltec became dominant. Upon establishing permanent settlements, including their capital city of Tula, the Toltec created a culture that borrowed many of the traditions and customs of other peoples in Mesoamerica. Unlike the Maya, the Toltec expanded via violent conquest. Their reign was a short one, however, and lasted only until around 1200 CE.

Aztec

The Aztec, or Mexica, rose to power after the fall of the Toltec. Originally a nomadic people from northern Mexico, the Aztec appeared as the Toltec civilization was nearing its end. The Aztec continued to move around the region for another hundred years before establishing a permanent settlement on an island in the center of Lake Texcoco. The Aztec believed this location was prophesied by one of their legends, and they called it Tenochtitlán.

As an agricultural society that was primarily dependent on the ability to cultivate maize, the Aztec soon found themselves faced without enough land for farming. To resolve this issue, they produced artificial plots of land called *chinampas*. These plots of land, which actually floated on the lake, were made by intertwining reeds and vines and covering the structure with soil brought up from the lake bed.

In time, the Aztec became a powerful empire. Using their military might, they forced surrounding peoples to pay tributes. Within just a few hundred years, the Aztec became a major force in the Mesoamerican world. Eventually, they allied with the city-states of Tlacopan and Texcoco to control the majority of the region.

Like the Mayan society, the Aztec society had a three-tiered class system. The Aztec class system, however, had slightly different class divisions, with nobles at the top, commoners in the middle, and slaves at the bottom. The Aztec also practiced a polytheistic religion. Perhaps the most defining feature of Aztec spirituality was their extreme penchant for human sacrifice, a ritual that was performed with frequency.

In the end, the Aztec's own violent tendencies ultimately brought an end to their civilization. In the early 1500s, internal protest against the Aztec's violent rule weakened their empire and left it vulnerable to conquest. The Spaniards arrived in the region in 1519 and overthrew the Aztec in a short period of time.

Inca

Further south, the Inca people were in the process of building what would soon become the largest empire anywhere in the Americas. Based in the highlands of the Andes Mountains, the Inca Empire began when the Quechua (later named *Inca* by the Spanish) entered the region surrounding Lake Titicaca, around the mid-thirteenth century. The Inca quickly established themselves as the dominant culture.

The early expansion of the Inca Empire was carried out under the leadership of Pachacuti, who conquered vast areas of land and took possession of coastal territory during his reign. By the beginning of the sixteenth century, the Inca Empire included an area more than 2,500 miles in length and ran along the western coast of South America.

The Inca were able to maintain control over their empire by constructing a network of roads. They used the roads to transport military personnel and transmit messages from one part of the empire to another.

In addition, instead of forcing conquered peoples to pay tributes, the Incas required them to submit to involuntary labor, often as part of various public works projects. Labor played a key role in the survival of the Incan community. Incan family groups were expected to work together on the projects that would make their society self-sufficient. Men and women were considered equally important in society, and both were entitled to inheritance through parallel descent.

Unlike other Mesoamerican cultures, the Inca did not have clear class distinctions. The large majority of Inca were peasants, and aristocrats, rulers, and priests accounted for only a small minority. The Inca were led by a ruler who was viewed as a deity. The Inca Empire began to decline in 1525 CE. Disputes over succession led to civil war. A weakened empire was unable to defend itself against the Spanish.

Review Questions

1. When the Mongols took control of China and established the Yuan dynasty, they did all of the following EXCEPT

    A. build their own communities separate from the Chinese
    B. adopt the Chinese form of centralized government
    C. attempt to invade Japan and Southeast Asia
    D. establish a new version of the civil service exam
    E. allow for greater religious freedom

2. The invasion of the Byzantine territory by the Seljuk Turks led to a weakening of the Byzantine Empire, primarily due to

    A. the political unrest and civil war that spread throughout the empire
    B. a reduction in both food supply and the ability to collect taxes
    C. a disruption of trade with other Mediterranean cultures
    D. a widespread religious upheaval and Islamic conversion
    E. the outbreak of epidemic disease that decimated the population

3. In the ninth century, the Vikings invaded other European communities primarily to

    A. decide territorial disputes
    B. incite religious fervor
    C. resolve food shortages
    D. establish trade embargoes
    E. cause economic distress

4. The reemergence of trade brought about by the Crusades was mainly facilitated through the shipping ports of which country?

    A. France
    B. Spain
    C. Greece
    D. Portugal
    E. Italy

5. Which of the following statements about how the Maya and the Aztec were similar is INCORRECT?

    A. They both had a three-tiered social class system.
    B. They both practiced ritual human sacrifice.
    C. They both occupied part of the Yucatán Peninsula.
    D. They both were conquered by the Spaniards.
    E. They both were made up of a collection of city-states.

Answer Explanations

1. **D.** Although the Mongols made a number of changes to traditional Chinese society when they took power, they did not establish a new version of the civil service exam. In fact, the Mongols chose to abandon the more bureaucratic aspects of the Chinese government entirely.

2. **B.** Once the Seljuk Turks took control of a large portion of Byzantine territory, food supplies shrank, as did collected taxes.

3. **C.** The Vikings invaded Europe in the ninth century primarily because of serious food shortages in their homeland of Scandinavia. The Vikings took to other communities to meet their own needs for survival.

4. **E.** The important role played by the Crusades in the reestablishment of trade in Europe was made possible by the shipping ports of Italy. Throughout the Crusades, the large ships of the Italian merchant fleet were used to transport troops to battle. They frequently returned to Italy

with a large supply of goods that then traveled through Europe. This practice helped reestablish patterns of trade across the continent.

5. **D.** The Maya were not conquered by the Spaniards. Rather, the Mayan culture ended for other reasons.

Review Chapter 4: Renaissance, Reformation, and Exploration

The Renaissance

The growing interest in the exchange of ideas that had been fostered in Europe as a result of the Crusades soon led to an era of increased scientific and artistic thought known as the *Renaissance*. The Renaissance was a celebration of humanity. During this period, many people began to challenge the teachings of the church and to experiment with scientific research and intellectual thought. Lasting from about 1300 to 1600 in most parts of Europe, the Renaissance bridged the gap between the Middle Ages and the early modern era.

One of the defining elements of Renaissance society was adherence to a school of thought known as *humanism*. Humanism placed a great deal of emphasis on the concept of reason and was chiefly concerned with the problems of everyday human life.

The Renaissance first emerged in Italy, where the Crusades had fostered the growth of many large cities with a wealthy citizenry, such as Florence, Naples, and Rome. Eventually, Renaissance ideas began to spread outward through the rest of Europe.

MAJOR FIGURES OF THE ITALIAN RENAISSANCE

FIGURE	ACCOMPLISHMENTS
Dante Alighieri	Authored *The Divine Comedy*
Leonardo da Vinci	Painter, inventor; excelled in arts and sciences; designed a flying machine, studied anatomy, painted famous works such as *Mona Lisa*
Donatello	Sculptor; modeled works after Greeks and Romans
Niccolò Machiavelli	Authored *The Prince*; advocated government by any means necessary
Michelangelo	Sculptor, painter; created *David*; painted the ceiling of the Sistine Chapel
Francesco Petrarch	Poet; supported full living over strict religious devotion
Raphael	Painter; created many papal frescos

By the fifteenth and sixteenth centuries, Renaissance ideas had reached much of Western Europe. The relatively quick spread of these ideas through such a vast area was due, in part, to Johannes Gutenberg's invention, around 1452 to 1453, of a printing press that used movable type, and the official publication of his Gutenberg Bible in 1455. As the concepts of humanism and realism that were such a large part of the Italian Renaissance began to permeate the rest of Europe, they were meshed with Northern Europe's religious devotion to create a unique variation on the original Renaissance known as the Northern Renaissance.

MAJOR FIGURES OF THE NORTHERN RENAISSANCE

FIGURE	ACCOMPLISHMENTS
Albrecht Dürer	Artist; known for works made from copper and wood
Desiderius Erasmus	Champion of humanism in northern Europe; authored *In Praise of Folly* to criticize the Catholic Church

FIGURE	ACCOMPLISHMENTS
Thomas More	Authored *Utopia*; described what he imagined to be the ideal society
Rembrandt	Painter; created works known for the contrast of light and shadow
William Shakespeare	Playwright and poet; wrote *Hamlet*, *Romeo and Juliet*, *Macbeth*, and many other great works

With the spread of Renaissance ideals throughout Europe, people became more aware of themselves as individuals. More important, they began to examine their religious beliefs and question the authority of the church. In time, this led to a major religious upheaval in Europe.

The Protestant Reformation

The changing attitudes of Europeans toward religion eventually culminated in the Protestant Reformation, which saw the emergence of several new variants of Christianity that were entirely separate from the Roman Catholic Church.

The early stages of the Protestant Reformation unfolded in Germany, where the sale of *indulgences* attracted the ire of Martin Luther. Indulgences, which were printed on Gutenberg's printing press, were sold to the faithful under the pretense that the buyer would receive less punishment in the afterlife. The funds from the sale of indulgences were used to pay for rebuilding St. Peter's Basilica. Martin Luther wrote the *Ninety-Five Theses* to decry the practice, and he nailed the document to the door of a church in Wittenberg, Germany, on October 31, 1517. Although he was later excommunicated from the Roman Catholic Church, Luther's teachings eventually earned him a great number of followers and led to the formation of the Lutheran faith.

Other religious reform movements followed. In Switzerland, John Calvin instituted a new Protestant faith based on the concept of *predestination*, or the belief that a person's fate is entirely predetermined by God and cannot be altered. In Scotland, John Knox established the Presbyterian Church. In England, Henry VIII, upset that the pope would not grant him an annulment of his marriage, established the Church of England.

The Protestant Reformation also led to some important changes in the Catholic Church itself. In 1534, the Society of Jesus, also known as the Jesuits, was formed by St. Ignatius of Loyola with the aim of supporting education, establishing missions, and stopping the spread of Protestantism. While the Jesuits approached their task in a peaceful manner, other factions of the Roman Catholic Church employed more violent strategies. During the Inquisition, torture was used to force heretics to confess their sins and convert to Roman Catholicism.

As a result of the Protestant Reformation, the political power of monarchies and other governmental states increased as the power of the pope declined. This encouraged the development of nation-states. In addition, religious disputes ignited a series of wars that would strengthen the cultural divide among the emerging European nations.

The Ottoman Empire

As the Byzantine Empire fell into decline, a new power emerged to seize control of the region: the Ottomans. The Ottomans were a tribe that had successfully defeated the Seljuk Turks and laid claim to Anatolia, the region of Asia Minor adjacent to the remains of Byzantium. The Ottomans were particularly forceful about conquering nearby non-Muslim cultures. In 1281, leadership of the Ottomans was assumed by Osman Bey, who was a *ghazi*, or Muslim warrior. He and his successors expanded the Ottoman Empire to a massive size; the Ottoman Empire remained in existence until 1923.

In 1453, the Ottomans successfully took control of Constantinople and formally ended the Byzantine Empire. The Ottomans rebuilt the fallen capital city of Constantinople and renamed it Istanbul. Expansion reached its maximum extent during the reign of Süleyman I (1520–66).

By 1529, his forces had advanced well into Europe, reaching the nations of Hungary and Austria. Much like the Mongols before them, the Ottomans were stopped at Vienna.

The Ottomans were not the only Islamic empire to emerge during this period, however. The Safavid Empire was a Muslim dynasty that conquered the majority of Persia in a military conflict led by a fourteen-year-old named Ismail Abu al-Muzaffar Safawi. The Safavids and the Ottomans, who were composed of Shia and Sunni Muslims, respectively, were often at odds with each other.

The Mughal Empire (1526–1707) rose to power in India after the fall of the Guptas. For a time, the Mughals worked to unite the people of India, who were largely split along the religious lines of Islam and Hindu. After a time, however, Muslim leaders began persecuting the Hindus, which led to unrest and a divided population. Eventually, the Mughal Empire collapsed under the weight of internal tensions caused by succession disputes.

European Exploration

By the fifteenth century trade activities between the East and West had increased significantly. At the same time, the emerging nations of Europe grew increasingly divided along national lines and began to compete with one another for commercial superiority. This competitive spirit drove many of Europe's leaders to look beyond their own borders for commercial opportunities that could increase wealth and improve international status.

The first steps of the Age of Exploration, as it is often called, were taken by Portugal. Having already established themselves as one of the leading maritime peoples of Europe, the Portuguese were eager to make their mark in the world of trade. At that time, Italy and the Muslims in the Mediterranean still dominated European trade with the East. The Portuguese believed that if they could find an alternative route to the East, they could end this stranglehold on trade. In 1498 their efforts paid off when Vasco da Gama successfully reached India by sailing around the southern tip of Africa and entering the Indian Ocean.

While Portugal traveled south to reach the East, Spain made the bold move of attempting to reach the East by sailing west. In 1492 the Spanish set their sights on finding a route to the East. When the Italian explorer Christopher Columbus suggested that he could reach India by traveling westward across the Atlantic Ocean, Ferdinand, the Spanish king, agreed to finance his journey in the hopes that Spain could reap financially from the potential trade route. Columbus's expedition culminated with his arrival at what he called the West Indies. Thinking that he had landed on some islands just east of India, he searched in vain, during several subsequent expeditions, to find the Indian mainland. In reality, he had landed in the Americas, specifically in the Caribbean nation now known as Haiti. Columbus's discovery introduced Europeans to the New World on the other side of the Atlantic.

These two discoveries made Spain and Portugal the dominant maritime nations in Europe and turned them into rivals. To avoid major disputes, the two nations agreed to the Treaty of Tordesillas in 1494. This agreement granted Spain exclusive trading rights to all lands discovered in the West, including the Americas, and gave Portugal exclusive trading rights to the East. The treaty was particularly advantageous to the Spanish, who would soon benefit from the massive stores of gold and silver in Mesoamerica.

Spain's entry into Mesoamerica began in 1519, when the conquistador Hernán Cortés arrived in Aztec territory. Although the relationship between the Spanish and the Aztec was initially agreeable, the Spanish eventually chose to seize control of the region. They successfully conquered the Aztec in 1521. The Incan civilization in South America suffered a similar fate when it was conquered by Francisco Pizarro in 1533. The new Spanish colonies in the Americas were operated through the use of the *encomienda* system, in which settlers could buy land grants that gave them the right to hire local natives to perform labor. This system was often abused, however, and natives were frequently exploited.

The American population also suffered and declined as the result of their susceptibility to various diseases, such as smallpox, brought to their shores by the Europeans.

The need for cheap, resilient labor in the Americas led to the African slave trade. European nations exported various goods to Africa in exchange for slaves. The slaves were brought to the Americas, where they were exchanged for commodities such as sugar and tobacco. This system continued to operate until 1807.

In time, England and France also launched expeditions to the New World. Both claimed territory in North America and established colonial settlements there. By the mid-eighteenth century, the two nations were players on the world stage and, with Spain, became embroiled in a bitter dispute over territorial control. Tensions reached their peak in 1756 with the outbreak of the Seven Years' War. The battle itself was fought on two different fronts. In North America and the Caribbean, the English engaged both France and Spain. In the Indian Ocean, England and Prussia allied themselves in a campaign against the French, the Austrians, and the Russians. After claiming victory in both theaters, England took its place as the world's dominant nation for the following 150 years.

The Rise of Monarchies

Two main types of monarchies emerged in Europe: constitutional monarchies and absolute monarchies. In a constitutional monarchy, the power of the monarch was limited by law. In an absolute monarchy, the monarch's power was unlimited, and the monarch exercised full control over the nation. Many absolute monarchs ruled by divine right, meaning they believed their authority came directly from a higher power.

Spain and France were among the leading nations governed by absolute monarchs. In the sixteenth century, Philip II of Spain led the expansion of the Spanish Empire both in the New World and in Europe, where he controlled Portugal and its assets. In France, Louis XIV, who reigned between 1638 and 1715, viewed himself as the ultimate authority and used his power to levy massive taxes to fund construction of opulent palaces and wage wars abroad. His abuses of power laid the groundwork for future political unrest in France.

In central Europe, various royal lines, such as the Hapsburgs of Austria and the Hohenzollerns of Prussia, ruled during this period. In Russia, powerful monarchs called *czars* came to power starting in the sixteenth century with the reign of Ivan the Terrible. In 1613, the Romanov family came to power, and they ruled until 1917.

Scientific Revolution and Enlightenment

Europe's dominance on the world stage was also solidified by a number of significant scientific advances during the Scientific Revolution. In the seventeenth century, interest in empirical scientific study grew considerably, and as a result, new research, technologies, and knowledge became available.

Along with these scientific advances came advances in philosophical thought. The philosophy of *deism*, in particular, became popular during the Scientific Revolution. Deists believed that the role of God in the universe was to set and enforce natural laws. Eventually, the change in philosophical thought that spread across Europe during this period led to the beginning of an intellectual movement called the *Enlightenment*.

Thinkers of the Enlightenment believed in general that humans were fundamentally good but could be improved through education. They also held that reason, as opposed to religious faith, was the best path to truth. Enlightened thinkers supported the application of scientific principles to society. The ideals of the Enlightenment had a profound effect on the world and played a major role in the development of modern society.

MAJOR FIGURES OF THE SCIENTIFIC REVOLUTION AND ENLIGHTENMENT

FIGURE	ACCOMPLISHMENTS
Copernicus	Proved that Earth was not the center of the universe
René Descartes	Developed the idea of natural laws and invented analytical geometry
Galileo Galilei	Confirmed Copernicus's theory
Johannes Kepler	Showed that planets orbited the sun in elliptical orbits
John Locke	Political theorist; wrote about the nature of society and government
Isaac Newton	Made important contributions to physics and discovered gravity
Andreas Vesalius	Advanced the study of human anatomy
Mary Wollstonecraft	Feminist; fought for political rights for women

Review Questions

1. Which factor was MOST responsible for the collapse of the Mughal Empire?

    A. Enemy invasion
    B. Religious unrest
    C. Economic distress
    D. Peasant revolts
    E. Succession disputes

2. The Northern Renaissance MOST differed from the Italian Renaissance in that it

    A. failed to significantly emphasize the visual arts
    B. placed greater importance on religious devotion
    C. largely rejected the concept of humanism
    D. did not increase the prevalence of secularism
    E. increased dissonance among Christians

3. Who developed and taught the doctrine of predestination?

    A. John Knox
    B. Martin Luther
    C. Ulrich Zwingli
    D. John Calvin
    E. Thomas More

4. Portugal's MAIN motivation for seeking an alternate route to the East was to

    A. establish a direct trading relationship with China
    B. compete with Spain and its holdings in the New World
    C. end the Italian and Muslim dominance of trade
    D. lay claim to all trade rights in the Indian Ocean
    E. begin colonizing key areas of Southwest Asia

5. The Seven Years' War was MOST beneficial for which nation?

    A. Britain
    B. France
    C. Russia
    D. Spain
    E. Italy

Answer Explanations

1. **E.** The collapse of the Mughal Empire in India was primarily caused by disputes over the line of succession. Although religious unrest between Muslims and Hindus divided the population and destabilized the empire, it was the dispute over the throne that was most damaging.

2. **B.** Over time, the ideas of the Italian Renaissance made their way into the rest of Europe. In northern Europe, the intellectual ideologies of the Renaissance were combined with the religious devotion of the region's inhabitants. As a result, the Northern Renaissance placed greater emphasis on religious devotion than did the Italian Renaissance.

3. **D.** The doctrine of predestination was the brainchild of John Calvin, who founded Calvinism. The cornerstone of Calvinism was the concept of predestination, or the belief that each person's fate was predetermined and could not be significantly altered by any earthly means.

4. **C.** Portugal's primary objective in finding a water route to India around the southern tip of Africa was to break the Italian and Muslim dominance of trade.

5. **A.** The Seven Years' War benefited Britain more than any other country. During this conflict, the British fought on two separate fronts, taking on the French and Spanish in the Americas and the French, Austrians, and Russians in the Indian Ocean. Ultimately, the British were victorious in both battles and, as a result, became the dominant world power for the following 150 years.

Review Chapter 5:
The Age of Revolutions

From the seventeenth through the nineteenth century, great political upheaval occurred in both Europe and the Americas. Several major revolutions during this period changed the political landscape of Europe and further encouraged the development of modern society.

The English Revolution

Although the nature of England's monarchy generally prevented most of the outrageous abuses of power committed by many of Europe's absolute rulers, there were still some questions over how much control the monarch should have. One of the first instances of stricter limitations being placed on the monarchy came in 1628, when Charles I requested funding for military campaigns against Spain and France. Seizing the opportunity to force Charles into a deal, Parliament agreed to finance his wars on the condition that he agreed to the Petition of Right. This petition would prevent the English monarch from imprisoning subjects without due cause, housing the military in private homes, enacting martial law in peacetime, and levying taxes without parliamentary approval.

After he refused to sign, civil war erupted. Charles was pitted against his non-Anglican subjects (the Scots) and Parliament. In the end, Charles was defeated and executed. In his place, the Puritan Oliver Cromwell was installed as dictator. Cromwell formed a new republican government and remained in power until his death in 1658.

Following Cromwell's demise, the monarchy was revived under the son of Charles I. When Charles II died in 1685 without an heir, the question of succession led to political division in England from which arose two separate groups, the Whigs and Tories. These groups would eventually evolve into England's modern political parties.

The question of succession led to the bloodless Glorious Revolution. Initially, James II, brother of Charles II and an ardent Catholic, was appointed as king. Later, the Protestant members of Parliament asked William of Orange and his wife, Mary (the daughter of James II), both of whom were Protestant, to take the throne. The most important event in the reign of William and Mary was their signing of the Bill of Rights, which further limited royal power by preventing the monarch from suspending a law of Parliament, levying taxes without parliamentary approval, hindering freedom of speech in Parliament, or preventing citizens from petitioning about grievances.

The American and French Revolutions

In 1776 Britain's colonies in North America rebelled against the colonizer, England. The ensuing American Revolution ended British colonial control of North America and resulted in the establishment of a new nation.

The French Revolution was brought on by inequities in the structure of French society, which was divided into three separate classes called *estates*. The First Estate included members of the clergy. The Second Estate was composed of the landed nobility. The Third Estate included merchants, peasants, and the rest of the French population. Although the clergy and nobility accounted for only a very small percentage of the population, they owned a large portion of the land and paid few, if any, taxes.

As a result, the Third Estate was heavily taxed and subject to poverty and poor living conditions. The civil unrest came to a head in 1789, when a meeting of the Estates-General, the French assembly, was called to address serious economic issues caused by Louis XVI's excessive spending. During this meeting, the Third Estate proposed a new system of voting that would give them an equal number of votes to the First and Second Estates combined. When the request was denied, the Third Estate founded its own legislature called the National Assembly. After being barred from their meeting place, the members of National Assembly met on a tennis court and took the so-called Tennis Court Oath, in which they vowed to write a new French constitution.

Eventually, the National Assembly adopted an important document called the Declaration of the Rights of Man. Much like the American Declaration of Independence, this document stated that all men were created equal and were naturally entitled to the rights of "liberty, property, security, and resistance to oppression."

The political battle for reform turned violent on July 14, 1789, when rebels stormed the Bastille, a major prison in Paris. The attack on the Bastille led to a period of civil unrest, known as the Great Fear, during which the country was plunged into chaos.

By 1791 the National Assembly had begun to lay the groundwork for a new government. They planned to adjust to a limited monarchy that would work in tandem with a new legislative body, the Legislative Assembly. The assembly was composed of three separate political factions, the radicals, the moderates, and the conservatives. The following year, in response to continued issues with Louis XVI, the Legislative Assembly and the limited monarchy were abolished and replaced with a republican government. As the monarchy crumbled, a violent political group known as the Jacobin Club rose to power. With France now under the control of the Jacobins, Louis XVI and his family were arrested. In 1793 Louis XVI was executed.

Louis XVI's death marked the beginning of the Reign of Terror, during which Maximilien de Robespierre, a powerful Jacobin, used the guillotine to execute anyone thought to be an enemy of the republic. Robespierre's rash of executions came to an end only with his own death by guillotine in 1794.

As peace began to return to France, another new government was formed. The Directory was composed of a two-house legislative body and a five-member executive branch. One of The Directory's most crucial decisions was to appoint Napoléon Bonaparte as the commander of the French army in 1796.

The Napoleonic Empire

Just three years after his appointment, Napoléon staged a coup d'état and installed himself as dictator of France. Early in his reign, Napoléon instituted a series of internal reforms intended to stabilize the country and restore its structural integrity. The centerpiece of Napoléon's government was the Napoleonic Code, a system of laws that ensured the legal equality of adult men, emphasized the patriarchal family, and placed limitations on the freedom of speech and the press.

Before long, however, Napoléon's attention turned to foreign matters. He was determined to build a French empire by any means necessary. To fund his plans, he sold off all of France's holdings in North America in 1803 in an economic deal called the Louisiana Purchase. Soon after, he declared himself emperor. His campaigns were initially successful. Within a year, only the British stood between him and total domination of Europe. A pivotal loss at the Battle of Trafalgar in 1805, however, prevented him from conquering England.

The Napoleonic Empire reached its zenith around 1812, but a series of costly miscalculations and key defeats led to its decline. In 1814 Napoléon was forced to abdicate and went into exile on the island of Elba, but he later returned. After some initial successes,

Napoléon's forces were finally defeated by the British and Prussians at the Battle of Waterloo in 1815. Following this critical defeat, Napoléon was exiled to the island of St. Helena, where he remained until his death.

After the final defeat of Napoléon, the major powers of Europe came together for the Congress of Vienna. The goals of this meeting were to establish European peace, to prevent France from committing further attacks, to restore the international balance of power, and to help restore Europe's monarchies. The actions taken by the congress restored the peace, increased the political power of conservatives, and encouraged the rise of nationalism. Britain and Prussia emerged as Europe's two most powerful nations.

Revolution in the Americas

The crisis in Europe and the subsequent changes made by the Congress of Vienna also led to revolutions in many of the remaining colonial territories in the Americas. Revolts in South America, Middle America, Mexico, and Haiti led to the end of European dominance of that region.

Most notable among the major figures who led these revolutionary efforts was Simón Bolívar, a Venezuelan general who played an important role in many of the early-nineteenth-century revolutions that unfolded in South America. His goal was to create a strong South American state, which he named Gran Colombia. In addition to leading his native Venezuela to independence in 1821, Bolívar also played a pivotal role in liberating Peru, Ecuador, and Chile. For a time, he also managed to make Gran Colombia a reality, but economic distress and other difficulties led to its dissolution into various nation-states after only a few years.

MAJOR REVOLUTIONS OF THE AMERICAS

LOCATION	COLONIAL POWER	DATES	KEY FIGURES
Haiti	France	1791–1804	Toussaint L'Ouverture
Venezuela, Argentina, Ecuador, Chile	Spain	1821–24	Simón Bolívar, José de San Martin, Bernardo O'Higgins
Brazil	Portugal	1822	Dom Pedro
Mexico	Spain	1810–21	Miguel Hidalgo y Costilla, José María Morelos, Agustín de Iturbide

Review Questions

1. Which of these was part of the French National Assembly's initial plan for government reform?

   A. Constitutional republic
   B. Dictatorship
   C. Limited monarchy
   D. Absolute monarchy
   E. Democracy

2. The Bill of Rights signed by William and Mary prevented the English monarch from doing all of the following, EXCEPT

   A. interfering with freedom of speech in Parliament
   B. levying taxes without legislative approval
   C. suspending any law passed by Parliament
   D. refusing to hear grievances made by citizens
   E. imprisoning subjects without due cause

3.   The Louisiana Purchase provided France with significant funding for

   A.   rehabilitating the economy after Louis XVI's extravagant spending
   B.   establishing a new republican government following the failure of the previous one
   C.   overthrowing the monarch and starting a new government under the Jacobins
   D.   financing Napoléon's campaign to conquer Europe and build a French Empire
   E.   rebuilding the nation after the defeat at the Battle of Waterloo

4.   Simón Bolívar was MOST interested in leading revolutions against Spain in the Americas because he wanted to

   A.   rule the entire region as a dictator
   B.   establish a unified Latin American state
   C.   force the Spanish into North America
   D.   isolate the region from outside influences
   E.   transfer colonial control from Spain to France

5.   In taking the Tennis Court Oath, the National Assembly vowed to

   A.   establish a republican government
   B.   overthrow the oppressive monarchy
   C.   boycott all unfair taxes
   D.   write a new state constitution
   E.   install a military dictatorship

Answer Explanations

1. **C.** The National Assembly initially planned to establish a limited monarchy in place of the absolute monarchy. This plan led to the establishment of the Legislative Assembly. The new limited monarchy lasted only a short time.

2. **E.** The Bill of Rights did not include a clause that restricted the

monarch's ability to imprison subjects without due cause. This matter was addressed in the Petition of Right, which was rejected by Charles I.

3. **D.** The Louisiana Purchase provided funding for Napoléon's empire-building ambitions. Napoléon recognized that his plans were costly and looked for means of raising funds in a short period of time. His solution was to sell the French holdings in North America to the United States.

4. **B.** Bolívar's main goal in leading some of the revolutions that occurred in South America in the nineteenth century was establishing a unified Latin American state. Bolívar wanted to build a strong nation in the area that he dubbed "Gran Colombia." Although Gran Colombia did come into existence for a time, the fledgling nation existed for only a few brief years.

5. **D.** In taking this oath, the National Assembly vowed to write a new constitution.

Review Chapter 6:
Industrialization and Imperialism

The political revolutions that so dramatically changed the face of Europe and the Americas in the eighteenth and nineteenth centuries gave rise to another type of revolution. The Industrial Revolution was equally transformative around the world.

Industrial Revolution

The Industrial Revolution got its start in England. Villagers in small communities had formerly relied on common lands to feed their flocks. These lands were available to all people to use, thus ensuring that all livestock had enough food to return a profit to its owner. In the eighteenth century, the "enclosure movement" allowed wealthy landowners to purchase large tracts of land and enclose the land with fences or other barriers. Common lands were no longer available for general use. As a result, many small farmers moved to urban centers to find new jobs.

This increase in the available workforce, advances in technologies, capital, and a spirit of entrepreneurship led to a phase of rapid industrialization around the country. One of the first industries to benefit from advances in technologies was the cotton textile industry. New, more efficient spinning machines improved production and increased profit. Other inventions, like James Watt's steam engine, also contributed to rapid growth by making it easier to move goods and people from one place to another.

Eventually, industrialization took hold in other countries as well. In the United States and continental Europe, railroads played a key role in the spread of industrialization. The same was true in Russia, where railroads connected the East to the West.

EFFECTS OF THE INDUSTRIAL REVOLUTION

DOMESTIC	GLOBAL
Encouraged growth of cities	Increased the economic gap between wealthy and poor nations
Increased the size of the middle class	Increased the rate of colonization
Led to unsafe working conditions	Increased Europe's economic power
Encouraged the use of child labor	Strengthened and politicized the middle class
Resulted in low wages and long hours	Increased interest in reform movements
Led to poor living conditions in urban tenements	Increased global trading
Increased standard of living and decreased costs	Led to closer connections between countries

Industrialization and Government Policy

With the increased prominence of industry came the question of the role government should play in its regulation. Several different theories emerged to answer this question.

Economist Adam Smith championed the *laissez-faire* approach, which held that government should not interject itself into the market. He believed government should not attempt to regulate industry at all. He argued that the economic system would naturally self-regulate as if an "invisible hand" was guiding it. Smith's theory was the perfect complement to and a major factor in the continued rise of *capitalism*, which was built on the concept of private ownership of business.

Other theorists held that government should be directly involved in the operation of industry. This view was supported by philosophers such as utilitarian John Stuart Mill and utopian socialist Robert Owen.

On the other end of the spectrum were those who believed that the factors of production naturally belong to the public and should be operated for the common good. This was known as *socialism*. Philosophers Karl Marx and Friedrich Engels introduced a radical form of socialism called *communism* in *The Communist Manifesto*. They argued that society was locked in an ongoing struggle between middle class employers (the *bourgeoisie*) and the working class (the *proletariat*). They believed the working class would inevitably rise up in response to poor working conditions and take control of the means of production. This, Marx and Engels said, would lead to the development of a proletariat-controlled government and, eventually, a classless society.

Imperialism

As European nations became increasingly industrialized, they found themselves in need of additional raw materials and markets to sell their goods. One solution to both of these problems was *imperialism*, or territorial acquisitions. At this time many European nations established colonial outposts in different parts of the world. These outposts allowed the nations to control trading rights. Some nations gained control by completely taking over a region's government. Other nations formed protectorates, which gave imperialist nations control while allowing the local government to continue operating. Still others would include regions in a "sphere of influence" over which they could claim exclusive trading rights. Finally, some regions were controlled via private businesses.

One of the first major regions to fall under imperialist control was Africa. Belgium established a strong presence in the Congo under King Leopold II. By the 1880s, the competition for land in Africa had become so fierce that some nations were concerned over the possibility of armed conflict in Europe. To address this issue, the imperialist powers came together in 1884 at the Berlin Conference, also known as the Berlin West Africa Conference, to peacefully divide Africa among themselves. Within thirty years, the entire African continent was under European control.

Another major region of interest was Southeast Asia, given its valuable natural resources. By the early 1800s, the British had established colonial control over India. Although the British made some effort to modernize India, the British occupation of India was met with resistance. Eventually, nationalist organizations such as the Indian National Congress and the Muslim League were established to fight for Indian independence.

The British also controlled Singapore, a major trading city located just off the Malay Peninsula, as well as Malaysia and Burma, which is known today as Myanmar. During the time the British controlled these regions, they encouraged Chinese workers to migrate there. This practice eventually led to a Chinese majority that still persists to this day.

Britain was not the only nation to establish imperialist control in Southeast Asia, however. By the nineteenth century, Indonesia was controlled by the Dutch, who established plantations and opened trading posts. The French controlled Vietnam, calling the region French Indochina. France's trading policies in the region were unpopular with the Vietnamese and eventually played an important role in fueling resistance.

Imperialism in China and Japan

As the imperialist nations of Europe were building vast foreign empires, China and Japan were attempting to isolate themselves from foreign influence. This proved a difficult challenge for both countries.

China's isolationist policies were first threatened by the British, who realized that they could profit from the opium trade. Widespread Chinese opium addiction led to two military conflicts that the British eventually won, the First Opium War (1839–42) and the Second Opium War (1856–60). British victory allowed England to control the port of Hong Kong. Within a few years, a number of other major nations were also given trading rights in China. In time, these countries capitalized on

China's internal weaknesses to establish spheres of influence in China. Many of the Chinese were unhappy with this arrangement. Political disorder was rampant and uprisings occurred. Perhaps the most notable of these uprisings was the 1900 Boxer Rebellion, in which a Chinese secret society known as the Boxers laid siege to Beijing before being swiftly defeated by American, European, and Japanese forces.

During the same period, Japan struggled to remain isolated by keeping its ports closed to foreign trade. This changed in 1853, when American Commodore Matthew Perry entered Edo Harbor in the city now known as Tokyo and forced the issue. When the Meiji government took over Japan in 1868, it began a period of modernization that strengthened the government and military and encouraged rapid industrialization. This, in turn, led to a period of Japanese imperialism and expansion into Taiwan, the Pescadores Islands, and Korea.

Review Questions

1. The beginning of the Industrial Revolution in England primarily resulted from

   A. widespread overpopulation
   B. increased trade
   C. national prosperity
   D. agricultural innovation
   E. abundance of resources

2. The Berlin Conference of 1884–85 was a meeting of European imperialist powers designed to peacefully negotiate

   A. terms of trade with China
   B. control over the African continent
   C. disputes over ports in Southeast Asia
   D. rights to former Ottoman territories
   E. international trading policies in Europe

3. The Boxer Rebellion of the late nineteenth and early twentieth centuries was a response to the

    A. forced opening of Japanese ports
    B. oppressive rule of the British in India
    C. foreign intrusion into China
    D. economic distress caused by the French in Vietnam
    E. dominance of the Dutch in Indonesia

4. Economist Adam Smith's laissez-faire theory supported the notion that governments should

    A. refrain from interfering with private business
    B. exercise direct control over private business
    C. regulate private business only in times of crisis
    D. maintain a set of minimal business regulations
    E. regulate only domestic businesses

5. Economic imperialism was different from other forms of colonial dominance in that the

    A. colonial territory was entirely dependent on the imperial power
    B. imperialist power directly controlled the government of the colonial territory
    C. region under imperialist influence was controlled by private businesses
    D. imperialist power held exclusive trading rights over a region
    E. colonial territory was allowed to operate its own independent government

Answer Explanations

1. **D.** The Industrial Revolution in England began primarily as the result of agricultural innovation. By the 1700s, the enclosure movement had changed the face of agriculture in England and caused many smaller landowners to sell their farms and move to urban areas.

2.   **B.** The Berlin Conference allowed Europe's major imperialist powers to reach an agreement over how they would control the African continent.

3.   **C.** The Boxer Rebellion was a Chinese revolt against foreign influence. By the late nineteenth century, China's policy of isolationism had been abused by the foreign imperialists who wanted to do business there. In 1899 a secret society of political activists called the Boxers led a revolt that culminated in the siege of Beijing in 1900.

4.   **A.** Smith's laissez-faire theory stated that governments should refrain from interfering with private business. Smith argued that governments should not attempt to influence the natural laws of supply and demand or regulate industry. The popularity of this theory helped to encourage the rise of capitalism.

5.   **C.** Economic imperialism was unique from other forms of colonial dominance because it involved controlling a region via private business.

Review Chapter 7:
Early Twentieth Century

By the early twentieth century, the forces of imperialism, nationalism, and militarism led to increasingly volatile relationships among the nations of Europe. The political disarray of Europe would lead to two devastating global wars.

World War I

In the years leading up to the outbreak of World War I, Europe was divided along political lines. Most notable among political divisions were the Triple Alliance (formed 1882) of Germany, Austria-Hungary, and Italy, and the Triple Entente (formed 1894) of Britain, France, and Russia. At the heart of these divisions was the belief of Germany's chancellor Otto von Bismarck that France was a serious threat to European security. With the Triple Alliance, the Germans hoped to isolate France from other nations. The Germans also entered an alliance with Russia, but when Kaiser Wilhelm II took power and ended the relationship between the two nations, Russia formed the Triple Entente with France and, later, Great Britain.

Compounding this tense situation was the decline of the Ottoman Empire, which led to the rise of several new rival states in the Balkans. The tensions between the nations of Europe were at a boiling point, and any incident had the potential to ignite a major conflict. Such an incident occurred on June 28, 1914, when the Austro-Hungarian Archduke Franz Ferdinand and his wife were assassinated during an official visit to the Bosnian capital of Sarajevo. In response, Austria-Hungary declared war on Serbia. Because of the alliances in place, the majority of Europe was drawn into battle. World War I had begun.

This conflict was fought between the Central powers and the Allied powers. The Central powers included Germany, Austria-Hungary, and, later, the Ottoman Empire and Bulgaria. The Allied powers included Britain, France, Russia, and Italy, which had broken its alliance with Germany after the German invasion of Belgium.

The bulk of the war was fought on separate fronts in Europe. In the west, the two sides engaged in the north of France. Both sides eventually employed trench warfare tactics. This strategy produced little in the way of territorial gains and caused massive casualties on both sides. In the east, the Germans and Austro-Hungarians fought the Russians. After initial losses, the Russians struggled to maintain their war effort and suffered significant human losses.

For the first several years of the war, the United States maintained a policy of *isolationism*, believing that the conflict was a matter that should be settled by Europeans. Two important events changed that stance. The first was the sinking of the British vessel, the *Lusitania*, in 1914, which resulted in the deaths of 128 American civilians. Later, in 1917, a German telegram outlining a plan to help Mexico recover territory it had lost to the United States in exchange for its support in the war was intercepted by British intelligence. This telegram, known as the Zimmermann telegram, convinced the Americans to join the war effort.

Just as the Americans entered the war, the Russians were leaving it. Food shortages and other hardships brought on by the war led to political unrest among the Russian people. Czar Nicholas II was forced to abdicate, and the new communist regime signed a treaty with Germany ending Russia's involvement in the war.

The arrival of American forces turned the war. As they began to advance on Germany, the Bulgarians and Ottomans surrendered, the Austro-Hungarian Empire collapsed, and the Germans began to turn against their government. After Kaiser Wilhelm II was forced from power, the war was officially ended. An armistice was signed on November 11, 1918.

Once the conflict ended, the process of establishing peace and rebuilding Europe began. The key element of European restoration was the Treaty of Versailles. This treaty was designed to ensure that Germany was disarmed and punished for its role in the war.

PROVISIONS OF THE TREATY OF VERSAILLES

Germany to return Alsace-Lorraine territory to France
Germany to relinquish its African and Pacific colonies
Germany to be restricted as to the size of its army
Germany to be restricted from making or importing weapons, operating an air force, or using submarine crafts
Germany to pay $33 billion in war reparations over thirty years
Germany to accept full responsibility for the war
The League of Nations to be formed, excluding Germany and Russia

The one-sided nature of the Treaty of Versailles did little to improve the situation in Europe. Germany was devastated, humiliated, and desperate for survival—a situation that made it vulnerable to extreme political movements. Other countries, notably Italy and Japan, were unsatisfied with the territorial gains granted to them in the treaty. Even at peace, Europe was still fractured.

Russian Revolution

The roots of the Russian Revolution were deeply influenced by Russia's attempts to modernize as well as by Marxism. As Nicholas II began industrializing the nation, economic challenges and difficult conditions arose. Two dominant Marxist revolutionary groups emerged, although each had different ideas on how a revolution should be undertaken. The Mensheviks were in favor of allowing industrialization to continue before organizing a proletariat revolution, whereas the Bolsheviks favored an immediate, radical revolution led by an elite group of revolutionaries.

The growing political crisis in Russia came to a head during World War I. The Russians' war effort placed a tremendous strain on the country's food and fuel resources and caused widespread shortages of both. These shortages prompted the people to call for the abdication of Nicholas II. When he did abdicate, a new provisional government was established. In the meantime, the leader of the Bolsheviks, Vladimir Ilich Lenin, who had been previously exiled to Germany, returned to Russia. Upon his arrival, Lenin and an army of factory workers overthrew the provisional government. Lenin instituted a communist system and pulled Russia out of the war.

Lenin then turned his attention to internal opposition. Russia was soon engulfed in a civil war that pitted Lenin's Red Army against the opposing White Army, backed by Western interests. Because many of the Russian people feared that the White Army would attempt to restore the czar, they supported the Reds, who eventually emerged victorious.

Firmly in control, Lenin set about restructuring the country. He divided the nation into self-governing republics under the control of a central government. He called his new nation the Union of Soviet Socialist Republics (USSR), or the Soviet Union. He instituted a series of social and economic reforms, including the "new economic policy," aimed to rapidly introduce communist life to Russia. His plans met with limited success.

After Lenin died in 1924, control of the Soviet Union transferred to Joseph Stalin, who immediately turned the nation into a totalitarian state. He also installed a command economy and launched an ambitious five-year plan to turn the Soviet Union into a major industrial power. His violent, dictatorial reign would continue until his death in 1953.

The Interwar Period

After World War I, Europe had to rebuild itself from the ground up. Initially, peace and order seemed to be returning to the continent. In particular, the signing of the Kellogg-Briand Pact in 1928, a largely symbolic treaty, established at least the willingness to coexist peacefully. Even Germany, which had been economically devastated by the outcome of World War I, showed signs of increased stability by the end of the 1920s. Unfortunately, the peace and stability was shattered by the onset of the Great Depression.

In 1929, the world was thrust into an economic meltdown. Although European economies had grown stronger since World War I, they were still fragile. When the U.S. stock market crashed in October, the world economy went into a tailspin that devastated and destabilized European nations as well as nations around the globe.

Desperate for economic relief, some European nations, notably Italy and Germany, turned to radical political movements whose charismatic leaders vowed to restore stability and economic prosperity. In Italy, the fascist dictator Benito Mussolini came to power after forcing King Victor Emmanuel III to abdicate.

In Germany, the political activist Adolf Hitler rose to prominence and eventually installed a totalitarian state. Hitler believed that the German people were the descendants of a master race called the Aryans. In an effort to promote the "purity" of the Aryan race and to punish those he felt were responsible for Germany's problems, Hitler initiated a systematic program of anti-Semitism that stripped Jewish Germans of their legal rights and led to significant ethnic violence. He also targeted Polish and Slavic populations, the Rom people (also known as Gypsies), the disabled or mentally ill, homosexuals, political prisoners, and Jehovah's Witnesses.

In Asia, the Great Depression encouraged Japan to turn to militarism as a solution to its economic problems. Under the command of Emperor Hirohito, the Japanese, who were struggling to sustain a booming population with insufficient raw materials, invaded Manchuria in 1931 with the intention of seizing control of their natural resources. In 1937 the Japanese continued their aggressive expansion by invading China.

As war erupted in the East, the seeds of war were planted in the West. In 1935 both Hitler and Mussolini took aggressive steps to assert their willingness to wage war. Mussolini, looking to establish an Italian colony in Africa, invaded Ethiopia. Hitler, meanwhile, began to mobilize troops in the Rhineland in defiance of the 1919 Treaty of Versailles. In 1938, he made the long-pondered unification of Germany and Austria, known as *Anschluss*, a reality through annexation. Hitler also began strategically positioning Germany for control of Czechoslovakia and Poland. Europe was on the brink of another major war.

World War II

In 1939 Germany and the Soviet Union signed a nonaggression pact. No longer faced with the threat of the massive Soviet army, Hitler was ready to begin his European campaign. On September 1 of that year, Hitler launched a surprise attack, the *blitzkrieg*, on Poland. After a brief struggle, the Polish were defeated and their nation divided between Germany and the Soviets.

Soon after, Europe was plunged into another major military conflict. As in World War I, the battle was fought between two major alliances. The Axis powers of Germany, Italy, and Japan allied themselves against the Allied powers of Britain, France, China, and, eventually, the Soviet Union and the United States. World War II had begun.

Early in the war, Hitler conquered Denmark and Norway and moved into Belgium, the Netherlands, and Luxembourg. In June 1940 he set his sights on France and successfully took the country in less than a month. Hitler then turned his attention to Britain, launching a prolonged series of air strikes on its major cities. The British were able to withstand the attacks and, with the help of new radar technology, managed to force the Germans to retreat.

In 1941 Hitler seized several additional Eastern European countries in preparation for attacking his next major target: the Soviet Union. Despite the nonaggression pact between the two nations, Hitler was determined to conquer the Soviet Union. His armies, however, met strong resistance from the Russians and struggled to survive harsh living conditions. Although they eventually reached Moscow, the Germans lost around five hundred thousand soldiers over the Russian winter. Hitler's Soviet campaign would prove one of his worst blunders of the war.

While Hitler waged war abroad, he also implemented genocide at home. Over time, Hitler's anti-Semitic policies became increasingly abusive as he placed further restrictions on the rights of Jews and forced them into segregated ghettos. Eventually, he began to relocate the Jews, along with any others he considered "undesirables," to concentration camps. In 1942 he implemented the "Final Solution": mass extermination of the Jewish people. Nazi forces began transporting the Jews to death camps, where they were killed in gas chambers and cremated in large ovens. By the end of the war, approximately 6 million Jews and others targeted by the Nazis had been killed in the camps.

As in World War I, the United States initially adhered to a policy of isolationism. That changed on December 7, 1941, when the Japanese launched a surprise attack on the American naval fleet at Pearl Harbor, Hawaii. The day after the attack, the United States declared war on Japan and officially entered World War II.

Soon after the Americans joined the war effort, the Allies began to make major progress. While the American navy worked its way across the Pacific toward Japan, the Allies forced the Axis powers out of Africa and defeated Mussolini in Sicily and Italy. In April 1945, Mussolini was assassinated.

On June 6, 1944, known as D-Day, the Allies invaded France through the beaches of Normandy and began to force the Germans into retreat. After France was liberated the following month, the allies continued to push the Germans back into their own territory. At the same time, the Soviets moved into German territory and advanced from the east. By

April 1945, the Soviets and Americans were both inside Germany and were rapidly approaching the capital city of Berlin. Faced with imminent defeat, Hitler committed suicide in an underground bunker. Germany surrendered on May 7, 1945, bringing an end to the war in Europe.

The war in the Pacific was still raging, however. American forces had pushed the Japanese back onto their mainland and were preparing for a ground invasion. Concerned that such an invasion would result in massive casualties, President Harry Truman opted for an alternative method to force surrender: the atomic bomb. In early August 1945, two atomic bombs were dropped on Japan, one on Hiroshima and one on Nagasaki. Within weeks, Japan surrendered. World War II was over.

Review Questions

1. Why were Hitler's attacks on Great Britain during World War II ultimately unsuccessful?

    A. The Luftwaffe was unable to inflict significant damage.
    B. American forces came to Britain's aid.
    C. The attacks were too costly for the Nazis to sustain.
    D. German forces could not carry out a ground attack.
    E. The British were able to track Nazi planes with radar.

2. In 1917, the United States entered World War I after learning of a German plot to

    A. seize control of U.S. territories in Southeast Asia
    B. launch a surprise attack on U.S. naval forces
    C. help Mexico retake land it had lost to the United States
    D. attack several U.S. major coastal cities
    E. destroy any U.S. ocean liners encountered

3. During the civil war in Russia, most of the people supported Lenin's
    Red Army because they

    A. feared the White Army would return the czar to power
    B. were promised great economic prosperity by Lenin
    C. wanted to isolate themselves from Western influences
    D. were coerced by aggressive communist propaganda
    E. believed the Red Army would attack them otherwise

4. What did the term *Anschluss* mean to Hitler and the Germans?

    A. A surprise attack on enemy forces
    B. The purification of the Aryan race
    C. An invasion of France and Britain
    D. The unification of Germany and Austria
    E. A secret police force

5. The American military resorted to the use of atomic weapons because

    A. American troops had no way to enter the Japanese mainland
    B. a ground invasion would result in too many casualties
    C. American forces would not be able to access necessary resources
        on the mainland
    D. Japanese ground forces were supported by additional Korean
        forces
    E. the American public wanted the war to end as quickly as possible

Answer Explanations

1. **E.** The German air strikes against Britain were unsuccessful because
the British were able to track Nazi planes using radar. This new technology allowed the British to track incoming German planes and attack
them before they reached the mainland.

2. **C.** The American entry into World War I was largely precipitated by
the interception of a telegram that outlined a deal between Germany and

Mexico. According to the agreement, the Germans would help Mexico to reclaim territory it had lost to the United States in return for Mexico's support in the European war. This direct threat to American security convinced the United States to forgo its policy of isolationism and enter World War I.

3. **A.** Lenin's Red Army enjoyed the support of most Russian people during the civil war primarily because many of the peopled feared the potential consequences of a victory by the White Army. Many Russian peasants believed the White Army would return the czar to power.

4. **D.** *Anschluss* referred to the unification of Germany and Austria. The idea of uniting Germany and Austria had been discussed for many years, but no such plan came to fruition until Hitler annexed Austria before World War II.

5. **B.** The American military opted to use the atomic bomb instead of ground attacks on the Japanese mainland because it believed that an invasion would produce too many American casualties.

Review Chapter 8:
Post–World War II

The Cold War

When World War II came to a close, the dividing lines of Europe were once again redrawn. The Soviet Union took control of several Eastern European countries, including Poland, Albania, Yugoslavia, Bulgaria, Romania, Hungary, and Czechoslovakia, and it installed communist regimes in each. Germany was divided, with the Soviets taking the eastern half of the country, and Britain, France, and the United States sharing control of the west. The city of Berlin was also divided between the Soviets and the West. The physical division of Europe between the communist-controlled East and the democratic West led to an ideological divide commonly referred to as the *Iron Curtain*.

The division of Europe also led to the beginning of a showdown between the Soviet Union and the United States. Fearing the potential consequences of the further spread of communism, the United States implemented a policy of containment, wherein it offered assistance to those nations that were most at risk of falling under communist control in order to "contain" the communist threat. The standoff between the two superpowers soon evolved into the Cold War.

The Cold War was not fought on a battlefield with weapons. Rather, it was waged through propaganda, diplomacy, and espionage. The possibility of the Cold War becoming a real conflict was a constant threat, however, and a number of military alliances were forged as a contingency plan. The United States, Canada, and Western European nations joined together to form the North Atlantic Treaty Organization (NATO), while the Soviet Union and its satellite nations allied themselves under the Warsaw Pact.

The most serious trend of the Cold War was nuclear proliferation. After the Soviets developed an atomic bomb in 1949, the United States countered by making a hydrogen bomb. This led to the mass production of nuclear weapons on both side of the Iron Curtain. With both superpowers in possession of a vast stockpile of nuclear weapons, the world hung precariously on the brink of a potentially globally devastating nuclear war.

Perhaps the most significant instance of the spread of communism came in 1949, when China came under the control of communist leader Mao Zedong. Following World War II, China was divided between nationalists and communists. Under Mao's leadership, the nationalists were defeated and forced out of mainland China to the island of Taiwan. Although communist China and the Soviet Union initially cooperated with each other, differences over political opinions soon drove the two apart.

The Korean War

Communism also spread into Korea and led to a major political split, with North Korea in the hands of communists and South Korea in the hands of a democratic government. The first major military conflict of the Cold War began in Korea on June 25, 1950, when North Korean forces crossed the border into South Korea. In response, the United Nations sent an international military force commanded by General Dwight D. Eisenhower to resolve the situation. Initially, the UN forces were successful in pushing the North Koreans back across the 38th parallel. Before they were able to totally defeat the North Koreans, however, China sent in a massive troop deployment to assist the North Koreans.

Seemingly deadlocked, the opposing sides were forced to agree to a cease-fire in July 1953. The terms of the agreement established a new border between the nations near the 38th parallel, with a demilitarized zone on either side of that border.

After the war, North Korea remained communist while South Korea remained democratic. Although there have been attempts to reunite the Koreas over the years since the Korean War, none has yet been successful.

The Vietnam War

One of the West's biggest concerns in the fight against communism was Southeast Asia. Many believed that if any Southeast Asian nation fell into communist hands, the rest would follow. In the 1950s no other Southeast Asian country seemed more at risk than Vietnam.

Communists first established a presence in Vietnam in the 1930s when they lent their support to Ho Chi Minh, a nationalist revolutionary who was one of the major figures in Vietnam's fight for independence from France. After a brief, self-imposed exile to avoid execution by the French, Minh returned to Vietnam in 1941 and founded the Vietminh resistance group. During World War II, Japan controlled Vietnam. When the Japanese were forced out in 1945, Minh declared Vietnam an independent nation.

In 1946 the French attempted to retake their former colony. After a war effort that lasted nearly ten years, the French were defeated. To limit the spread of communism in Vietnam, delegates at the 1954 Geneva Conference divided the country in half, leaving the north in the hands of Minh and the south under the control of an anticommunist government led by Ngo Dinh Diem, who was backed by France and the United States.

This arrangement did not play out as the West had envisioned. The land redistribution polices of Ho Chi Minh made him popular in North Vietnam, whereas the oppressive reign of Diem made him unpopular in South Vietnam. Diem's dictatorial leadership led to the formation of the Vietcong, a band of communist guerillas who operated in South Vietnam. To regain control, the United States cooperated with several South Vietnamese generals to assassinate Diem. The new government was not much more effective than Diem's had been, however, and the threat of communist invasion loomed large.

Eventually, the United States was forced to supply South Vietnam with military equipment and advisers so that they could defend themselves against communist forces if necessary. In August 1964, the United States began sending troops into Vietnam to fight the North Vietnamese and the Vietcong.

As the Vietnam War dragged on, it became increasingly unpopular among American citizens, who were shocked by the violent, graphic realities of the conflict. For the first time, the public could experience warfare firsthand through the television. Faced with increasing domestic resistance and the reality that the war in Vietnam could not be won, President Richard Nixon began to gradually withdraw the troops. The last of the American military forces left Vietnam in 1973. By 1975 the North Vietnamese had toppled the remnants of South Vietnam's government and seized control of the entire country.

The Formation of Israel

One of the most significant events of the post–World War II era was the founding of Israel, the Jewish state in Palestine. The movement to establish a Jewish state in Palestinian territory, known as *Zionism*, originated early in the twentieth century, when the first Zionists immigrated into the region. At that time, the Ottomans controlled Palestine. When the Ottoman Empire collapsed, the League of Nations tasked Great Britain with governing the region until it was stable enough to become an independent state. To that end, in 1917 the British issued the Balfour Declaration, which called for the formation of an independent Jewish state and attempted to protect the rights of the Arabs who were currently settled there.

Over time tensions between the Jewish settlers and the Arabs escalated. The Arabs became particularly concerned when Jews began to enter Palestine en masse during the 1930s and 1940s to escape Nazi persecution. Once World War II came to a close, the United Nations divided Palestine and created separate Jewish and Palestinian states within its borders. The United Nations designated Jerusalem, a sacred city for both Jews and Muslims, independent. Israel officially came into existence on May 14, 1948.

Almost immediately, Israel came under fire from its neighbors. On the very next day after Israel was formed, an Arab coalition with forces from Egypt, Saudi Arabia, Iraq, Syria, Jordan, and Lebanon attacked Israel. With support from the United Nations, Israel was able to win the war, and it ultimately claimed half the land that originally had been parceled out to the Palestinians. After Jordan and Egypt claimed parts of that land as well, the Palestinians were left with virtually no land of their own. In many cases, people were forced to live in refugee camps. Hostilities between the Israelis and Palestinians have continued since that time.

IMPORTANT EVENTS IN ISRAELI HISTORY

EVENT	YEAR	IMPORTANT NOTES
Suez Crisis	1956	Gamal Abdel Nasser of Egypt seized control of the Suez Canal from Israel
Six-Day War	1967	Led to Israeli occupation of Jerusalem, the West Bank, the Sinai Peninsula, and the Golan Heights
October War	1973	Brief war between Israel and Egypt
Camp David Accords	1978	Peace treaty between Israel and Egypt; Egypt recognized the legitimacy of Israel and was granted control of the Sinai Peninsula

IMPORTANT EVENTS IN ISRAELI HISTORY, CONT.

EVENT	YEAR	IMPORTANT NOTES
Declaration of Principles	1993	Peace treaty between Israel and the Palestine Liberation Organization (PLO); Palestinians were granted the right to self-rule in the West Bank and the Gaza Strip

The Fall of the Soviet Union

In 1985 Mikhail Gorbachev became leader of the Soviet Union. Gorbachev realized that traditional Soviet policies of censorship and restricted civil rights were unpopular among the people. He attempted to implement reforms that not only would make the government more transparent but also would grant the people greater freedom. His policy of *glasnost* ("openness") encouraged open discussion about the ways that Soviet society could be improved. His policy of *perestroika* ("restructuring") was aimed to rework the economic structure to improve productivity. For many of the people under Soviet control, however, Gorbachev's reforms were insufficient. Opposition to the government continued.

The first major sign of the decline of Soviet power came in 1989, when the Soviets closed the borders of East Germany to prevent citizens from escaping to the West. East Germans began to rebel. Civil unrest continued until November 9, 1989, when officials in East Germany were forced to open the Berlin Wall, which had divided Germany's capital city since 1961. Shortly thereafter, the East German government collapsed.

The fall of communism in East Germany inspired similar revolts in other Soviet-controlled countries. Anticommunist movements and civil unrest in Eastern Europe weakened Soviet control over its satellite nations and diminished the power of the Communist Party in Russia itself. A major blow against communism came in 1991, when the Soviets elected Boris Yeltsin as president.

Looking to reassert their dominance, Communist Party officials hatched a plan to overthrow Gorbachev and launch a military attack on Parliament. When the army refused to carry out the attack, Gorbachev exited the Communist Party and Parliament officially suspended its activities. Communism in Russia had come to an end.

Gorbachev resigned on Christmas Day in 1991. Yeltsin, meanwhile, disbanded the Soviet Union, replacing it with the Commonwealth of Independent States (CIS), which united Russia with a number of the former Soviet states. With the collapse of both communism and the Soviet Union, the Cold War came to an abrupt conclusion.

Review Questions

1. What is the primary reason the Soviet Union installed communist regimes in Eastern Europe after World War II?

   A. To prevent the spread of democracy
   B. To insulate itself from the West
   C. To take control of trade in the region
   D. To increase its supply of natural resources
   E. To help spread communism through Europe

2. Why did the Korean War ultimately end in a stalemate?

   A. Because UN forces were unable to penetrate North Korean territory
   B. Because the South Korean government was not supported by the Korean people
   C. Because Soviet forces threatened to enter the battle on North Korea's behalf
   D. Because the Chinese entered the war and forced UN troops to retreat
   E. Because the North Koreans did not have the resources to take South Korea entirely

3. In response to Ho Chi Minh's victory over the French in 1954, the Geneva Conference

    A. formally condemned Ho and called for his removal
    B. recognized Vietnam as an entirely independent nation
    C. split Vietnam into a communist north and democratic south
    D. enacted international economic embargoes against Vietnam
    E. petitioned the United Nations to send troops to restore French control

4. The war that followed the formation of the Jewish state of Israel resulted in all of the following, EXCEPT

    A. Israeli control of the West Bank
    B. the establishment of Palestinian refugee camps
    C. Israeli seizure of land intended for the Palestinians
    D. Egyptian control over the Gaza Strip
    E. Israeli victory over Arab forces

5. Mikhail Gorbachev's policy of *perestroika* was an attempt to stabilize the Soviet Union by

    A. encouraging discussion about government
    B. reducing political corruption
    C. restructuring the economy
    D. allowing more foreign trade
    E. promoting the further spread of communism

Answer Explanations

1. **B.** The Soviet Union was primarily interested in establishing satellite nations in Eastern Europe to protect itself from any further attacks by the West. The satellite nations in Eastern Europe created a buffer zone between mainland Russia and Western Europe.

2. **D.** The Korean War ended in a stalemate because of intervention by

China. Initially, UN forces were successful in pushing the North Koreans out of South Korea and into their own territory. The tide turned when China got involved. With a massive influx of Chinese troops, the North Koreans forced the UN army to retreat. The war ended when both sides later agreed to a cease-fire.

3.   C. The Geneva Conference divided Vietnam into a communist north and a democratic south. Hoping to limit the spread of communism in the newly independent nation, the Geneva Conference divided Vietnam at the seventeenth parallel, thereby allowing Ho to maintain his communist regime in North Vietnam while installing a democratic government in the south.

4.   A. Although the victorious Israelis claimed a considerable amount of land after they defeated the Arabs, they did not control the West Bank. At the conclusion of the war, the West Bank went to Jordan. Israel would not reclaim the West Bank until after the Six Day War in 1967.

5.   C. Gorbachev's *perestroika* policy aimed to stabilize the Soviet Union through economic restructuring. By allowing the Soviet people to own small businesses and exercise more control over farms and factories, Gorbachev hoped to stabilize the state and keep communism alive.

Review Chapter 9:
A Globalized World

T he world has become an increasingly globalized community. Where various cultures were once strongly divided by differences, modern communities have formed closer ties than have ever existed before. A global culture of interdependence has emerged and ushered in an era of heightened international relations and global awareness.

Technologies

One of the major reasons for globalization is advancement in communication and media technologies. Inventions such as radio, television, telephones, and the Internet have drastically changed the way the world communicates, allowing people to connect with one another instantaneously from nearly any location. This increased ability to communicate has led to a world that is more connected and more closely related than at any other time in history.

Other technological advancements have also played a key role in the development of the global community. In the 1950s, 1960s, and 1970s, technological competition between the United States and the Soviet Union led to rapid advances in the field of space exploration as both superpowers attempted to become the first to enter outer space. In time, the "space race" turned into a cooperative international effort, beginning with the docking of American and Soviet spacecraft in 1975. By the turn of the twenty-first century, a global team of scientists and astronauts had constructed an international space station.

Technological advances in the medical field have been equally important. The increased availability and use of vaccines, antibiotics, and insecticides have increased the population and made people healthier. International health-care organizations, such as the World Health Organization (WHO), have been established to ensure that people around the world have access to quality medical care and a healthier way of life.

Trade

One of the most significant factors in the emergence of a globalized world has been trade. A large global trading market plays a major role in creating a global community. One of the primary reasons trade has flourished in recent history is the breakdown of national trade barriers, such as protective tariffs. Various trade organizations have also been formed to help promote free trade among nations, including the European Economic Community (EEC). Founded in 1957, the EEC later became known as the *European Union* (EU). The management of free trade was improved by the formation of the World Trade Organization (WTO) in 1995. In some places, such as Europe, trade communities were able to introduce a single currency across many countries. This simplifies transactions and facilitates trade.

Regional trade organizations have also emerged. In 1994 the United States, Canada, and Mexico agreed to end tariffs as part of the North American Free Trade Agreement (NAFTA). In 1960 several South and Middle American countries signed a similar agreement called the Latin American Free Trade Agreement (LAFTA). Looking to increase the economic stability of their region, the countries of Indonesia, Thailand, Singapore, and the Philippines formed a trade alliance in 1967 called the Association of Southeast Asian Nations (ASEAN).

Environmental Issues

The globalized culture is also driven by awareness of global environmental issues. As the world has become increasingly industrialized, it has also become more dependent on fossil fuels for energy. The burning of these fuels produces pollution and damages Earth's ozone layer. The widespread use of fossil fuels, along with other forms of air pollution, have also contributed to a significant increase in the amount of carbon dioxide in the atmosphere, which has led to an increase in global temperatures, commonly referred to as *global warming.*

Global warming has elicited an international response and a cooperative attempt to find a solution. In 1997 the United Nations organized a conference in Japan to discuss the climate crisis. This conference produced the Kyoto Protocol, an environmental treaty aimed to establish regulations to control the amount of greenhouse gases in the atmosphere.

Concerns about global warming have also led to greater interest in renewable energy sources that could serve as alternatives to fossil fuels. Nations around the world have explored solar, wind, hydroelectric, geothermal, and other forms of power to meet energy needs in a more environmentally friendly way.

Terrorism

Not all aspects of globalization have been positive, of course. Recent years have seen the emergence of sophisticated international terrorist organizations. These groups commit violent attacks to spread hate and destabilize governments. Terrorists commit bombings, political assassinations, hijackings, and hostage taking to spread terror in the population. Extremists favor these types of attacks because of the media attention they attract.

One of the earliest examples of a terrorist attack that received major media attention was the kidnapping and murder of eleven Israeli athletes at the 1972 Olympic Games in Munich, Germany. Another example is the September 11, 2001, attack that occurred in the United States.

Terrorist operatives hijacked several commercial airliners and flew two of them into the Twin Towers of the World Trade Center in New York and one into the Pentagon in Washington, DC. A fourth plane bound for another target crash-landed in a field in Pennsylvania after passengers attempted to overpower the terrorists. Nearly three thousand people were killed in the attacks.

Global terrorism continues to be a significant threat to safety and security around the world.

Civil Rights

Of all the advances made since the World War II era, perhaps none has been as significant as those made in the area of civil rights. In the wake of World War II and the horrors of the Holocaust, the United Nations developed the Universal Declaration of Human Rights in 1948. This important document states that all human beings have the right to "life, liberty, and security of person."

One of the most important civil rights activists of the twentieth century was Dr. Martin Luther King Jr., who led the movement for equal rights for African Americans in the United States in the 1950s and 1960s. The African American civil rights movement inspired similar movements among other minority groups in the United States.

The struggle for women's rights, which has been ongoing throughout history, met with a number of successes in the twentieth century. The Civil Rights Act of 1964, which was beneficial for both racial minorities and women, outlawed sexual and racial discrimination. In the modern world, women in many countries enjoy the same legal rights and social standing as their male counterparts and have become a major part of the global workforce and the political arena.

Around the world, nongovernmental human rights organizations, such as Amnesty International, work to ensure that all people in the global community enjoy basic human rights.

Review Questions

1. Which of these has been the MOST important factor in the rise of globalized trade?

    A.   Increase in world population
    B.   Emergence of multinational corporations
    C.   Decline in regional national resources
    D.   Breakdown of protective tariffs
    E.   Enhancement of communications technologies

2. The Declaration of Human Rights issued by the United Nations in 1948 explicitly stated that all human beings have the right to

    A.   freedom, equality, and justice
    B.   life, liberty, and security of person
    C.   liberty, self-governance, and protection of the law
    D.   freedom, security, and religious tolerance
    E.   life, liberty, and the pursuit of happiness

3. Which terrorist incident was the first to receive major mainstream media attention?

    A.   Oklahoma City bombing
    B.   Iran hostage crisis
    C.   Israeli athletes at Munich
    D.   First World Trade Center bombing
    E.   September 11, 2001

4. Which of these is the MOST significant cause of global warming?

    A.   Global overpopulation
    B.   Increased urbanization
    C.   Nuclear energy
    D.   Burning of fossil fuels
    E.   Widespread deforestation

5. In 1997 the United Nations attempted to address the issue of global warming by

    A. producing a treaty meant to help control greenhouse gases
    B. conducting its own independent study of the phenomenon
    C. asking industrial leaders to reduce their carbon dioxide emissions
    D. encouraging the development of alternative energy sources
    E. launching a worldwide global-warming awareness campaign

Answer Explanations

1. **D.** The most significant factor in the rise of globalized trade has been the breakdown of protective tariffs between nations. The breakdown of these tariffs over the course of the latter half of the twentieth century made it much easier and less costly for nations around the world to engage in trade with one another. In many cases, the breakdown of protective tariffs was made possible through trading agreements such as LAFTA and NAFTA.

2. **B.** Since its inception, the United Nations has been committed to preserving basic human rights around the world. To this end, the organization issued the Universal Declaration of Human Rights in 1948. This landmark document explicitly states that all human beings have the natural right to "life, liberty, and security of person."

3. **C.** The murder of Israeli athletes at the 1972 Munich Olympic Games was the first terrorist incident to receive major mainstream media attention. Angered over the establishment of the Jewish state of Israel in their homeland, a group of Palestinian terrorists kidnapped eleven members of the Israeli Olympic team and murdered them. The incident played out on live television. The media attention encouraged other terrorist groups to commit similar public atrocities to attract the same kind of attention.

4. **D.** The most significant cause of global warming is the burning of

fossil fuels. As Earth's population has grown and the planet has become increasingly industrialized, communities have become more reliant on the burning of fossil fuels for energy. This practice results in the release of a number of harmful gases, including carbon dioxide, which builds up in the atmosphere.

5. **A.** The United Nations attempted to address the issue of global warming in 1997 by producing a treaty meant to help control greenhouse gases. Specifically, the United Nations adopted the Kyoto Protocol, which aims to control the greenhouse gases in the atmosphere. The treaty went into effect in 2005.

THE BIG PICTURE: HOW TO PREPARE YEAR-ROUND

No matter how far in the future you plan to take the SAT World History Subject Test, the time to start preparing is *now*. And this part of the book is here to help. Here you will learn how to register for the test, how to make the most of your preparation time both in the classroom and outside of it, and how to manage the stress a test of this magnitude may bring. As you get closer to your test date, make sure you are using all of the materials provided in this book. That way, when the day of the test arrives, you'll be ready to earn your top score!

Step 1: Get Registered

The SAT World History Subject Test is offered twice a year, once in June and once in December. The College Board recommends taking the test as soon as possible after completing your course of study in the subject, because the material will be fresher in your mind.

Test locations and registration requirements vary by location, so visit the College Board website (go to www.collegeboard.org and search for SAT Subject Test in World History, or follow the links) as soon as possible to figure out how you should register for the test and where you will be able to take it. You also want to check admissions requirements with the colleges and universities you're interested in attending; if you plan to pursue a degree in the sciences, you may be required or recommended to take one test or the other, or to achieve a particular score.

Note that SAT subject tests are available to homeschooled students as well as those in traditional high schools. Advance registration is required, and you may need to pay a fee if you do not register far enough in advance. Check the College Board's website for the information that applies in your circumstances.

Here are some important points to keep in mind as you get started:

- **Do you know what you need to know?** We can't emphasize enough how important it is to make sure you have accurate information about this test. Refer to the College Board's official website (www.collegeboard.org) for current information about the test, including eligibility, late testing, special accommodations for students with disabilities, and reduced testing fees for low-income students. This site also allows you to register (and gives alternative registration options, such as how to register by phone or mail) and tells you how your score will be reported to the colleges and universities you're interested in attending. Don't depend on getting this information from anyone else! Since you purchased this book, obviously you're interested in doing well on the examination, so don't risk losing points by not knowing what you need to know. Time spent on early research can pay off for you down the road.

- **It's all about the timing.** The tricky thing about an examination like the SAT World History Subject Test is that you really don't want to take it more than twice, and you do want to take it somewhere close to your relevant coursework. You should try to take the test once in your junior year and a second time in your senior year. If you're worried about coordinating the testing date around your studies, don't be! The test is actually offered twice a year; as long as you do some advance planning, you should be able to get a test date that works for you.

- **Be proactive.** If you're *not* enrolled in a suitable class at school, take the initiative! Do some reading to refresh yourself on the topic. Borrow some suitable books from the library. Review the study guide carefully and determine exactly what you need to know.

- **Remember, it's worth it!** You might be worried about your anxiety level for this test. You might be thinking that in the overall scheme of senior year and college prep, this test is less important than others you need to worry about. You might be concerned about not doing well. If your thought process is running in this direction, slow down for a minute! Consider how little you have to lose if you score poorly on the test, and how much you have to gain if you do well. Plus, you may do better than you expect if you make the best use of study time and material at your disposal. (Consider especially the resources in this book!) Even if, after all is said and done, you *don't* do well, remember, a low score doesn't have to be devastating—you can take the test again if you wish. Plus, if you're concerned, the Score Choice service allows you to choose the particular scores you want to share with the colleges of your choice.

Step 2: Become an Expert Student

To do well on the test, you must retain a ton of information both in and out of the classroom. You will have to work hard and study. Did you know that studying is a discipline in and of itself that many people just don't know how to do well? It's true. Even the smartest people need to learn *how* to study to maximize their ability to learn.

One of the most critical study skills involves notes. More specifically, it involves taking effective notes rather than just writing down every-thing your teacher says. Don't underestimate how important good note taking is both during class and while you're studying alone or with a partner. Good note taking serves several purposes. First (and most obvi-ously), note taking is important for making sure you have recorded the key points being made by your teacher (or your study partner). Since this person is very familiar with the material and the test, he or she knows where you should focus your time, so you should glean as much knowledge as you possibly can. Second, effective note taking is impor-tant because the process of working on notes can actually help you retain the material. For example, the deceptively simple act of writing and rewriting reinforces your memory just from doing the activity. In addi-tion, writing in conjunction with listening or reading helps reinforce the information, which makes it more likely that you will remember it.

Here are some tips for taking great notes:

- **Listen actively**. The first key to taking good notes is to practice *active listening*—that is, listening in a structured way to understand and evaluate what's being said. Active listeners are not distracted, thinking about other things or considering what they will say next (in the classroom, this means opening up your mind rather than thinking about some question you might ask your teacher). Active listening also does not involve writing down every single thing the teacher says. Rather, it means listening in a structured way so that you hear the main ideas, pay attention to cues that impart meaning, and keep your eyes on the speaker (not on your notebook).

    ◦ Listen for main ideas. Before you even begin the note-taking process, consider the topic under discussion and be ready to organize your notes around that topic. Is it a person, place, movement? Is it a particular era or concept? Do some thinking beforehand about the topic and work from that angle. Also listen for transitions into new topics as the teacher works his or her way through the material.

○ Pay attention to cues. If you're taking notes in class, certain words and phrases tend to reflect the way the discussion is organized. For example, the teacher usually starts with an introduction, and this introduction generally provides the framework around how the topic will be treated. For example, "Today we will evaluate the results of the French Revolution and think critically about how it influenced the emergence of modern society." Listen for transition words such as *next* and *the following,* and look out for numbered or bulleted lists.

○ Don't just stare at your notebook. Information is conveyed by speakers in a number of ways, many of them nonverbal. Keep an eye on the instructor's body language and expressions. These are the types of nonverbal cues that will help you determine what's important and what's not.

- **What do good notes look like?** Good notes are not just a jumbled mass of everything. It's unrealistic and ineffective to try to write down everything there is to say about a topic. Instead, you should learn to focus on key words and main ideas. Here are some tips on how to proceed:

○ Start with a clean sheet. Indicate today's date and the main or primary topic. This will jog your memory later on when you study these notes.

○ If the instructor is using slides, don't just copy word for word what's on the slide. Instead, jot down the title of the slide and the key idea, concept, or overall topic under discussion (this should be apparent from either the title of the slide deck, the title of the slide itself, or the instructor's introduction).

○ Listen actively to your instructor's treatment of the material and his or her points of emphasis. Try to *really listen* to what your instructor is saying. Then, as your teacher makes important points, write them down in bullet-point or summarized fashion. Don't worry too much about organization in the moment. Just do your best to capture the discussion in a way that makes sense to you.

- If you're confused about something, ask for clarification. Many students make the mistake of not asking for help when the teacher makes a statement that is confusing or unclear. Sometimes even the best teachers go too fast or fail to transition you through the material plainly. It's much better to ask for help than to write down a bunch of information that makes no sense to you later.

- This is an important and often-overlooked point: once class is over, *rewrite* or *retype* your notes, using the opportunity to also fold in information from your textbook or other resources. This is your opportunity to bring real organization, clarity, and understanding to the material. You should rewrite or retype your notes regularly (preferably daily, but if that's not possible, at least weekly). You'll be amazed at how much more sense the material makes if you take the time to look at it critically and rework it in a way that makes sense to you on a regular basis.

- Take notes from your books and other resources as well as your class notes—see the section later here on "reading to understand." This test covers *a lot* of material. Paying attention to what gets attention in resources can help you focus.

- Review your notes before class every day. Doing so serves as a reminder of where you are chronologically and helps you transition from concept to concept and era to era. Work mindfully to make connections among the material that you're learning. Those connections will serve you well later.

- **How do you read to understand?** Material such as this book and your class textbook can make the difference between a passing and failing grade, or between a so-so and an excellent score. However, you need to understand what you're reading so that you can supplement your class notes:

- Do a complete read-through. Start with the objectives of the chapter. Review the questions at the end.

- Map out the main ideas. Once you've read through the material and have an overall understanding, write down the main ideas and leave space to fill in details. Wherever possible, find your own words. Avoid copying text exactly from the book. Paraphrasing the material in your own words helps you engage with the material and facilitates your learning.

- Reread the material. Once you have the main ideas mapped out, you should reread the material with an eye toward filling in details under each of the main ideas.

- Fill in the details. Now that you've reread, write details under each main idea—again, do not copy the words exactly from the book, but use your own words so that you retain the information. Use details from the book or other resource and from your class notes.

- Put the book aside, and read through your notes. Do you understand what you've written? Have you accurately represented the main ideas? Did you fill in the appropriate level of detail?

- Review, review, review. Read your notes over and over again. That's how you get the information to stick.

Step 3: Create a Realistic Study Plan

If you're like many students with challenging classes, extracurricular activities, and other priorities, you may have only a limited amount of time to review for this test. This section will help you get the most out of your limited test preparation time and make it really count. You need a plan specifically for you—one that addresses *your* needs and considers the time you have available. No two people will have exactly the same plan or use this book in exactly the same way. To develop a personalized test prep plan, you'll need to identify your weak points and then allocate time to address them efficiently and effectively.

Here are the three basic steps to creating a personalized test prep plan:

1. **Identify your weak points**. Start by taking the **Diagnostic Test** (page 53) in this book. This will show you what you're up against. It will also help you get a feel for the test and identify the subject areas in which you need to focus. On the basis of your performance, you can prioritize the subjects to review, starting with the areas in which you are weakest. If your time is limited or if you feel you're not ready to take a complete practice test, focus your review by skimming the diagnostic test and identifying those areas in which you have the most difficulty with understanding.

2. **Develop a review plan and a schedule.** Figure out how much time you can devote each week to test preparation and reserve specific blocks of time for this purpose. Create a written schedule that includes specific time slots and activities or content areas for review. This will help you pace yourself to get through all of the material you want to review. You'll likely find that there are content areas or question types you want to focus on more than others. Also make sure your plan includes time to master test-taking strategies and actually take the practice tests.

3. **Marshal your self-discipline**. The hard part about a plan for test prep is making yourself stick to it. Schedule your test prep time actively in your calendar. Don't let it get pushed aside by more seemingly urgent activities. You've come a long way; don't blow the test by failing to prepare for it. Develop a plan for your needs in the time you have available and then stick with it.

For some people, it helps to have a study partner. A partner may make it easier to hold to the schedule and it may also help you to study more effectively. You and your partner can quiz each other, share information, and exchange ideas. However, for other people, having a study partner makes it harder to stay on topic and focus on studying. Try to figure out, by thinking about past experience, how you can best enforce your study plan and most effectively use your time.

Step 4: Use All the Resources at Your Disposal

This book is an excellent way to prepare for this test. It includes not only the diagnostic test but also two *full* practice tests. Each test has unique questions so you get the opportunity to address all different areas of the content in all different ways.

In addition, another practice test is available to you free of charge at mymaxscore.com.

Check out the website for the College Board (www.collegeboard.org). At this site, you can find actual released tests that are no longer in circulation along with general information about the test and testing advice.

You'll also find lots of other test resources in your library, at the local bookstore, or online. Look around to see what's available and figure out ways to work that material into your study time if you can.

Good luck! Happy studying!

This book contains two practice tests. Visit mymaxscore.com to download your free third practice test with answers and explanations.

SAT World History Subject Test Practice Test 1

SAT Subject Test in World History
Time—60 minutes
95 questions

Directions: Each of the questions or incomplete statements is followed by five answer choices. Choose the answer choice that best answers the question or best completes the incomplete statement.

Note: This test uses the chronological designations BCE (before the Common Era) and CE (Common Era). These designations correspond to BC (before Christ) and AD (*anno Domini*), which are used in some history texts.

1. The Mauryan emperor Ashoka's reign was characterized by

    A. honest proclamations and positive behavior
    B. incessant warfare and brutality toward citizens
    C. oppressive and ascetic totalitarian government
    D. construction of expansive monuments and buildings
    E. drastic rejection of Buddhist principles

2. Socialists such as Friedrich Engels argued that

   A.   society is necessary to protect individuals from the chaotic brutality inherent to human nature
   B.   governments can be truly just only when they directly represent the people under their rule
   C.   nations must compete for power and fortune just as animals compete for supremacy in nature
   D.   financial wealth and resources should be distributed evenly among the citizens of a nation
   E.   every citizen has a duty to devote his or her life to the betterment of the nation or culture

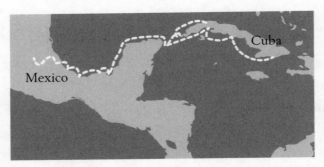

3. In the map shown, the dotted line approximates the path of

   A.   the Spanish silver trade
   B.   Portuguese colonization
   C.   the Cortés conquest of the Aztec
   D.   Mayan expansionism
   E.   the Pizarro conquest of the Inca

4.   Which of these describes Hammurabi's most significant contribu-
     tion to civilization?

     A.   The defeat and destruction of Assyrian invasion armies around
          675 BCE
     B.   A precedent of peaceful negotiations with the rulers of
          Southwest Asia
     C.   The ushering of Egypt into the period known as the Old Kingdom
     D.   The design and construction of the legendary Hanging Gardens
          of Babylon
     E.   A comprehensive system of laws by which a kingdom could
          be governed

5.   What was Sigmund Freud's intent with his breakthrough publica-
     tion *Die Traumdeutung?*

     A.   Reconciling taboo desires
     B.   Interpreting the meaning of dreams
     C.   Exploring societal and gender roles
     D.   Debunking theories of hypnosis
     E.   Treating emotional hysteria

6.   The nomadic practices of the Mongols proved MOST beneficial to
     the conquering of other peoples in that these practices

     A.   helped the Mongols to amass great stores of riches, food,
          and weapons
     B.   encouraged toughness and endurance among the Mongols
     C.   improved Mongol horsemanship and mobility and allowed
          them to strike quickly
     D.   enhanced the Mongols' ability to survive in different environments
     E.   served to increase the Mongol population and its armies

7. The Green Revolution was important in modern times because it

    A. raised global support for environmental preservation initiatives
    B. encouraged the development and use of renewable energy sources
    C. aggressively advocated for equal rights for women and children
    D. brought greater political stability to the nations of Eastern Europe
    E. increased crop yields to combat starvation in developing nations

8. Which event marked the first year in the Muslim calendar?

    A. Muhammad completed the Koran.
    B. Muhammad was born.
    C. Muhammad joined a caravan to Syria.
    D. Muhammad died.
    E. Muhammad journeyed from Mecca to Medina.

9. Which of these is symbolically represented by the sculpture of a mother wolf feeding two children?

    A. Founding of the city of Rome
    B. Greek dominance of the ancient world
    C. Myths of the demigod Hercules
    D. Importance of ancient philosophy
    E. Rise of neoclassicism in Europe

10. The South African policy of apartheid was specifically designed to

    A.   prevent the spread of communism into the region
    B.   limit foreign influence on internal political matters
    C.   encourage trade with Europe and the Americas
    D.   ensure Afrikaners political dominance of the country
    E.   stabilize the nation in its early years of independence

11. Which modern fields have been most affected by the accomplishments of the ancient Greeks and Romans?

    A.   Ethics and religion
    B.   Medicine and hygiene
    C.   Politics and government
    D.   Finances and trade
    E.   Science and technology

12. In European history, the term *Lebensraum*, or "living space," most commonly refers to the

    A   German desire for expansion in the twentieth century
    B   forced relocation of ethnic minorities into ghetto towns
    C   rejection of industrialization and urbanization
    D   celebration of the bucolic ideal in art and literature
    E   immigration to North America in the twentieth century

13. Conflicts between which two religions resulted in the Edict of Nantes (1598)?

    A.   Jainism and Islam
    B.   Calvinism and Lutheranism
    C.   Roman Catholicism and Protestantism
    D.   Hinduism and Buddhism
    E.   Sikhism and Orthodox Judaism

14. What was the primary motivation for most Irish citizens who immigrated to North America in the nineteenth century?

    A.   Find freedom of religion
    B.   Locate support for Irish independence
    C.   Escape national famine
    D.   Avoid conscription in the British army
    E.   Protest British imperialism

15. In the Hindu caste system, members of the Shudra caste originally served as

    A.   servants and workers
    B.   kings and nobles
    C.   traders and merchants
    D.   soldiers and courtiers
    E.   priests and teachers

16. The Olmec civilization occupied the modern-day lands known as

    A.   Baja California Peninsula
    B.   Western Mexico's Pacific Coast
    C.   Guatemala and Northern Belize
    D.   Southern Mexico's Gulf Coast
    E.   Amazon basin and rainforest

"Whatsoever therefore is consequent to a time of war, where every man is enemy to every man, the same consequent to the time wherein men live without other security than what their own strength and their own invention shall furnish them withal. In such condition there is...continual fear, and danger of violent death; and the life of man, solitary, poor, nasty, brutish, and short."

17. The above statement expresses the views of which historical figure?

   A.   Thomas Hobbes
   B.   John Calvin
   C.   Jean-Jacques Rousseau
   D.   Niccolò Machiavelli
   E.   Thomas Aquinas

18. Japan underwent change during the Meiji Restoration that most closely resembled change in

   A.   Persia under the rule of the Hephthalites
   B.   Russia during the reign of Czar Peter I
   C.   Judea under Roman occupation
   D.   Sri Lanka prior to British colonization
   E.   France during the Revolutionary era

19. The Duma, active in Russia from 1906 to 1917, can BEST be described as a/an

   A.   revolutionary secret society
   B.   anticommunist political party
   C.   elected legislative body
   D.   secret government police force
   E.   union of industrial workers

20. The Byzantine Empire collapsed after more than one thousand years in existence primarily because of the

    A.   ascension of Frederick III to Holy Roman Emperor in 1452

    B.   Great Schism that began around 1378

    C.   Ottoman conquest of Constantinople in 1453

    D.   end of Russian tributes to the Golden Horde in 1462

    E.   French victories that ended the Hundred Years' War in 1453

21. Books such as George Orwell's *Nineteen Eighty-Four* and Aldous Huxley's *Brave New World* are major twentieth-century examples of what literary form?

    A.   Tragicomedy

    B.   Satirical fiction

    C.   Epistolary fiction

    D.   Dystopian novel

    E.   Feminist novel

22. The practice of offshoring by industrialized countries in the twentieth century generally values all of the following EXCEPT

    A.   increased availability of raw materials

    B.   domestic economic development

    C.   reduction of overall business costs

    D.   overall lowering of labor costs

    E.   less stringent labor and environmental laws

23. The introduction of agriculture most significantly affected formerly nomadic societies by

    A.   creating a gender-based separation of responsibilities

    B.   increasing the density of the population

    C.   necessitating the frequent migration of humans

    D.   decreasing the chance of food surpluses

    E.   eradicating the traditional specialization of labor

24. Which country claimed the colony of Madagascar as a possession until an ongoing freedom movement led to its independence in 1960?

    A. France
    B. Germany
    C. United States
    D. Portugal
    E. Britain

25. When issued in 1215, the Magna Carta established the legal principle of

    A. due process of law
    B. burden of proof
    C. statute of limitations
    D. judicial deference
    E. sovereign immunity

26. Which religion developed in India alongside Buddhism around the sixth century BCE in response to religious speculation over Hinduism?

    A. Jainism
    B. Rastafarianism
    C. Shintoism
    D. Sikhism
    E. Zoroastrianism

27. In the Paraguayan War beginning in 1864, Paraguay fought against the combined forces of

    A. Spanish and British colonizers
    B. Uruguay, Argentina, and Brazil
    C. Chile, Peru, and Bolivia
    D. Peru and British colonizers
    E. Bolivia and Spanish colonizers

28. In what year were Upper and Lower Canada united?

    A. 1755
    B. 1776
    C. 1813
    D. 1841
    E. 1913

29. The medieval African empire of Ghana thrived because of its inter-
    mediary position between the

    A. intellectuals of Europe and Africa
    B. traders of salt and traders of gold and ivory
    C. Silk Roads and the spice routes
    D. fishing towns and agricultural communities
    E. Christian and Muslim settlements

30. The Chinese imperial palace used by rulers from the Ming through
    the Qing dynasties was known as the

    A. Forbidden City
    B. Wumen
    C. Potala Palace
    D. Xanadu
    E. Outer City

31. The ziggurats of ancient Mesopotamia most closely resembled the

    A. Vedas of the Aryans
    B. pyramids of the Egyptians
    C. aqueducts of the Romans
    D. pueblos of the Native Americans
    E. pagodas of the Chinese

32. A twentieth-century territorial dispute over control of the province of Kashmir resulted in conflict between India and

   A. Russia
   B. China
   C. Pakistan
   D. Japan
   E. Bangladesh

33. Which of these was NOT true of the pharaohs of ancient Egypt?

   A. They owned most of the kingdom's land.
   B. They were said to become divine after death.
   C. They typically delegated duties to viziers.
   D. They were required to be male.
   E. They were believed to control nature.

34. The opium trade between Britain and China arose primarily due to

   A. lack of Japanese participation in trade
   B. European interest in trading with China
   C. the belief that opium was medicinally beneficial
   D. Chinese desire for European manufactured items
   E. the increasing scarcity of natural resources in Europe

35. How was the Great Schism in Roman Catholicism resolved in the fifteenth century?

   A. Church electors installed a second and third pope.
   B. The Council of Constance chose to recall popes.
   C. Scholars translated the Bible into vernacular English.
   D. Scholasticism changed belief systems in Europe.
   E. The papacy temporarily relocated to Avignon in France.

36. The theology of Judaism MOST differed from other early religions due to its belief in

    A.   monotheism
    B.   Gnosticism
    C.   nihilism
    D.   divine right of monarchs
    E.   religious rites and rituals

37. What was the primary difference between the artistic movements of romanticism and classicism?

    A.   Romanticism alluded to the art and thought of ancient civilizations.
    B.   Romanticism stressed the importance of feelings and emotions.
    C.   Classicism was inspired by the forms and essences of nature.
    D.   Romanticism was founded on principles of reason and rationale.
    E.   Classicism rejected science and symmetry in its compositions.

38. Which of these was an important virtue in Daoism?

    A.   Focusing on secular advancement
    B.   Fostering community-mindedness
    C.   Separating spirituality from culture
    D.   Adhering to strict moral duties
    E.   Eliminating all earthly desires

39. The Rosetta stone was important in

    A.   understanding currency and trade rates in ancient North Africa
    B.   deciphering Egyptian hieroglyphics using Greek translations
    C.   tracing the milestones of Roman occupation in Southwest Asia
    D.   translating written inscriptions in the Linear A and B forms
    E.   providing a written record of the laws of ancient Mesopotamia

40. Pope Benedict VIII made a lasting change to Roman Catholic doctrine in 1022 when he passed a declaration that

   A.   instituted a celibacy requirement for clergy
   B.   forbade the sale of indulgences to laymen
   C.   instituted the practice of selling church offices
   D.   forbade the use of torture during inquisitions
   E.   instituted the practice of electing multiple popes

41. Which ancient civilization most likely pioneered the production and use of iron around 2500 BCE?

   A.   Persians
   B.   Hebrews
   C.   Hittites
   D.   Babylonians
   E.   Sumerians

42. The individual political struggles of Nelson Mandela and Mahatma Gandhi were MOST similar in that they

   A.   worked to secure the independence of their nations from colonial rule
   B.   fought against oppressive governments that encouraged racism
   C.   eventually became high-ranking officials in their governments
   D.   protested injustice through prolonged hunger strikes
   E.   founded militant revolutionary organizations

43. By the year 1100 CE, the strongest Norman influence was felt in which modern regions?

   A.   Norway, Sweden, and England
   B.   Africa and the Mediterranean
   C.   Russia and the Baltic region
   D.   Germany, Austria, and Italy
   E.   England, Italy, and France

44. The Paleolithic Era was distinguished by the use of stone tools, while the Neolithic Era was distinguished by

    A. metalworking capabilities
    B. cavalry as part of warfare
    C. advanced architectural construction
    D. advances in agriculture
    E. marked empire building

45. The medieval cities of Venice, Italy, and Tenochtitlán, Mexico, were MOST similar in that they

    A. hosted populations of about 400,000 citizens
    B. served as major seaports for international trade
    C. were sacked by invaders in the sixteenth century
    D. prospered because of their industrial capacities
    E. were constructed on top of islands

46. Which of these is the BEST example of the practice known as "total war"?

    A. Extension of armed conflict beyond traditional land battles into the sea and air
    B. Use of extensive espionage and reconnaissance networks within enemy territory
    C. Use of cutting-edge technology and propaganda to influence public sentiments
    D. Bombing of civilian centers to destroy an enemy's ability to continue fighting
    E. Inability to end a conflict without the complete destruction of the enemy's army

"Respectfulness, without the rules of propriety, becomes laborious bustle; carefulness, without the rules of propriety, becomes timidity; boldness, without the rules of propriety, becomes insubordination; straightforwardness, without the rules of propriety, becomes rudeness."

47. The above excerpt expresses the viewpoint of

   A. Machiavelli
   B. Socrates
   C. Erasmus
   D. Confucius
   E. Lao Tzu

48. Which of these statements about the practice of slavery in ancient and medieval civilizations is NOT true?

   A. Slavery was rarely pursued among hunter-gatherer populations.
   B. Enslaved people were put to work in a wide variety of occupations.
   C. Slavery existed within Africa before European colonization.
   D. Enslaved people were important to ancient Greece and Rome.
   E. Enslaved people were almost exclusively black Africans.

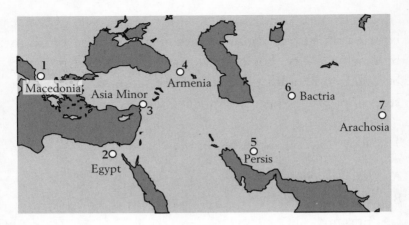

49. In the map shown, the numbered dots correspond to cities. Which cities most closely represent the East-West limits of the territories conquered or controlled by Alexander the Great?

   A.   1 and 6
   B.   1 and 7
   C.   2 and 6
   D.   2 and 7
   E.   3 and 7

50. The main goal of the 1848 meeting among liberal leaders in Frankfurt am Main was to

   A.   destroy the autonomy of the German states
   B.   win political favors from German princes
   C.   abolish the system of hereditary monarchy
   D.   promote the unification of German states
   E.   overthrow Frederick William of Prussia

51. European imperialist powers competed for influence in Egypt during the nineteenth century primarily because of the

    A.   importance of the Suez Canal

    B.   desire to exploit the Nile River valley

    C.   ease of moving armies through Egypt

    D.   interest in utilizing industrial capabilities

    E.   abundance of labor and resources

52. Which of these religions does NOT view the state of nirvana as the ultimate spiritual goal?

    A.   Buddhism

    B.   Hinduism

    C.   Islam

    D.   Jainism

    E.   Sikhism

53. The White Lotus society, most active in China between the seventeenth and twentieth centuries, is BEST characterized as a

    A.   civilian militia

    B.   religious sect

    C.   Manchu tribe

    D.   political party

    E.   economic alliance

54. Which two countries did James I rule concurrently from 1603 to 1625?

    A.   England and France

    B.   England and Wales

    C.   England and Scotland

    D.   Denmark and Norway

    E.   Ireland and Scotland

55. Which of these was the MOST significant accomplishment of the Phoenician civilization?

    A. Creation of intricate and accessible legal codes
    B. Discovery of significant celestial bodies
    C. Development of the idea of compensatory damages
    D. Study of the stars and their relationship to the zodiac
    E. Invention of an alphabet for syllabic writing

56. The nation called Ceylon by British colonizers became known in the postcolonial period as

    A. Sri Lanka
    B. Cambodia
    C. Laos
    D. Bhutan
    E. Myanmar

"We intend to begin on the first of February unrestricted submarine warfare. We shall endeavor in spite of this to keep the United States of America neutral. In the event of this not succeeding, we make Mexico a proposal of alliance on the following basis: make war together, make peace together, generous financial support and an understanding on our part that Mexico is to reconquer the lost territory in Texas, New Mexico, and Arizona."

57. In what document did the above excerpt originally appear?

    A. *The Communist Manifesto*
    B. Final Solution
    C. Five-Year Plan
    D. Zimmermann telegram
    E. Schlieffen Plan

58. All of these led to the Industrial Revolution in Britain EXCEPT a

    A. consumerist society
    B. number of technological advancements
    C. decrease in the agricultural workforce
    D. lack of being a colonial power
    E. major international trading partner

59. The Taiping Rebellion was similar to the communist takeover in China in that both events

    A. were generally unaffected by religious doctrine
    B. originated from radical Marxist political views
    C. were driven by discontent with the Versailles Treaty
    D. involved minimal physical conflict and bloodshed
    E. called for the equal distribution of property and rights

60. Which world calendar was created most recently?

    A. Julian calendar
    B. Egyptian calendar
    C. Coptic calendar
    D. Gregorian calendar
    E. Mayan calendar

61. The actions of the Luddites MOST strongly supported the social perspective that

    A. hereditary nobility is ordained by a divine power
    B. freedom of religion could not exist in monarchical government
    C. traditional gender roles are the foundation of a healthy economy
    D. public education should be limited to the higher classes
    E. industrial technology may be a detriment to workers

62. The medieval African emperor Mansa Mūsā was most notable for his

    A.   cruelty to ambassadors from neighboring lands
    B.   frequent violent incursions into Europe
    C.   role in establishing the Atlantic slave trade
    D.   opulence and enrichment of Timbuktu
    E.   religious fervor and support of Christianity

63. The Silk Roads were indirectly responsible for spreading

    A.   slavery in Europe
    B.   diseases in Africa
    C.   Buddhism in China
    D.   socialism in Asia
    E.   manorialism in India

64. Which system of writing was primarily used in the languages of Hindi, Sanskrit, and Nepali?

    A.   Arabic
    B.   Cuneiform
    C.   Latin
    D.   Cyrillic
    E.   Devanagari

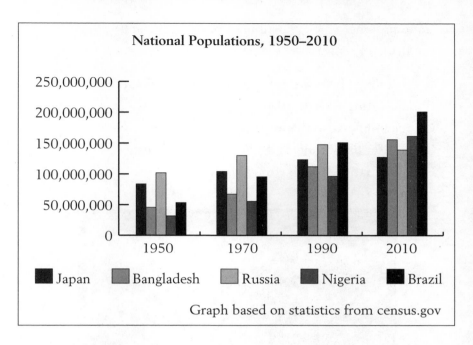

National Populations, 1950–2010

Graph based on statistics from census.gov

65. The information shown in the graph BEST supports which of the following statements?

   A. The birthrate of the developed nations in East Asia is on a rapid increase.

   B. Improvement of medical technologies in South America has increased the life span there.

   C. The population on the Indian subcontinent has been significantly reduced by natural disasters.

   D. An HIV epidemic in the late twentieth century claimed a significant number of African lives.

   E. The migration of Eastern Europe workers searching for employment has risen since the fall of the Soviet Union.

66. Captain James Cook contributed most significantly to the power of the British Empire by

    A. leading a British campaign in the Seven Years' War
    B. defeating French forces at Quebec
    C. claiming Australia for the British crown
    D. legislating for increased British industrialism
    E. negotiating British control in India

67. Which style is demonstrated in the architecture of the buildings shown?

    A. Gothic
    B. Pueblo
    C. Baroque
    D. Spanish colonial
    E. American colonial

68. In the twentieth century, Manfred von Richthofen came to be generally recognized as a symbol of the

    A. excesses of landed aristocracy
    B. spread of colonial expansionism
    C. last vestiges of military chivalry
    D. desire to separate church from state
    E. movement for German unification

"O, my brothers, love your Country!...It is only through our country that we can have a recognized collective existence...Let each man among you strive to incarnate his country in himself. Let each man among you regard himself as a guarantor, responsible for his fellow-countrymen, and learn so to govern his actions as to cause his country to be loved and respected through him."

69. Which theory is best exemplified in this excerpt from the work of Giuseppe Mazzini?

   A.   Absolutism
   B.   Conservatism
   C.   Utilitarianism
   D.   Nationalism
   E.   Liberalism

70. Which philosopher died after being convicted of corrupting the youth of Athens in 399 BCE?

   A.   Xenophon
   B.   Socrates
   C.   Plato
   D.   Aristotle
   E.   Heracleides Ponticus

71. Mumbai was a world leader in which industry during the middle of the nineteenth century?

   A.   Silk production
   B.   Cotton textiles
   C.   Opium manufacture
   D.   Slave trade
   E.   Spice trade

72. The primary result of the Third Crusade was the

    A.   Muslim sacking of Constantinople

    B.   removal of Islamic rule in Spain

    C.   Christian failure to regain Jerusalem

    D.   foundation of the Latin Empire

    E.   Christian capture of Jerusalem

73. All of these took place in Brazil during the reign of Pedro II (1831–89) EXCEPT a/an

    A.   backlash against the "coffee government"

    B.   focus on producing coffee instead of sugar

    C.   abolition of slavery throughout Brazil

    D.   modernizing of railroads and telegraphs

    E.   military coup that overthrew the monarchy

74. Which of these leaders was MOST influential in the establishment of an Islamic government in modern Iran?

    A.   Reza Shah Pahlavi

    B.   Nader Shah Afshar

    C.   Ayatollah Rūḥallāh Khomeynī

    D.   Mohammad Reza Shah Pahlavi

    E.   Āghā Moḥammad Khān

75. In African tradition, elaborately carved and decorated wooden masks are most likely to be employed during

    A.   ceremonies of spirits and religion

    B.   tribal battles and other warfare

    C.   family gatherings and clan meetings

    D.   theatrical and social entertainments

    E.   trade and diplomatic missions

76. In 212 CE, Roman citizenship was extended to

    A.   slaves and indentured servants
    B.   all free inhabitants of the Republic
    C.   all military personnel and veterans
    D.   educated native-born landowners
    E.   all free inhabitants of the empire

77. The events that took place at Masada in 72–73 CE showed that the early Jews of Israel were

    A.   great reformers in economy and society
    B.   fierce conquerors of opposing kingdoms
    C.   mediators of conflicts between neighbors
    D.   determined defenders of their homeland
    E.   enlightened scholars of philosophy

78. Which of these shows the correct chronological order in which different types of metals were discovered and used?

    A.   Bronze, iron, steel, copper
    B.   Copper, bronze, iron, steel
    C.   Iron, steel, copper, bronze
    D.   Steel, copper, iron, bronze
    E.   Bronze, copper, steel, iron

79. London was originally developed from a village into a major walled city by the

    A.   Vikings, circa 865 CE
    B.   Normans, circa 1066 CE
    C.   Anglo-Saxons, circa 670 CE
    D.   Celts, circa 50 BCE
    E.   Romans, circa 43 CE

80. The kingdom of Great Zimbabwe was most notable in the African Iron Age for its extensive system of

    A. military formations
    B. walls and stonework
    C. ports and markets
    D. silver mines
    E. salt mines

81. The Russo-Japanese War became the first event in modern history in which

    A. colonial and imperial ambitions led to armed conflict
    B. an Asian nation achieved victory over a European power
    C. two major world powers clashed over territory
    D. a conflict took place simultaneously on the land and sea
    E. territory rather than ideology was the motivating factor

82. The writings of Charles Dickens were BEST known for their criticism of

    A. apparent hypocrisy in religious ethics
    B. universal suffrage movements
    C. British colonial ambitions and trade
    D. economic inequality and poverty
    E. racist practices and world slavery

83. In ancient times, the most common route for the Chinese to trade with the Roman Empire and Europe was

    A. Via Maris
    B. Silk Roads
    C. Appian Way
    D. Middle Passage
    E. King's Highway

84. The Four Noble Truths, traditionally believed to have been articu-
    lated by the Buddha in his first sermon after enlightenment, include
    all of the following EXCEPT

    A. suffering is caused by desire and other negative actions
    B. dissemination of beliefs is necessary to a religion
    C. human life is inevitably filled with sorrow
    D. nirvana may be reached via the path of the Middle Way
    E. cessation of desires can lead to the peace of nirvana

85. Chinese leader Kublai Khan was known for all of the following,
    EXCEPT

    A. introducing Buddhism to China
    B. completing the Mongol conquest of China
    C. establishing a capital city in Beijing
    D. serving as host and benefactor to Marco Polo
    E. launching unsuccessful invasions of Japan

86. In seventeenth-century Holland, a major economic bubble resulted
    from speculative frenzy over the sale of

    A. artwork
    B. religious relics
    C. Chinese silks
    D. houses
    E. tulips

87. This embroidery of England's King Harold was created to memorialize the

    A. invasion of the Anglo-Saxons
    B. Roman takeover of England
    C. Irish resistance to English oppression
    D. Norman takeover of England
    E. English domination of Wales and Scotland

88. Which of these was the primary obstacle to French construction of the Panama Canal in the 1880s?

    A. Diseases carried by mosquitoes
    B. Negotiations with labor unions
    C. Encroachments by the British
    D. Conflicts with the natives
    E. Battles of the Spanish-American War

89. The Chinese concept of *t'ien ming,* or mandate of heaven, most closely resembled the European ideal of

    A. indentured labor
    B. feudal manorialism
    C. the "city on the hill"
    D. divine right of kings
    E. royal appanage

90. Which of these does NOT describe one of the reasons Mexico declined an alliance with Germany during World War I?

   A. British blockades would prevent armament shipments to Mexico.
   B. Americans in former Mexican territories would refuse to assimilate.
   C. Mexican ships felt too threatened by German U-boats.
   D. Attacking the United States would endanger South American alliances.
   E. The United States would be too powerful an enemy for Mexico.

91. Ancient imperialism MOST differed from modern imperialism in that

   A. modern imperialism focuses more on taxation of conquered people
   B. ancient imperialism was undertaken mostly by Britain and France
   C. modern imperialism has generally involved very few nations
   D. ancient imperialism focused more strongly on Asia and Africa
   E. modern imperialism is focused primarily on industrialist pursuits

92. The Songhai Empire in Western Africa collapsed in 1591 as an immediate result of

   A. attempts to promote trade on the Niger River
   B. an invasion by Morocco into the Songhai territory
   C. fluctuations in the trading of gold and salt
   D. conflict between Islam and traditional religions
   E. the conquering of Gao by the Mali Empire

93. Alchemy is best defined as the practice of

   A. paying reparations for damages caused by warfare
   B. banning religious services in a particular region
   C. making a government's political processes transparent
   D. manufacturing interchangeable parts on assembly lines
   E. attempting to transform metals and find immortality

94. The 1955 Warsaw Pact created a communist counterbalance to the

    A.   European Union
    B.   United Nations
    C.   Union of Soviet Socialist Republics
    D.   European Economic Community
    E.   North Atlantic Treaty Organization

95. The Zapatista National Liberation Army, which arose in Mexico in the 1990s, chose the name Zapatista to evoke the

    A.   glories of Mexican monarchs
    B.   spirit of peasant rebellion
    C.   fervor of Islamic extremists
    D.   plight of migrant workers
    E.   anger of South American warriors

END OF PRACTICE TEST 1

Practice Test 1 Answers and Explanations

Answer Key

1. A	26. A
2. D	27. B
3. C	28. D
4. E	29. B
5. B	30. A
6. C	31. B
7. E	32. C
8. E	33. D
9. A	34. B
10. D	35. B
11. C	36. A
12. A	37. B
13. C	38. E
14. C	39. B
15. A	40. A
16. D	41. C
17. A	42. B
18. B	43. E
19. C	44. D
20. C	45. E
21. D	46. D
22. B	47. D
23. B	48. E
24. A	49. B
25. A	50. D

51. A	74. C
52. C	75. A
53. B	76. E
54. C	77. D
55. E	78. B
56. A	79. E
57. D	80. B
58. D	81. B
59. E	82. D
60. D	83. B
61. E	84. B
62. D	85. A
63. C	86. E
64. E	87. D
65. B	88. A
66. C	89. D
67. B	90. C
68. C	91. E
69. D	92. B
70. B	93. E
71. B	94. E
72. C	95. B
73. A	

Answer Explanations

1. **A.** Ashoka, the last emperor of the Mauryan culture who reigned in present-day India around 250 BCE, was known for his promotion of Buddhist principles. Although his reign was marked by early fighting, he

soon denounced violence and dedicated himself wholly to the Buddhist principle of dharma, or right living. He became a successful proponent of the religion even though he did not openly discuss it. Instead, he modeled its ideals and hoped his people would follow.

2. **D.** Socialist philosophy holds that all of a nation's wealth—both money and resources—should be shared equally among the people. It is an opposing position to capitalism, which encourages private enterprise. Friedrich Engels, a German English social theorist, helped create a form of socialism known as Marxism in the 1840s.

3. **C.** The dotted line on this map shows the approximate course of Hernán Cortés and his forces during their conquest of the Aztec civilization, which occurred between 1519 and 1521. Unlike other colonizers, Cortés took a methodical approach by exploring the coastal areas, communicating with native groups, and stopping to found the city of Veracruz to ensure his political independence. Cortés was able to gather allies to supplement his tiny military force as they entered the enormous empire of the Aztec.

4. **E.** Hammurabi was one of the most noteworthy kings of the ancient civilizations, primarily because of his crafting of the Code of Hammurabi, one of the world's earliest known written systems of law. It includes 282 case laws that deal with a variety of legal areas, such as criminal law, civil law, economic law, and family law. Leaders and citizens alike could refer to the code to learn their rights and recourses in many legal situations. Historians have noted that this comprehensive set of rules abandoned many primitive practices and was an early step toward more modern forms of government.

5. **B.** Freud's 1900 book *Die Traumdeutung,* or *The Interpretation of Dreams*, is perhaps his most famous and celebrated written work. In this volume, Freud describes his belief that dreams are "the royal road to knowledge of the unconscious." In the book, he presented examples from his own dreams and those of his patients, and he showed how these dreams could be deciphered.

6. **C.** Before the thirteenth century, the Mongols roamed freely through the plains in search of grass for their herds. This hardy lifestyle created expert riders. Their comfort with and large supply of horses allowed the Mongols to travel long distances and strike enemies with stunning speed and ferocity. While the Mongols did not generally have much wealth or equipment, or the ability to engage in protracted battles with large armies, their terror strikes broke their opponents' wills and caused nation after nation to flee upon their approach.

7. **E.** The so-called Green Revolution was a period of agricultural innovation in the mid-twentieth century during which global production of grains increased as a result of the use of high-yield crops and chemical fertilizer. Although the Green Revolution increased the world's food supply and helped combat starvation in many regions, critics have pointed out some negative effects, including potential environmental harm.

8. **E.** The initial year in the Muslim calendar is 622 CE, the year in which Muhammad migrated from Mecca to Medina. That pivotal act is seen as the origination of the Muslim faith. The first day on the calendar is July 16, as it is the first day of the year, according to the Koran. The Muslim calendar observes 354 days per year, as well as 29 or 30 days per month.

9. **A.** According to legend, Rome was founded by twins Romulus and Remus, the sons of the war god Mars. Jealous enemies ordered that the twins be drowned, but they survived and were raised by wild animals, including a she-wolf.

10. **D.** Apartheid strictly segregated the white and nonwhite populations of South Africa. It was designed to ensure the political dominance of the country's white minority, the Afrikaners, who were South Africans of Dutch heritage. To solidify their political control over South Africa, the white members of the National Party enacted apartheid laws after gaining power in 1948.

11. **C.** The ancient Greeks and Romans made important and long-term

advances in many areas, but their most enduring developments were in the field of politics and government. The Greeks and Romans were among the first societies to introduce democratic elements into government.

12. **A.** *Lebensraum*, or "living space," was a geographical concept that became a major point in Nazi ideology during the 1920s. This concept held that German people needed more land in order to grow and fulfill their destiny as world leaders. Hitler and others felt that the territory in question was land occupied by primarily Slavic peoples, including Poland, Russia, and the Ukraine. The call for *Lebensraum* attempted to justify the invasion of these lands and the cruel treatment of their occupants.

13. **C.** Throughout much of the sixteenth century, France was gripped by a series of religious wars between Roman Catholics and French Protestants known as Huguenots. In 1598 King Henry IV of France issued the Edict of Nantes. This proclamation attempted to settle the religious tension and grant Huguenots, a repressed Protestant minority, substantial rights in French society.

14. **C.** One of the most devastating events in Irish history was the potato blight, a massive crop failure that swept through Ireland from 1845 to 1849. Since potatoes were a staple crop in Ireland and the main food source for many poor families, widespread famine followed. Many died of starvation, malnutrition, and disease. Others immigrated to North America to avoid the famine.

15. **A.** The Hindu caste system contained four major divisions: Brahmans, Kshatriya, Vaishya, and Shudra. The social roles of these groups descend in importance, with Shudra being the lowest in the social hierarchy. Members of the Shudra had the lowest social distinction and the least desirable roles. Generally, they were considered servants.

16. **D.** The Olmec people, whose civilization lasted from approximately 1200 to 400 BCE, built their villages on lowlands in what is now Southern Mexico, specifically in the regions of Tabasco and Veracruz. This location gave them access to the Gulf Coast but brought year-round heat

and humidity. The oldest Olmec building discovered is near present-day San Lorenzo in Veracruz.

17. **A.** This excerpt comes from *Leviathan*, published in 1651 by philosopher Thomas Hobbes. In this work, Hobbes expresses his beliefs about human nature and the need for society and government. In contrast to philosophers such as Rousseau, Hobbes believed that humans are essentially brutes. Government becomes necessary to prevent chaos. In an era when many were speaking out against repressive governments, Hobbes believed that government needed to be powerful or risk the people destroying themselves.

18. **B.** Emperor Meiji strove to open the previously isolated Japan to global development. Japan underwent a series of drastic changes in society, economics, and politics. By the end of the Meiji era, Japan was more modernized, industrialized, and Westernized. These developments were similar to what occurred in Russia under Peter the Great.

19. **C.** The Duma was an elected legislative body established in 1906 by Czar Nicholas II as a result of the 1905 revolution. Nicholas presented the legislature as a representative body whose participation would be required in all future lawmaking, thus giving the Russian people a stake in crafting government policy. The Duma briefly became a lower house of the Russian Parliament. However, a series of laws quickly whittled away the power of the Duma. It was dissolved in March 1917.

20. **C.** The Byzantine Empire, which thrived for more than a millennium, lost its power as a result of internal dissent, competition with neighboring powers, and territorial loss. It was weakened during a series of civil wars in the 1300s. In the fifteenth century, a disastrous conflict against the Ottomans led to defeat. The Byzantine Empire crumbled, and the Ottoman Turks annexed its territories in 1453.

21. **D.** Dystopian novels, also known as anti-utopian novels, are works of fiction that deal with a negative future. The future is typically characterized by a repressive government, environmental damage,

destructive war, and increased human cruelty. Dystopian literature became popular in the twentieth century as many people looked ahead with trepidation at a future that often seemed uncertain thanks to two world wars, the spread of communism, the threat of nuclear annihilation, and other issues.

22. **B.** Offshoring, also known as outsourcing, occurs when companies in industrialized nations hire workers in other countries, particularly developing countries. Offshoring generally seeks out locations with fewer regulations, lower costs, cheap raw materials, and proximity to low-wage workers.

23. **B.** Agriculture caused lasting change for civilization. One of the most important was in human population. Whereas nomadic people typically lived in small bands that moved frequently, agriculture led to more stable and sedentary populations. Sedentary peoples had more time and resources to raise families, which led to a sharp rise in population. As a result of the gathering of people around farms and the eventual growth of villages, population density increased significantly. In some cases, ancient farming communities developed over thousands of years into today's major cities.

24. **A.** French troops invaded Madagascar in a series of invasions beginning in 1883. By 1896 France had annexed Madagascar into its colonial empire. In the twentieth century, freedom movements challenged the colonial domination. After World War II, France had little choice but to surrender its claim to the colony. After a transitional period, Madagascar declared independence in 1960.

25. **A.** The English Great Charter, or Magna Carta, was first issued by King John in 1215. Although this charter was first celebrated as a victory against oppressive government, it was soon recognized for its importance in outlining the rights of citizens. Clause 39 states that "no free man shall be…imprisoned or [dispossessed]…except by the lawful judgment of his peers or by the law of the land," effectively establishing the modern principle of due process.

26. **A.** Like Buddhism, Jainism developed in India around the sixth century BCE as a result of changing perspectives regarding religion. After the arrival of the Aryans in the Indus River valley, Hinduism had become the dominant religion in India. By around the sixth century BCE, there were a growing number of people who took issue with the Hindu belief system and the sociopolitical environment it fostered. This led to the development of Buddhism and Jainism.

27. **B.** The Paraguayan War, also known as the War of the Triple Alliance, lasted from 1864 to 1870. Paraguay was pitted against Uruguay, Argentina, and Brazil. The war began after various political, economic, and boundary disputes led Paraguayan leader Francisco Solano López to declare war on Brazil. Brazil quickly brought its allies into the conflict, overwhelming Paraguayan forces. The aggressive actions of López would lead to a devastating loss to Paraguay, including the deaths of more than half the country's population and the loss of thousands of square miles of territory.

28. **D.** In Canada's early history, the nation was divided into the regions of Upper and Lower Canada. After rising tensions and a series of attempted rebellions underscored the problems of this arrangement, leaders began to examine how to unite the country. In 1841 the British government consented to unite the regions. Citizens of both French and British backgrounds were given representation in the new government, although the British citizens received proportionately more.

29. **B.** Ghana was a primary trading power in medieval times. Its people, mostly of the Soninke clans, were situated between the booming salt trade in the north and the gold and ivory producers in the south. Leaders in Ghana negotiated transactions between the two groups, bringing prosperity and wealth.

30. **A.** The Forbidden City was a massive complex used by China's rulers from the Ming dynasty through the Qing dynasty. Located in Beijing, the Forbidden City was built after 1406 and occupied in 1420. It gained its unusual title because entry into the palace was forbidden to most

regular citizens. A person could gain admittance only with permission of the emperor.

31. **B.** Ziggurats were built from about 2200 to 500 BCE. They were four-cornered stepped structures that were somewhat similar to pyramids. They had religious significance to the people who built and used them. However, their construction was different from that of pyramids, as they were usually made from mud brick rather than carved stone. In addition, ziggurats did not have internal chambers.

32. **C.** Kashmir is a region of the northwestern Indian subcontinent. Since 1947, several nations, primarily Pakistan and India, have contested control of Kashmir. Pakistan controls the northern and western districts, whereas India has incorporated the southern regions. This disagreement between Pakistan and India culminated in brief wars in 1948 and 1965.

33. **D.** The pharaohs, the rulers of ancient Egypt, were believed to be all-powerful mediators between gods and humans. Although most pharaohs were male, in rare instances women ascended to this position of power. Some early female pharaohs had themselves depicted as masculine, but others did not. Hatshepsut took on the pharaoh's role during her reign beginning in 1473 BCE. Later, and more famously, Cleopatra ascended to rule over Egypt just before the Roman takeover of the kingdom. Other, lesser-known female pharaohs included Ankhesenamen, who shared the throne with Tutankhamen, and Sebeknefru, who reigned in the final years of the Middle Kingdom.

34. **B.** The opium trade began after a trade imbalance occurred between China and Europe. Europeans prized many Chinese exports, including porcelain, tea, and silk. However, the Chinese generally had low interest in European goods. Chinese industry was on par with most European nations and could produce comparable or superior manufactured goods, a traditional export for Europe. The only European commodity consistently valued in China was precious metal, which Europeans were hesitant to part with. In desperation, British traders arranged to import addictive opium drugs to China to create a new and bustling market.

35. **B.** The Great Schism was a troubled period for the Roman Catholic Church; at times, there were two or even three popes. They gathered supporters and competed for power and influence. The schism began in 1378 when the papacy moved to Avignon, and it created turmoil in many nations. From 1414 to 1418, the Council of Constance met to debate a course of action to resolve the problem. Ultimately, the council chose to recall the three standing popes, John XXIII, Gregory XII, and Benedict XII. In their place, the council elected a single and preeminent pope, Martin V, on November 11, 1418. With those acts, the Council of Constance ended the Great Schism.

36. **A.** Most ancient religions were polytheistic, or characterized by a belief in many gods. However, Judaism showed a marked transition away from this view. Monotheism is the belief in the existence of only one god.

37. **B.** Ancient classical notions of philosophy and art were revived by the neoclassicists, who favored allusions to the great civilizations of the Greeks and Romans and based their compositions on science, order, and reason. In the eighteenth century, the neoclassicist movement met with opposition from a new style of art and thought in romanticism. Romantic artists took virtually an opposite stance from the classicists. Romantics emphasized the wildness of nature and celebrated expressions of human feeling and emotion in their works.

38. **E.** Daoism revolves around the belief that the universe is unified by a mysterious force called Dao. Humans must eliminate the distractions caused by earthly desires—such as wealth, knowledge, social advancement, and power—to clear their hearts and minds enough to connect with the Dao life force.

39. **B.** The Rosetta stone was a carved stone tablet crafted in ancient Egypt. On it were recorded phrases in both Egyptian and Greek. The Rosetta stone allowed modern researchers to understand and decipher Egyptian hieroglyphics.

40. **A.** Pope Benedict VIII was a short-reigning pontiff who entered the papacy in 1012. His time as pope was marked by his aristocratic leanings as well as his participation in frequent military campaigns. His most lasting action took place during a council in 1022 at Pavia, where he introduced a doctrine aimed to coerce the clergy into following a previously mandated policy of celibacy that had not been properly enforced or practiced.

41. **C.** The Hittites most likely pioneered the production and usage of iron. They mined iron from the mountains near the Black Sea and used it to produce implements of war. Iron weapons and tools were generally superior to those of bronze, copper, and stone, and they gave the Hittites an advantage in battle.

42. **B.** Mahatma Gandhi was an Indian nationalist leader who struggled with an oppressive British colonization of his homeland. His situation was similar to that of Nelson Mandela, the South African rights activist. Both leaders were known for diplomacy and nonviolent methods of protest.

43. **E.** The Normans established a homeland in northern France. From there, they launched successful conquests into Italy and England. Their pinnacle of success came in 1066, when they invaded and conquered England. In subsequent generations, Norman forces would spread throughout the British Isles.

44. **D.** The defining milestone of the Paleolithic era was the use of stone tools; in fact, the term *Paleolithic* means "old Stone Age." *Neolithic* means "new Stone Age," and stone tools continued to be used almost exclusively during this time. The primary advancement of the Neolithic period was in agriculture. At that time, people first discovered methods of farming. They cultivated crops, planted fruit trees, and domesticated animals.

45. **E.** Venice and Tenochtitlán were both major cities constructed on islands. Tenochtitlán was established as the Aztec capital around 1325

CE. It originated as a settlement on two islands in Lake Texcoco. Venice, an island town in northern Italy that became a major seaport in medieval times, was built in the Laguna Veneta, near the Adriatic Sea.

46. **D.** "Total war" is a phrase used to describe conflicts in which the participants are willing to mobilize all of a nation's resources and make unlimited sacrifices to achieve victory. In such wars, even civilians are viewed as part of the enemy's war effort. Combatants may bomb civilian centers to demoralize the nation and disrupt industry and government.

47. **D.** Confucius, the premier philosopher of ancient China, lived from 551 to 479 BCE. Many of the guiding principles of his philosophy, Confucianism, dealt with the importance of the social order, moral conduct, proper actions, and political organization. To Confucius, these things were roots of a productive and peaceful world. This excerpt comes from a compilation of his writings and sayings known as the *Analects of Confucius*.

48. **E.** Slavery was a common practice in many cultures worldwide throughout history. In early times, there were no widespread racial designations on slaves. In ancient times, individuals were enslaved for a number of reasons.

49. **B.** Alexander the Great embarked on a conquest spanning much of the ancient world. His campaign began in Macedonia and took him through Egypt, Asia Minor, Mesopotamia, Persia, and Bactria. In 327 BCE, Alexander and his armies arrived in India, where they successfully battled King Porus and his elephant-mounted warriors.

50. **D.** The meeting in Frankfurt am Main beginning in 1848 was conducted by the Frankfurt National Assembly, a short-lived parliamentary organization that attempted to unify the German states. The assembly, led by Heinrich von Gagern, was largely guided by liberal principles and empowered by liberal leaders. It spent much of its existence debating plans for German unity and went so far as to draft a constitution for the unified kingdom.

51. **A.** The Suez Canal, built by a French engineering company in the 1850s and 1860s, was immensely valuable to Europe's imperial powers. The canal spanned the Isthmus of Suez in Egypt and provided a shortcut between Europe and Asia. With the advent of the Suez Canal, the distance of the average sea trip was reduced significantly.

52. **C.** Nirvana is a spiritual state of bliss that is considered the highest goal of meditation among many Indian religions. It is most famously connected with Buddhism, but it is also present in other Indian faiths, such as Hinduism, Jainism, and Sikhism. Islam does not share the belief in nirvana.

53. **B.** The White Lotus society was a religious sect formed in medieval times. It had been largely dormant in central China until the sixteenth century, when it reemerged in response to a takeover by Manchurian Manchu tribes. The White Lotus members opposed the Manchu, and by the end of the eighteenth century, the society began rebelling against them.

54. **C.** James I, who supported the authorized English translation of the Bible popularly known as the King James Bible, began his reign in Scotland in 1567 and went on to become the first Stuart king of England in 1603. He held both thrones concurrently until 1625. James was known for his absolutist policies in both countries. His practices led to conflicts with the British Parliament, which was beginning to assert power independent of the monarchy.

55. **E.** Prior to the Phoenicians, writing generally consisted of pictographs, or symbols that portrayed objects, people, and ideas. Around 1000 BCE, the Phoenicians invented a new form of writing based on syllables.

56. **A.** Sri Lanka is an island nation located in the Indian Ocean, close to the southeastern edge of the Indian subcontinent. Although inhabited since prehistoric times, Sri Lanka was generally known to the world by names that outsiders gave it. Arab, Greek, and Portuguese traders all had their own names for this land. When Britain colonized Sri Lanka,

British leaders transliterated a previous name and called the island nation Ceylon. This name held well into the twentieth century and persisted even after the nation gained independence from Britain. In 1972, however, national leaders officially changed the name to the Democratic Socialist Republic of Sri Lanka.

57. **D.** Arthur Zimmermann was a German foreign secretary whose aggressive style contributed to the scale and severity of World War I. In 1916 Zimmermann hatched a plan in which Germany would make secret agreements with Mexico and Japan to attack the United States. Zimmermann believed that this would keep the United States occupied and out of the European conflict. On January 16, 1917, Zimmermann sent a coded telegram to the German minister in Mexico proposing such a scheme. The telegram was intercepted and led to the United States' entry into the war.

58. **D.** The Industrial Revolution began in Britain in the closing years of the eighteenth century. Britain's textile, coal, and steel industries grew sharply, and British manufactured goods were exported all over the world. The factor that did not apply was a lack of colonial power; on the contrary, at this time, Britain was one of the world's most powerful global empires.

59. **E.** The communist movement in China, beginning around the 1920s, followed through on some of the ideological demands of the Taiping Rebellion. In particular, both movements advocated for equality in the distribution of land, goods, and liberties. However, in other ways, the revolts were quite different.

60. **D.** Many of the great civilizations of ancient times developed their own calendars, some of which were relatively accurate. The Romans introduced the Julian calendar, which became one of the world's most widely accepted records of time until the sixteenth century. In 1582, Pope Gregory XIII replaced the Julian calendar with the Gregorian calendar, also called the New Style calendar.

61. **E.** The Luddites were an organization of craftsmen in nineteenth-century England. They were disturbed by the development of automated industrial machines, particularly power textile looms, which threatened to take away their jobs and livelihoods. The Luddites quickly became known for the sabotage and destruction of such machines.

62. **D.** Mansa Mūsā was a West African *mansa*, or emperor, of the Mali kingdom. He ruled from about 1307 until his death in the 1330s. Musa was a gifted and generally benevolent ruler who encouraged great developments in trade, education, and architecture. In particular, he is remembered for turning Timbuktu into a large, successful city that included the Great Mosque, built under his orders. He is also known for his vast personal wealth.

63. **C.** The Silk Roads were a land trade route between China and the Roman Empire. A branch of the Silk Roads reached into India and allowed Indian merchants to share their religion, Buddhism, with China. Indian monks even joined the trade caravans to bring Buddhist holy texts to the Chinese. Buddhism took hold in China and, within the next few centuries, became the dominant religion in that country. After that, trade networks and other international relations spread the faith to other parts of Asia including Korea and Japan.

64. **E.** Devanagari, sometimes referred to as Nagari, is a type of script that developed from the Brāhmī Gupta writing system around the seventh century CE. Over the following four centuries, it developed into the form still widely used today.

65. **B.** The information in the chart is best used to support the statement that "improving medical technologies in South America has increased the life span there." Although the chart does not contain any direct evidence to this effect, it does show that the population of the South American nation of Brazil has grown considerably since 1950. This population boom could be used as indirect evidence to suggest that health-care services have improved in the region.

66. **C.** Captain James Cook, the famed British explorer, spent much of his life at sea and explored more miles of the world's coastline than any of his contemporaries. Many of his voyages and discoveries were in the South Pacific. In 1768 Cook led the *Endeavour* on a scientific mission during which he mapped the coasts of New Zealand and Australia. His work led the British to claim ownership over those lands. Cook even named New South Wales, a region of eastern Australia, in honor of his home country, believing that the two places looked similar.

67. **B.** Pueblo architecture originated with the Pueblo Indians of the American Southwest. This style is derived from the appearance and functionality of the cliff dwellings built by early Pueblo peoples. As shown, Pueblo architecture involves small attached homes arranged in multiple stories. They are often arranged in an almost pyramidal step formation around a central courtyard.

68. **C.** Manfred von Richthofen, better known to history as the "Red Baron," was a German fighter pilot in World War I. Born to a family of minor aristocracy, Richthofen became a career military officer in the Prussian army. In World War I, after a brief stint in the cavalry, Richthofen became a pioneer of early aerial combat. His many successes, along with his refined and chivalric personal style and the fact that he daringly painted his plane bright red, captured the public imagination in countries around the world.

69. **D.** Nationalists believe that citizens owe their highest loyalty to the nation. In the nineteenth and twentieth centuries, nationalism was prevalent in many European nations, and it commingled with militarism, imperialism, and other philosophies to produce deadly conflict. Giuseppe Mazzini was an Italian revolutionary active in the mid-1800s. He helped establish an organization called the Risorgimento that pushed for the unification of Italy. His dedication to and love of Italy helped inspire a tide of nationalism that rose in Europe, uniting fragmented countries such as Italy and Germany in the late nineteenth century and then sending them to war in the twentieth.

70. **B.** Socrates, born around 470 BCE, was famous for philosophy and conversation, which he spread around the streets of Athens. Typically going barefoot and dressed simply, Socrates habitually engaged strangers in dialogues that relied on questions to reveal philosophical leanings, faulty arguments, and prejudices. Although he became a lasting figure in philosophy and oratory, his critical and questioning methods made him many enemies, particularly among Athenian leaders. In 399 BCE, some of his foes brought serious charges against him, including "corruption of the young." Socrates subsequently died by drinking poisonous hemlock.

71. **B.** Mumbai, previously known as Bombay, is one of India's premiere business and industry centers. The city began its rise to industrial prominence in the 1850s, when it became a major player in the cotton textile industry. This move was encouraged by the British, who came to rely on India for its cotton materials after its former supplier, the United States, became embroiled in tensions that would eventually lead to the American Civil War.

72. **C.** Beginning in 1096, Christians from across Europe began participating in a long series of military actions, or Crusades, meant to wrest control of the "Holy Land" in Palestine from the Muslims. When Muslim leader Saladin conquered Jerusalem, Christians undertook the Third Crusade, which lasted from 1189 to 1191. After some early victories, infighting among Crusaders led to a Christian withdrawal.

73. **A.** Pedro II of Brazil, emperor from 1831 to 1889, was one of the country's longest-reigning, most successful, and most widely supported leaders. During Pedro's reign, Brazil made considerable advances in many fields. Brazil saw population growth, economic development, and infrastructure improvement. However, although Brazil was faring well, many people remained dissatisfied. Conflicts over social hierarchies and the abolition of slavery contributed to growing unrest and an eventual military coup in 1889. Pedro's rule included all of the listed events except for the backlash to the so-called coffee government, which occurred in the 1920s.

74. **C.** All of these leaders were important to Iranian history. However, Ayatollah Rūḥallāh Khomeynī was the leader who did the most to reinvent government on the basis of a stricter interpretation of Islamic law. A leader of the Shia sect, Khomeynī led a revolution in 1979. He eventually declared himself ruler and created a new set of stricter laws based closely on interpretation of the Koran.

75. **A.** Traditional African masks were typically made of wood and decorated with paint, grass, and other materials. Masks often took human, animal, or abstract forms. Some were intentionally grotesque. Although the masks had many different uses, their primary role was in religious ceremonies and other rituals of spirituality. In African tradition, the wearer of a mask temporarily takes on the spirit represented by the mask, thus becoming a medium between the worlds of the living and the nonliving. Many of the ceremonies were so sacred and mysterious that only a select few from a community were allowed to participate or even watch.

76. **E.** The question of citizenship had long been a difficult issue for the Romans, particularly as their empire grew to encompass many lands and peoples. At first, Roman subjects in distant regions had few enumerated rights, and the Latin people around Rome had a set of rights called *jus Latii* but lacked full citizenship. During the reign of Emperor Caracalla, however, reforms took place in the citizenship laws. Under the Edict of Caracalla in 212 CE, almost all people living within the Roman Empire were granted Roman citizenship. The Romans' largely fair treatment of subject peoples stands in contrast to most modern imperial policies and was one of the reasons for the Roman Empire's long reign and diverse accomplishments.

77. **D.** Masada was a fortified city built by the Hasmonean dynasty on top of a high mountain in Palestine. Herod, one of the chief proponents of the fortification, equipped it with strong walls, citadels, irrigation systems, and royal palaces. Following the death of Herod, Romans began their domination of the region and briefly took control of Masada. In

66 CE; however, Jewish rebels called Zealots won it back from Roman control and held it for several years. When Jerusalem fell to the Roman invaders, Masada became the Jews' last stronghold in Palestine, and the small band of Zealot defenders fought for two years to resist invasion by some fifteen thousand Roman legionaries.

78. **B.** The Copper Age was the first major period in the discovery and use of metal, occurring from approximately 5000 to 3000 BCE. Bronze was the next metal to be put into use. An alloy of copper, bronze proved sturdier and stronger, and it soon replaced copper in most tools and weapons. The Bronze Age began around 3200 BCE. About two thousand years later, around 1200 BCE, the Iron Age began in Europe. This was followed around 475 BCE by the creation of steel, a hardened form of iron, in India.

79. **E.** When England came under the rule of the Roman Empire around 43 CE, Roman scouts found a small village near the mouth of the Thames River. This village, Lud Hill, stood near the location where London is today. The Romans chose to expand this site into a great city they called Londinium. They fortified the city with strong walls, constructed the first London Bridge to facilitate travel, and promoted trade with other regions of England.

80. **B.** Great Zimbabwe, a civilization that originated during the African Iron Age, was located in what is today southeastern Zimbabwe. Great Zimbabwe is known for its stonework, particularly its stone walls and houses. In fact, the word *Zimbabwe* derives from a Shona term for stone homes.

81. **B.** After a Japanese victory over China, Japan took control of Port Arthur on the Liaodong Peninsula. This created international tension, and when Japan relented, Russian forces took over the peninsula in 1898. Further Russian encroachments in Asia pushed Japan to the brink of war, and in 1904 Japanese forces began torpedoing Russian ships in Port Arthur. The Japanese then engaged the Russians and defeated them in several land and sea battles. The Russians ultimately had to withdraw.

For the first time in modern history, an Asian nation had defeated a European power.

82. **D.** One of the most distinguishing characteristics of Charles Dickens's writings was his treatment of issues concerning economic class and poverty. Many of Dickens's most enduring characters, such as Oliver Twist, are on the lowest rungs of the socioeconomic ladder. These characters struggle against poverty and oppression while demonstrating virtues that are often lacking in more affluent characters.

83. **B.** One of the most important developments in early international trade was the establishment of the Silk Roads, a landed pathway connecting China to Europe. This approximately four-thousand-mile-long road allowed the passage of trade caravans bringing silk, a prized textile produced by silkworms in China, to Europe. In exchange, Europeans sent back precious metals, wool, and other products.

84. **B.** After years of study and fasting, Buddha felt that he had achieved a state of spiritual enlightenment. He identified his accomplishment as being based on the Four Noble Truths, concepts that could be used to guide an individual to enlightenment. These truths included the inevitability of suffering, the roots of suffering in desire and negative actions, the possibility of reaching a state of peace (nirvana), and the Middle Way as a path to reach it. Buddha's Four Noble Truths dealt with personal spirituality and did not directly address organized religion.

85. **A.** Kublai Khan, grandson of Genghis Khan, was a Mongol leader in China who helped unify the nation and bring it under Mongol control. Ultimately, the world would know him best for his role in the life and memoirs of Venetian explorer Marco Polo, who lived at the khan's court for twenty years. Kublai Khan was not, however, responsible for bringing Buddhism to China.

86. **E.** Tulips were introduced to Europe by Turkish merchants around 1550 CE. In Holland, tulips became immensely popular; in the years following their introduction, they became valuable status symbols. Some

rare varieties of tulip bulbs were traded for the equivalent of thousands of dollars, new homes, or successful businesses. Around 1633 all classes of Dutch society began trading in tulips, and many people took on extensive mortgages so they could increase their investments in the flower trade. The assumed value of tulips so exceeded their actual value that an economic "bubble" became inevitable; the bubble exploded in 1637.

87. **D.** The embroidery is just one scene in the large Bayeux Tapestry, a seamless linen sheet some 231 feet long. The tapestry includes images representing eleventh-century history, particularly the Norman takeover of England. Each scene portrays one event in the story, ending in the 1066 Battle of Hastings, in which William the Conqueror and the Norman invaders routed the native forces under King Harold. The tapestry was stored for centuries in the Bayeux Cathedral before its discovery by scholars in the 1700s.

88. **A.** The Panama Canal project faced many obstacles. Construction was undertaken by a French company led by Ferdinand de Lesseps; the main challenge quickly became the thick swaths of mosquitoes and the diseases they carried. Unprepared for such conditions and lacking medical knowledge to deal with the situation, the French workers suffered greatly. As many as twenty-two thousand men died during the construction attempt, and the project was ultimately abandoned. Later, a U.S. company would complete the task.

89. **D.** *T'ien ming* was a fixture of Chinese social, political, and religious thought that was derived from the philosophy of Confucianism. The concept, enacted around 1000 BCE, held that heaven mandated the emperor, or the so-called son of heaven, to rule. The concept is similar to the European divine right of kings. A subtle but important difference was that, whereas many European monarchs took their divine mandate as an invitation for oppressive rule, in China the *t'ien ming* actually held the monarchs to moral behavior.

90. **C.** In 1917, Germany worried about the United States getting involved in World War I. A German statesman offered Mexico a secret alliance

in which Mexico would attack the United States to divert its attention. Not only was Germany's secret solicitation discovered; Mexico rejected it for a number of reasons. Mexican President Venustiano Carranza had asked his military leaders to examine Germany's offer, and they reported that the terms offered and the overall benefits would not make the plan feasible.

91. E. Imperialism has existed since prehistoric times, and its influence has spanned almost all regions of the world. The basic tenets of imperialism have changed little since the time of ancient civilizations such as the Persians, Greeks, Assyrians, and Romans. However, the nature of the colonizers' intentions has changed significantly. In ancient times, colonization was often undertaken with the intent to gain wealth by taxing conquered people and frequently enslaving them. In modern times, imperialism is usually undertaken to support industrial goals, such as accessing raw materials and opening new markets.

92. B. The Songhai Empire was a flourishing trade power in West Africa in the 1400s and 1500s that gained considerable wealth from gold and salt. Despite clashes with the Mali Empire and the temporary loss of the city of Gao, the Songhai people were generally successful at controlling their territory. However, in the late sixteenth century, a Moroccan army began a campaign in the Sahara. Employing superior weapons and tactics, the Moroccans overwhelmed the Songhai and captured their cities, which led to the collapse of their empire.

93. E. Alchemy is an ancient form of pseudoscience in which people attempted to transform metals—particularly lead into gold—and to find magical or supernatural methods of achieving eternal life. Various forms of alchemy were practiced in Asia, India, Europe, and the Middle East.

94. E. The Warsaw Pact, formally known as the Warsaw Treaty of Friendship, Cooperation, and Mutual Assistance, was arranged by the Soviet Union and signed on May 14, 1955. The members of the pact included the Soviet Union, Czechoslovakia, East Germany, Hungary, Poland, Romania, and Albania. This organization primarily served

as a buffer between the Soviet sphere and the Western democracies. This latter faction was best represented by the North Atlantic Treaty Organization (NATO), established in 1949 as a defense against the Soviet Union and its associated states.

95. **B.** The Zapatista National Liberation Army (EZLN) became a dynamic force in Mexican politics in the early 1990s. After starting an armed revolt in the state of Chiapas, the group made claims and demands concerning Mexican politics and economics. The EZLN believed that Mexico's financial partnerships and policies would cause native Mexicans to suffer greater poverty. The Zapatistas named their organization after Emiliano Zapata, a rebel guerrilla during the Mexican Revolution who battled for the rights of Mexican Indians, peasants, and poor farmers.

This book contains two practice tests. Visit mymaxscore.com to download your free third practice test with answers and explanations.

SAT World History Subject Test Practice Test 2

SAT Subject Test in World History
Time—60 minutes
95 questions

Directions: Each of the questions or incomplete statements is followed by five answer choices. Choose the answer choice that best answers the question or best completes the incomplete statement.

Note: This test uses the chronological designations BCE (before the Common Era) and CE (Common Era). These designations correspond to BC (before Christ) and AD (*anno Domini*), which are used in some history texts.

1. The Aztec built their capital city Tenochtitlán on an island in the middle of Lake Texcoco primarily because the site

    A. was ideally located for trade purposes
    B. provided protection from outside attackers
    C. fulfilled a prophecy about where they should settle
    D. was rich with natural deposits of gold and other minerals
    E. was sacred to the people conquered by the Aztec

2. Early civilizations in Mesopotamia and Egypt were MOST similar in that they both

    A. developed a code of retaliatory punishment
    B. viewed women as socially equal to men
    C. developed a government of separate city-states
    D. were invaded and occupied by the Hyksos
    E. depended on the annual flooding of a river for survival

3. Which of these nations was the first to establish a trading presence in Asia by finding a sea route to India?

    A. Spain
    B. England
    C. France
    D. Portugal
    E. Italy

4. Claudius Ptolemy's geocentric theory of astronomy was not disproved until the sixteenth century, when the heliocentric theory was introduced by

    A. Aristotle
    B. Copernicus
    C. Galileo
    D. Kepler
    E. Brahe

5. Which of these statements MOST accurately describes the Bantu people of sub-Saharan Africa?

    A. They initially organized into a stateless society composed of numerous villages.
    B. They developed a class system that divided people along the lines of social importance.
    C. They relied on a trans-Saharan gold and salt trade for economic and physical survival.
    D. They practiced a monotheistic religion similar to that of the Hebrews.
    E. They experienced violent clashes with the Muslim population in Africa.

6. The Treaty of Versailles contained all of the following provisions EXCEPT a

    A. demand that Germany cede the territory of Alsace-Lorraine to France
    B. condition that placed permanent restrictions on the size of the Germany army
    C. clause that required Germany to be held solely responsible for starting the war
    D. stipulation that forced Germany to pay for the right to retain its African colonies
    E. requirement that prevented Germany from manufacturing or importing weapons

7. Respect for elders and ancestors, emphasis on effective government, and the belief that order and harmony can exist only if leaders cooperate with the most highly educated are all major philosophical tenets of

    A. Daoism
    B. Confucianism
    C. Shintoism
    D. Buddhism
    E. Legalism

8. The departure of Alexander the Great and his forces from India in 325 BCE led directly to the

    A. rise of the Mauryan Empire
    B. decline of Indian Buddhism
    C. reemergence of Hinduism
    D. formation of the Gupta Empire
    E. decentralization of Indian government

9. Which twentieth-century school of art produced works that were primarily whimsical in tone and devoid of any single specific meaning?

    A. Surrealism
    B. Dadaism
    C. Expressionism
    D. Functionalism
    E. Cubism

10. Which of these was primarily responsible for the tensions between China and Great Britain that led to the Anglo-Chinese War in 1839?

   A. Chinese desire for independent self-rule
   B. British importation of opium into China
   C. Westernization of Chinese society
   D. Territorial control over Hong Kong
   E. Spread of communist influence

"The heart of the idea of the social contract may be stated simply: Each of us places his person and authority under the supreme direction of the general will, and the group receives each individual as an indivisible part of the whole."

11. Which of these would be LEAST likely to agree with the statement above?

   A. John Locke
   B. Voltaire
   C. Thomas Hobbes
   D. Montesquieu
   E. Jean-Jacques Rousseau

12. The Crusades had all of the following effects on Europe EXCEPT a/an

   A. increase in the power of European monarchs
   B. elevation in the social status of women
   C. emergence of a middle class in society
   D. decline of trade between Europe and the East
   E. increase in the political strength of the church

13. Japan and the countries of Western Europe were most similar around the thirteenth century in that both

   A. established strong centralized governments
   B. experienced a series of civil wars
   C. developed intricate feudal systems
   D. advanced the social status of women
   E. endured invasion by Mongol forces

14. The stone carving pictured is a type of calendar created by which of these civilizations?

   A. Mauryan
   B. Phoenician
   C. Harappān
   D. Aztec
   E. Zhou

15. The influence of Minoan culture on Mycenaean culture was MOST evident in the Mycenaean

    A. written language
    B. interest in metallurgy
    C. system of trade
    D. social class structure
    E. religious practices

16. In 1975, the Khmer Rouge, led by Pol Pot, attempted to establish communist rule in which country?

    A. Thailand
    B. Cambodia
    C. Laos
    D. Malaysia
    E. Burma

17. The Balfour Declaration, issued by Britain in 1917, clarified England's position on the

    A. Indian movement for independence from British rule
    B. discriminatory South African policy of apartheid
    C. establishment of a Jewish state in Palestine
    D. formation of the Soviet Union under Lenin
    E. proposed terms of German surrender in World War I

18. In 1908, facing international criticism for his harsh treatment of the Congolese in the Congo Free State, King Leopold II was forced to

    A. agree to Congolese independence and abdicate
    B. relinquish his control and pay reparations
    C. surrender his authority in the Congo to British forces
    D. cede control of the Congo Free State to the Belgian government
    E. adopt humanitarian policies that ended hostilities

19. The Upanishads contain the core philosophy and central teachings of which world religion?

    A. Buddhism

    B. Hinduism

    C. Jainism

    D. Shintoism

    E. Zoroastrianism

20. Which of the following was a significant change instituted during the reign of the 'Abbāsid Empire?

    A. Non-Arab Muslims were allowed to hold civil and military office.

    B. The Islamic capital was moved from Mecca to Damascus.

    C. A hereditary method of succession was put in place.

    D. Islam was divided into the major sects of Sunni and Shia.

    E. The Byzantine capital of Constantinople was conquered.

21. Early human cultures in the Paleolithic Age were characterized by all of these EXCEPT the

    A. development of language

    B. prevalence of hunter-gatherers

    C. emergence of agriculture

    D. appearance of artwork

    E. practice of funereal rituals

22. The Ottoman policy of *devşirme* primarily served to

    A. cement governmental control

    B. increase military manpower

    C. maintain religious freedom

    D. improve agricultural productivity

    E. ensure economic stability

23. Which of these was NOT one of the global effects of the Industrial Revolution?

    A. Decline in the colonization of foreign territories by industrial powers
    B. Widening of the divide between industrialized and non-industrialized nations
    C. Lessening of isolation between distant world cultures
    D. Increase in Europe's economic power
    E. Strengthening of the political influence of the middle class

24. Who led the South American struggle for independence from Spain?

    A. Benito Juárez
    B. Porfirio Díaz
    C. Emiliano Zapata
    D. Simón Bolívar
    E. Miguel Hidalgo

25. What was the purpose of this late-eighteenth-century French cartoon?

    A. To criticize the insolence of the lower class
    B. To illustrate the size imbalances of the three estates
    C. To encourage the reversal of the French class system
    D. To decry the inadequacy of the French aristocracy
    E. To demonstrate the strength of the Third Estate

26. After solidifying his control over Russia following civil war in 1918,
    Lenin's immediate goal was to

    A. create a new communist government
    B. reclaim Russian territory lost in World War I
    C. eliminate any remaining political dissidents
    D. institute his own totalitarian political regime
    E. stabilize the Russian economy

27. Early Vietnamese resistance to the French imperialists who controlled their country was primarily a response to

    A.   abusive labor practices
    B.   destructive agricultural policies
    C.   racially discriminatory governance
    D.   suppression of native religion
    E.   violent police tactics

28. The city of Great Zimbabwe and the kingdom of Aksum were MOST similar in that both

    A.   became predominantly Christian societies
    B.   were located along the banks of the Red Sea
    C.   were eventually toppled by Muslim invaders
    D.   thrived on income derived from trade routes
    E.   incorporated Greek as their primary language

29. During the expansion of the Muslim Empire in the seventh century, all of these were true EXCEPT

    A.   conquered people who converted to Islam were not required to pay a poll tax
    B.   the ability to read Arabic was highly valued in regions conquered by Muslims
    C.   pagan members of conquered societies were expected to convert to Islam or face death
    D.   conquered people of Christian or Jewish faiths were required to submit to military service
    E.   conquered people who refused to convert to Islam were prevented from spreading their faith

30. The native Japanese religion of Shinto is primarily focused on

    A. deity worship
    B. personal enlightenment
    C. ancestral veneration
    D. dogmatic occultism
    E. penitent self-denial

31. Which of these was NOT true of the spread of Islam in eastern and central Africa?

    A. The conversion of Africans to Islam was largely the result of trade.
    B. African women readily accepted Islam's traditional attitudes toward women.
    C. The elite of the African business community saw conversion as commercially valuable.
    D. Many Africans who converted to Islam were allowed to retain some tribal customs.
    E. The agricultural population was more reluctant to convert than others.

32. The spread of ancient Greek culture throughout the Mediterranean region was primarily the result of Greece's

    A. unique geography
    B. military conquests
    C. diverse population
    D. democratic government
    E. economic prosperity

"It is the State which educates its citizens in civic virtue, gives them a consciousness of their mission and welds them into unity."

33. This quote was most likely spoken by a leader who supported what philosophy of government?

   A. Republicanism
   B. Absolute monarchism
   C. Enlightened despotism
   D. Fascism
   E. Constitutional monarchism

34. The concept of the mandate of heaven provided a rationalization for

   A. maintaining strict standards of morality
   B. invading and conquering foreign civilizations
   C. transferring power from one dynasty to another
   D. believing in the moral superiority of the Chinese
   E. adopting largely male-dominated gender roles

35. The Incan civilization was unique among pre-Columbian civilizations most notably because the Inca

   A. used irrigation systems to increase agricultural yield
   B. practiced a polytheistic form of religion
   C. developed a complex written language
   D. expanded their empire through conquest
   E. built an advanced system of roads

36. For the majority of the eighteenth century, South Africa was controlled by the

    A. Dutch
    B. English
    C. Spanish
    D. French
    E. Portuguese

37. Fear over the "domino theory" led the United States to enter which military conflict?

    A. World War I
    B. World War II
    C. Korean War
    D. Vietnam War
    E. Persian Gulf War

38. Which of these Roman authors produced both the *Annals* and *Germania?*

    A. Cicero
    B. Tacitus
    C. Virgil
    D. Seneca
    E. Horace

39. Both England and Egypt experienced all of the following as a result of the Industrial Revolution, EXCEPT

    A. improved communication methods
    B. expertise in glassmaking
    C. increased levels of foreign trade
    D. thriving cotton textile factories
    E. commercial agriculture profits

40. The earliest significant civilization in Mesoamerica developed around the settlement of

    A.   Tenochtitlán
    B.   Cuzco
    C.   Chichén Itzá
    D.   Tula
    E.   Tikal

41. Japan turned to militarism in the 1930s primarily as a result of the

    A.   series of Chinese threats along the borders
    B.   belief that democracy had failed
    C.   desire to retake control of nearby foreign colonies
    D.   rash of violent civil unrest in the cities
    E.   desire to be completely isolated from the West

42. In order to restore peace in Europe after the Napoleonic Wars, the Congress of Vienna did all of the following EXCEPT

    A.   formally recognize Swiss independence
    B.   introduce the German Confederation
    C.   require France to disband its military
    D.   create the Kingdom of the Netherlands
    E.   restore the legitimacy of the monarchy

43. The Later Ly dynasty incorporated many aspects of the Chinese bureaucratic and civil service practices as it established a new centralized form of government in present-day

    A.   Vietnam
    B.   Cambodia
    C.   Korea
    D.   Thailand
    E.   Laos

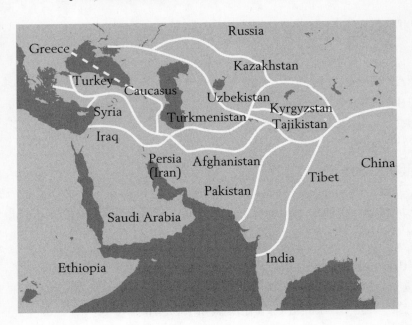

44. What famous trade route is shown on the map?

    A. Via Appia
    B. Silk Roads
    C. Via Maris
    D. Amber Road
    E. King's Highway

45. During his reign, Alexander the Great conquered all of the following EXCEPT

    A. Syria
    B. Egypt
    C. Mesopotamia
    D. India
    E. Asia Minor

46. The Maoist version of communism practiced in China during the 1950s and 1960s differed from the concurrent Soviet version of communism in that it

   A.   promoted a peaceful coexistence with capitalist countries
   B.   viewed the proletariat as a nation rather than a class
   C.   favored the redistribution of wealth among the peasantry
   D.   advocated the censorship of artistic and literary endeavors
   E.   espoused the value of state-run agricultural programs

47. Which civilization's code of law was written in the Twelve Tables?

   A.   Greece
   B.   Egypt
   C.   England
   D.   France
   E.   Rome

48. Which of these BEST describes the Taiping Rebellion?

   A.   National uprising against imperialist rule
   B.   Militant communist insurgency
   C.   Battle for dynastic control of China
   D.   Religious and political civil war
   E.   Revolt against the Mongol occupation

49. Among the Bantu-speaking peoples of Africa, the term *griots* referred to

   A.   leaders
   B.   storytellers
   C.   priests
   D.   warriors
   E.   slaves

50. The navigator Ferdinand Magellan is most famous for

    A. leading the first expedition around the Cape of Good Hope
    B. being the first European to reach the Pacific Ocean
    C. leading the first attempt to locate the Northwest Passage
    D. making the first landing in the New World
    E. being the first person to circumnavigate the globe

51. Which of these BEST describes the Mensheviks and the Bolsheviks in early-twentieth-century Russia?

    A. The Mensheviks believed in working with the bourgeois, while the Bolsheviks believed in immediate revolution against them.
    B. The Mensheviks supported an elitist political system, while the Bolsheviks supported a more inclusionary approach.
    C. The Mensheviks favored an altered form of Marxism, while the Bolsheviks favored pure Marxism.
    D. The Mensheviks were a proactively radical political group, while the Bolsheviks were comparatively reactionary in approach.
    E. The Mensheviks supported Russia's involvement in World War I, while the Bolsheviks were against it.

52. In the mid-1800s, the southeastern port of Singapore was controlled by the

    A. Dutch
    B. French
    C. Germans
    D. British
    E. United States

53. The campaign for Mexican independence from Spain was different from other political revolts in the Americas in that it was

   A. diplomatic in nature and did not involve violence
   B. ultimately decided by events in Europe
   C. started by mestizos instead of the Creole class
   D. undertaken to install a new monarchy
   E. conducted with the help of other nearby countries

54. The signing of the Treaty of Tordesillas served to

   A. end hostilities in the Spanish Civil War and affirm nationalist control
   B. grant Spain exclusive rights to all land discovered in the New World
   C. free the colony of Brazil from Spanish imperial governance
   D. formally and permanently abolish the Spanish Inquisition
   E. establish a trade agreement between Spain and the United States

"Whose government is unostentatious, quite unostentatious, his people will be prosperous, quite prosperous. Whose government is prying, quite prying, his people will be needy, quite needy."

55. The above quotation reflects the central view of government espoused by which spiritual philosophy?

   A. Confucianism
   B. Buddhism
   C. Legalism
   D. Shintoism
   E. Daoism

56. From which region did the cuneiform method of writing emerge?

    A. Egypt
    B. Mesoamerica
    C. India
    D. Mesopotamia
    E. China

57. The African kingdom of Ghana fell into decline during the eleventh century primarily as a result of

    A. invasion by foreign conquerors
    B. internal political strife
    C. poor agricultural practices
    D. weak government leadership
    E. violent religious disputes

58. In 1935, Italian forces under the command of Benito Mussolini invaded the nation of

    A. Somalia
    B. Ethiopia
    C. Egypt
    D. Libya
    E. Nigeria

59. Which crop's cultivation led to the rise of the Khmer Empire in the region known today as Cambodia?

    A. Tea
    B. Opium
    C. Rice
    D. Sugar
    E. Corn

60. What was the primary reason Russia ended its involvement in World War I?

    A. The population devastation wrought by massive casualties
    B. The diplomatic agreement signed with Germany for territory in East Europe
    C. The adversarial nature of the relationship with the French and British allies
    D. The internal political dissent against the czarist government
    E. The severe economic strain placed on the country by its war efforts

61. All of these emerged during the reign of the Gupta Empire in India EXCEPT

    A. funerary custom of sati
    B. common Arabic numeral system
    C. Sanskrit poems of Kalidasa
    D. discovery of Earth's circumference
    E. tradition of viewing cows as sacred

62. The ancient African city of Meroe became a major trading center between 250 BCE and 150 CE due to production of

    A. gold
    B. spices
    C. iron
    D. silver
    E. grains

63. All of the following were true of the Roman army EXCEPT

    A.   all citizens who owned land were expected to serve in the army

    B.   each army legion consisted of several thousand foot soldiers

    C.   the government was responsible for providing the army with weapons

    D.   every army legion was complemented with a regiment of cavalry

    E.   all peoples allied with Rome were required to provide army troops

64. In the eighteenth century, Prussia rose to prominence under the leadership of the

    A.   Hapsburgs

    B.   Bourbons

    C.   Romanovs

    D.   Hohenzollerns

    E.   Carolingians

65. The culture of the Bantu people evolved and spread throughout Africa primarily as a result of

    A.   warfare

    B.   trade

    C.   migration

    D.   agriculture

    E.   religion

66. Which of these BEST describes *parallel descent* as it was practiced by the Inca in the sixteenth century?

    A. Males inherited separately from the mother and father.
    B. Males inherited from the father, while females inherited from the mother.
    C. Males inherited from the mother and father, while female were not eligible to inherit.
    D. Females inherited from the mother and father, while males were not eligible to inherit.
    E. Females inherited only monetary wealth and not land or property.

67. Which issue did the 1997 Kyoto Protocol address?

    A. Nuclear disarmament
    B. World poverty
    C. Energy crisis
    D. Global warming
    E. Water shortage

68. The Korean and Vietnam wars of the twentieth century were MOST similar in that they

    A. produced significant territorial gains for communist forces
    B. ended with the establishment of a neutral demilitarized zone
    C. resulted from a desire to prevent the spread of communism
    D. originated in nationalistic fervor to be free of colonial control
    E. broke out as a result of invasions of democratic territories

69. After being installed as dictator, Julius Caesar did all of the following EXCEPT

   A.   declared himself a monarch
   B.   established a new solar calendar
   C.   decreased the power of the Senate
   D.   granted citizenship to inhabitants of provinces
   E.   offered public land to soldiers who had served him

70. When Spanish conquistadors entered South America in the 1500s,
they were able to conquer the Inca with relative ease because of the
Inca's weakness from

   A.   natural disasters
   B.   famine
   C.   disease
   D.   prior invasion
   E.   civil war

71. Which of these was true of both Sparta and Athens?

   A.   They were democratic governments.
   B.   They denied female participation in politics.
   C.   They made significant contributions to the arts.
   D.   They prohibited the use of gold and silver.
   E.   They required all men to serve in the military.

72. The overthrow of the Qing dynasty in China in 1912 was primarily
the result of

   A.   severe governmental oppression
   B.   excessive taxation of imports
   C.   rising nationalistic sentiment
   D.   increased foreign pressure
   E.   widespread poverty and famine

73. In the 1500s, which Southeast Asian nation was a Spanish colony that helped facilitate trade with Mexico?

    A. Burma
    B. Indonesia
    C. Siam
    D. Vietnam
    E. Philippines

74. The collapse of the Carolingian dynasty in the 800s quickly led to the

    A. rise of European nation-states
    B. introduction of the feudal system
    C. beginning of the Renaissance
    D. establishment of the Protestant church
    E. onset of widespread industrialization

75. Lutheranism and Calvinism were LEAST similar in regard to views on the

    A. degree of corruption in the Roman Catholic Church
    B. importance of religion in everyday life
    C. sale of indulgences
    D. ability of individuals to affect their fate
    E. importance of celibacy outside marriage

76. With which statement would an adherent to the philosophy of cynicism be MOST likely to agree?

    A. All human beings are part of a common brotherhood.
    B. Inner peace can be found by seeking pleasure and avoiding pain.
    C. Individuals have an inherent responsibility to help others.
    D. Life should be lived simply and without material attachments.
    E. Conducting oneself virtuously is the key to living a good life.

77. The world peacekeeping organization known as the League of Nations and its successor, the United Nations, are MOST different in that the

    A. League of Nations originated with many more nations
    B. League of Nations excluded the nations it viewed as troublesome
    C. United Nations formed a military division to enforce its policies
    D. United Nations was founded to help bring an end to an active war
    E. League of Nations included several separate administrative bodies

78. In 1521 Hernán Cortés led the Spanish conquest of which Mesoamerican culture?

    A. Aztec
    B. Inca
    C. Olmec
    D. Maya
    E. Toltec

"Wild and blasphemous ideas of God are formed because man has wandered away from the unchangeable laws of science, and the right use of reason; and because something called revealed religion was invented."

79. The above statement MOST reflects the ideology of which intellectual movement?

    A. Humanism
    B. Materialism
    C. Deism
    D. Utilitarianism
    E. Idealism

80. The Greater East Asia Co-Prosperity Sphere was primarily designed by Japan to

    A. end Japanese reliance on Western support
    B. limit the spread of communism in Asia
    C. free Asian nations from imperial control
    D. establish its own empire throughout Asia
    E. secure an adequate supply of raw materials

81. The Greek philosopher who developed a teaching methodology based on systematic questioning was

    A. Aristotle
    B. Epicurus
    C. Plato
    D. Democritus
    E. Socrates

82. While they controlled China, the Mongols were unsuccessful in their attempts to extend their empire into Southeast Asia primarily because

    A. their incursions were met with heavy resistance
    B. the terrain was too difficult to navigate
    C. they lacked the manpower to overcome local forces
    D. the regional climate was extremely inhospitable
    E. they had insufficient resources for long campaigns

83. The written language of the Mycenaeans was based on that of the

    A. Minoans
    B. Phoenicians
    C. Babylonians
    D. Hittites
    E. Assyrians

84. Which of these BEST describes the type of protectorate commonly found in imperial-controlled Africa?

    A. A region directly controlled by a foreign power
    B. A region considered an administrative subdivision of another country
    C. A region allowed to maintain its government while under imperial control
    D. A region controlled by a private business instead of a foreign government
    E. A region over which another nation holds exclusive trade rights

85. Which of these does NOT accurately describe a similarity between the peoples of ancient Egypt and the Indus River valley?

    A. They practiced polytheistic religion.
    B. They drove out a foreign occupation force.
    C. They developed a stratified social structure.
    D. They made significant architectural advances.
    E. They depended on agriculture for survival.

86. During their conquest of Mesoamerica, the Spaniards utilized the encomienda system, which allowed them to

    A. compel the natives out of settlements and off the land
    B. require the natives to pledge allegiance under penalty of death
    C. pay the natives to fight on Spain's behalf
    D. require the natives pay tribute and perform labor
    E. encourage mass migration of the native peoples

87. Which of these was the most important point of agreement between Woodrow Wilson's Fourteen Points and the Treaty of Versailles?

    A. Germany should relinquish control of its African colonies.
    B. An international peacekeeping organization should be established.
    C. Trade barriers between nations should be reduced.
    D. Germany should be forced to accept full responsibility for the war.
    E. Freedom of the seas should be guaranteed in both peace and wartime.

88. The separation of the Shia sect of Islam from the larger Sunni sect was primarily the result of disputes over the

    A. treatment of women in Muslim society
    B. differing interpretations of the Koran
    C. Umayyad preoccupation with wealth acquisition
    D. trade practices with nearby cultures
    E. line of succession following the death of Muhammad

89. Which factor contributed the MOST to the rise of the Fascist Party under Benito Mussolini in Italy?

    A. Increased sense of nationalism among Italians
    B. Oppressive policies of the existing Italian government
    C. Frustration with Italy's lack of territorial gains after World War I
    D. Widespread opposition to Italian monarch Victor Emmanuel III
    E. Concern over the fragile state of international relations in Europe

90. Which of these was NOT true of the Han dynasty?

    A. It engaged in extensive trade with Europe.
    B. It introduced the civil service examination.
    C. It began early construction on the Great Wall.
    D. It created roads and canals to improve transportation.
    E. It funded bureaucracy and army through taxes.

91. What was the major goal of the Concert of Europe?

    A. To redraw the boundaries of Europe after World War I
    B. To restrict the spread of communism to Eastern Europe
    C. To prevent future revolutions by maintaining the status quo
    D. To establish new nation-states after the fall of the Roman Empire
    E. To develop continental trade relationships and business partnerships

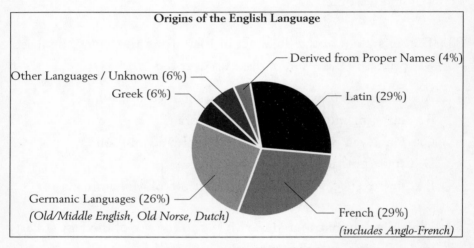

92. What inference can BEST be made from the information in the chart shown?

    A. Slavic languages strongly influenced the development of the English language.
    B. The Roman occupation of England significantly influenced the development of the English language.
    C. The English language developed through a blend of Germanic, French, and Greek influences.
    D. The classical languages strongly influenced the development of both English and French.
    E. The English language primarily developed during the Middle Ages and the Renaissance.

93. Why did the government installed in South Vietnam in 1954 by France and the United States ultimately fail?

    A. The government was corrupt and unpopular with the Vietnamese people.
    B. The Vietnamese people preferred Ho Chi Minh's communist regime.
    C. The Vietnamese people distrusted the government because of its French backing.
    D. The government was unable to procure the resources necessary for independent existence.
    E. The Vietnamese people were angered by the government's communist policies.

94. In which way were the ancient Chinese philosophies of Confucianism and legalism MOST similar?

    A. They divided educational standards by class.
    B. They emphasized the importance of strong government.
    C. They promoted respect and reverence of elders.
    D. They emphasized life in harmony with the natural world.
    E. They discouraged most independence of thought.

95. The concept of humanism was a key characteristic of the

    A. Enlightenment
    B. Protestant Reformation
    C. Renaissance
    D. Scientific Revolution
    E. Impressionism movement

END OF PRACTICE TEST 2

Practice Test 2 Answers and Explanations

Answer Key

1. C		24. D	
2. E		25. C	
3. D		26. E	
4. B		27. B	
5. A		28. D	
6. D		29. D	
7. B		30. C	
8. A		31. B	
9. B		32. A	
10. B		33. D	
11. C		34. C	
12. D		35. E	
13. C		36. A	
14. D		37. D	
15. A		38. B	
16. B		39. E	
17. C		40. E	
18. D		41. B	
19. B		42. C	
20. A		43. A	
21. C		44. B	
22. B		45. D	
23. A		46. B	

47. E	72. C
48. D	73. E
49. B	74. B
50. E	75. D
51. A	76. D
52. D	77. C
53. C	78. A
54. B	79. C
55. E	80. E
56. D	81. E
57. A	82. D
58. B	83. A
59. C	84. C
60. D	85. B
61. E	86. D
62. C	87. B
63. C	88. E
64. D	89. C
65. C	90. C
66. B	91. C
67. D	92. B
68. C	93. A
69. A	94. B
70. E	95. C
71. B	

Answer Explanations

1. **C.** The Aztec chose to build their capital city, Tenochtitlán, on an island in the middle of Lake Texcoco primarily because the site fulfilled an ancient prophecy that gave them specific instructions as to where they should settle. Originally a nomadic people, the Aztec migrated from northern Mexico southward and eventually into the Valley of Mexico. According to legend, the Aztec believed that the site on which they should permanently establish themselves would be marked by a cactus on which would be perched an eagle with a snake in its mouth. Having found this sign on the island in Lake Texcoco, they built a permanent residence there that would become their capital city of Tenochtitlán.

2. **E.** The early civilizations that emerged in both Mesopotamia and Egypt were most similar in that both depended on the annual flooding of a river for survival. Each year, the Tigris and Euphrates rivers in Mesopotamia and the Nile River in Egypt would flood, leaving behind a fertile layer of silt. This silt was crucial for agriculture.

3. **D.** For most of the fifteenth century, Western trade with Asia was dominated by Italy and the Muslims. However, in 1498, Portugal found a sea route to India. The discovery of this crucial maritime trading route came when navigator Vasco da Gama sailed around Africa's southern tip and into the Indian Ocean, where powerful monsoon winds took him to India.

4. **B.** Claudius Ptolemy's geocentric theory of astronomy was based on the belief that Earth was at the center of the galaxy. This theory was the most widely accepted astronomical model from the second century until Nicolaus Copernicus published the heliocentric theory in the sixteenth century. Copernicus argued that the sun, in fact, was at the center of the galaxy, not Earth.

5. **A.** Following their early migratory period, the Bantu settled into numerous small villages that coexisted within a large, stateless society. Unlike other societies that were led by bureaucratic government bodies, the first permanent Bantu societies were governed individually by kinship groups. Each group was led by a selected family member.

6. **D.** Although the Treaty of Versailles did contain a provision related to Germany's colonial holdings in Africa, it did not involve any sort of payment for the right of retention. Rather, the treaty required Germany to completely relinquish its African and Pacific colonies.

7. **B.** First introduced by the Chinese philosopher Confucius between the sixth and fifth centuries BCE, Confucianism believed reverence toward elders, good government, and education were a vital pathway toward order and harmony. Confucian philosophy became prominent near the end of the Zhou dynasty.

8. **A.** Alexander the Great's departure from India in 325 BCE led directly to the rise of the Mauryan Empire. Shortly after Alexander left the country, Chandragupta Maurya, a local leader from the agricultural and trading hub of Magadha, rose to prominence. He created an empire that united most of India, with a centralized government for the first time in India's history.

9. **B.** Prominent during the period from 1916 and 1924, the Dada movement was marked by artistic works that were noted for their whimsical tone and lack of explicit meaning. The prevailing theme of Dadaism, and one of the main reasons for its meaningless nature, was the idea that the violent, destructive events of World War I had stripped all traditions of meaning and relevance. However, there were other themes and ideas that also inspired the Dadaists.

10. **B.** Also known as the First Opium War, the 1839 Anglo-Chinese conflict was primarily the result of rising tensions over Britain's importation of opium into China. By the 1830s, the opium trade in China had led to such widespread opium addiction among the Chinese that its very importation was a serious political issue. China made the trafficking of opium illegal in 1836, but the British continued to import it, and the crisis persisted. Three years later, in a desperate attempt to stop the flow of opium into their country, the Chinese turned British trading ships away from their ports. In response, the British launched a naval attack.

11. **C.** This quote is taken from *The Social Contract* (1762), in which the author Jean-Jacques Rousseau argued in favor of direct democracy. Rousseau viewed the social contract as an agreement reached among free individuals to form a society and a government and supported the belief that all people were equals. These viewpoints were in stark contract with those of Thomas Hobbes, who argued in *Leviathan* that people were naturally incapable of self-government and should submit to the will of a ruler as a means of ensuring law and order.

12. **D.** The primary effect of the Crusades on Europe was an increase in trade that, in turn, stimulated many changes. The revival of trade following the Crusades had a significant influence on European society, leading to a decline of the barter system in favor of a monetary one; an increase in the population of urban cities; and the emergence of the middle class, which was comprised largely of merchants and bankers.

13. **C.** During the Middle Ages, the countries of Western Europe and Japan both developed intricate feudal systems that replaced more centralized forms of government. In Europe, the decline of the Carolingian dynasty and the constant threat of invasion led to the emergence of a feudal system based on protection. In Japan, a similar feudal system emerged as the result of the collapse of the Heian court and the presence of dangerous bandits in the Japanese countryside.

14. **D.** The carving pictured is the Aztec calendar, which was based on the earlier Mayan calendar. The calendar was composed of a 260-day ritual cycle and a 365-day civil cycle. The calendar seen in the image was discovered in 1790 and features, at its center, the image of Tonatiuh, the Aztec sun god.

15. **A.** The influence of the preceding Minoan culture on the Mycenaean civilization is most clearly seen in the Mycenaean written language. The Mycenaean written language, known as Linear B, is a derivative of the Minoan written language, Linear A. Both languages are adapted from Egyptian hieroglyphics.

16. **B.** Political activist Pol Pot and his communist regime, known as the Khmer Rouge, attempted to establish a communist government in Cambodia in 1975. Pol Pot's political coup was initially successful, though his violent methods led to the slaughter of an estimated 2 million people. The Khmer Rouge was overthrown by the Vietnamese in 1978, but continues to maintain a presence in Cambodian politics.

17. **C.** The Balfour Declaration outlined Britain's position on the establishment of a permanent Jewish state in Palestine. The declaration was a response to the ongoing Zionist movement. In it, Britain announced support for the establishment of a new home for Jewish people in Palestine. The declaration also attempted to account for the rights of those Arabs already living in the region.

18. **D.** After gaining personal control of the Congo in the late nineteenth century, King Leopold II of Belgium constructed large rubber plantations in the region and forced the native Congolese to work as laborers. During his reign, Leopold's policies destroyed the Congolese economy and led to the deaths of more than 10 million Congolese people. As international awareness of Leopold's abusive tactics spread, public outcries forced the Belgian government to seize control of the Congo from the king.

19. **B.** The Upanishads are the sacred texts of the Hindu religion. As part of the larger collection of Hindu texts known as the Vedas, the Upanishads primarily cover Hinduism's philosophical teachings. While the major Upanishads were written between 800 and 200 BCE, some texts were composed as recently as the sixteenth century.

20. **A.** During the reign of the 'Abbāsid Empire, a new era of cooperation between Arab and non-Arab Muslims was ushered in. The 'Abbāsids allowed non-Arab Muslims to hold civil and military offices alongside Arab Muslims. This increased the influence of conquered peoples on Islamic culture and encouraged intermarrying between Arabs and non-Arabs.

21. **C.** Although language, hunting-gathering techniques, artwork, and

funereal rituals emerged during the Paleolithic Age, agricultural development did not occur until the Neolithic Age.

22. **B.** The main purpose of the Ottoman policy of *devşirme* (gathering) was to increase military manpower. Under *devşirme*, young non-Muslim boys were removed from their homes, educated, taught the Islamic belief system, and trained for military service. This policy ensured that leaders had the necessary military resources to expand the empire.

23. **A.** The Industrial Revolution had a significant global impact throughout the eighteenth and nineteenth centuries. During this period, industrialization increased Europe's economic power, widened the gap between industrialized and nonindustrialized nations, increased the political power of the middle class, and brought various world cultures closer together. The Industrial Revolution did not, however, decrease the rate at which industrial powers, such as Europe and Japan, colonized foreign territories.

24. **D.** Venezuelan general Simón Bolívar led the South American independence effort, along with Argentinean generals José de San Martín and Bernardo O'Higgins. Starting in 1821, Bolívar and his forces secured Venezuelan independence while San Martín and O'Higgins began their own campaigns in Ecuador, Argentina, and Chile.

25. **C.** The main purpose of this political cartoon was to encourage the reversal of the French class system. Around the time of the French Revolution, French society was divided into three classes known as estates. The First Estate included the clergy, the Second Estate included the aristocracy, and the Third Estate included the remaining lower classes. The cartoon suggests that the order of the estates should be reversed.

26. **E.** Lenin's first goal after the Bolshevik's victory over the White Army in the Russian Civil War was to stabilize and restore the Russian economy. Within a year of the war's conclusion, Lenin unveiled his "new economic policy" (NEP), which was intended to help the Russian economy recover from the destruction of industry and trade caused by

the war. Under the NEP, Lenin permitted a limited amount of capital-ism, allowing peasants to sell surplus crops and profit from the indi-vidual sale of various goods. At the same time, the NEP allowed the government to take over the operation of banks, large industrial opera-tions, and communications.

27. **B.** The initial Vietnamese resistance to French imperialism was a direct result of the destructive agricultural and trade policies that affected the supply of rice available to the Vietnamese people. The French, who assumed control of Vietnam in the sixteenth century, established a num-ber of agricultural and exportation policies that reduced the amount of rice available. This shortage was a major factor leading to the Vietnamese independence movement.

28. **D.** Great Zimbabwe and Aksum were most similar in that both thrived on income derived from trade routes. Great Zimbabwe rose to prominence in Africa after taking control of a key trade route. Likewise, Aksum established itself as a major civilization after taking control of part of the southwestern region of the Arabian Peninsula through which ran trading routes between Egypt and Meroe, as well as routes to the Mediterranean and the Indian Ocean.

29. **D.** During the Muslim expansion of the seventh century, conquered people of the Christian or Jewish faith were not explicitly required to submit to military service. At the time, the Muslims viewed Christians and Jews as fellow "people of the book" who believed in the same God and followed written scriptures similar to the Koran. As such, the Muslims allowed these individuals to avoid military service in return for the payment of a yearly tax.

30. **C.** As a form of spirituality, Shintoism is primarily focused on the veneration of both ancestors and spirits of nature (*kami*). Shintoism is a spiritual way of life in which simple devotion to ancestral spirits and *kami* are believed to bring good fortune and happiness. Shintoism is rarely practiced outside Japan.

31. **B.** The spread of Islam across eastern and central Africa was met with numerous cultural obstacles, one of the most prominent being resistance against the traditional Islamic views about the role of women. In many sub-Saharan African communities, women enjoyed a considerably greater degree of gender equality than did women in Muslim countries. As Islam spread, many of these women refused to accept traditional Muslim gender roles.

32. **A.** The most important factor in the spread of ancient Greek culture across the Mediterranean region was unique geography. The mountains surrounding the landscape meant that numerous isolated city-states arose. Equally important, Greece's geography was ideal for trading, which helped spread its culture.

33. **D.** This quote is attributed to Italian dictator Benito Mussolini and indicates his support of fascist philosophies. This philosophy places the good of the state above all else, including the rights of individual members of society. In most cases, fascist governments are led by totalitarian dictators who control the inhabitants of their state through regimented social and economic structures, mass indoctrination, forcible suppression of resistance, and other similar means.

34. **C.** The mandate of heaven played a crucial role in Chinese culture because it provided a rationalization for the transfer of power from one dynasty to the next. The mandate of heaven first emerged in the twelfth century BCE, when it was created by the Zhou dynasty to rationalize their assumption of power from the declining Shang dynasty. Subsequent dynasties used the mandate similarly.

35. **E.** While other pre-Columbian civilizations developed basic road systems, the Incan system was elaborate and efficient. Spanning the entire length of the empire, the Incan road system consisted of two main routes: one through the mountains and one through the lowlands. The roads allowed for the transportation for military forces, messengers, merchants, and others.

36. **A.** Throughout much of the eighteenth century, the colony of South Africa was controlled by a group of Dutch settlers known as the Boers. The Boers retained imperial control over South Africa until the British overtook their holdings in 1795.

37. **D.** A phrase coined by President Dwight D. Eisenhower, "domino theory" led to U.S. involvement in the Vietnam War. Eisenhower's domino theory was based on the idea that communism in Southeast Asia would spread easily if any nation came under communist rule.

38. **B.** The *Annals* and *Germania* were both written by the Roman historian Tacitus between the first and second centuries CE. The *Annals* is a history of the Roman Empire during the reigns of four emperors. *Germania* is a historical review of the Germanic tribes that lived along the imperial borders.

39. **E.** Commercial agriculture was a profitable venture for Egypt but not for England. As part of his program of industrial reforms, the Egyptian leader Muḥammad ʿAlī instituted a system in which village farmers were forced to give up private plots and work on commercial plantations. These plantations produced cash crops that were then sold to European nations.

40. **E.** The earliest significant Mesoamerican civilization, the Maya, developed around Tikal in what is today known as Guatemala. First established as a small Mayan village around 900 BCE, Tikal evolved into a major center of ceremonial importance between 300 BCE and 100 CE. Over the course of its history, Tikal grew into the urban core of the Maya Empire and was home to an array of plazas, pyramids, and other important structures.

41. **B.** Japan turned to militarism in the early 1930s as a result of the widespread belief that the democratic government was responsible for the country's dire economic state. In the 1920s, the then-democratic Japanese government ushered in an era of economic prosperity and committed itself to peace with the signing of the Kellogg-Briand Pact. When the Great Depression struck, however, the economy collapsed. The

Japanese people blamed the government, which was subsequently taken over by the military.

42. **C.** While the Congress of Vienna did take steps to ensure that France would no longer be a serious threat to European peace, it did not require the French military to disband. Most notably, the Congress of Vienna required France to cede all the territories it had seized during Napoléon's campaigns. In effect, this stripped France of its stranglehold over Europe.

43. **A.** The Later Ly dynasty reigned in Vietnam between 1009 and 1225 CE. Leaders adopted the Chinese style of government and replaced the traditional Vietnamese local lords with a bureaucracy of civil servants and state officials. They also established educational programs for civil servants and introduced universal military service.

44. **B.** The map illustrates trade routes of the Silk Roads. The Silk Roads were a critical trading route linking China and the Far East with Europe and the West. The route was primarily used for trading silk with the West, and gold, silver, and wool with the East.

45. **D.** During his thirteen-year campaign in the fourth century, Alexander the Great conquered the lands of Egypt, Syria, Mesopotamia, and Asia Minor. He attempted to conquer India but was unsuccessful.

46. **B.** Although the form of communism practiced in China under Mao Zedong was based on the same fundamental concepts as the form practiced in the Soviet Union, Maoism included uniquely Chinese ideology. Among the most notable differences was the Maoist view of the proletariat as a nation rather than a class. In Mao's view, China's struggle was that of a proletarian nation exploited at the hands of the bourgeois of capitalist nations.

47. **E.** The Twelve Tables were the written code of laws of the ancient Romans. The Twelve Tables was written in 451 BCE and established the fundamental precepts of Roman law. The Twelve Tables also granted Roman citizens the right to the protection of the law.

48. **D.** The Taiping Rebellion, fought between 1850 and 1864, was a

violent religious and political uprising that ultimately claimed the lives of approximately 20 million Chinese. The rebellion was led by Hong Xiuquan, who was disgruntled with the Chinese civil service system. He claimed to have had a series of visions in which he learned that he was a son of God and destined to bring reform to China. Hong led his followers through a bloody revolt against the Qing dynasty and proclaimed the formation of his own Taiping Tianguo dynasty. Hong's forces were eventually defeated, and the rebellion largely came to an end after Hong committed suicide in 1864.

49. **B.** Among the Bantu-speaking people, the term *griots* referred to storytellers. The Bantu were followers of animism, a form of spirituality founded on the belief that spirits inhabit the various features of the natural world. Of particular importance to the Bantu were the spirits of one's deceased ancestors. The *griots* were responsible for passing on these traditions from one generation to the next via stories.

50. **E.** The Portuguese navigator Ferdinand Magellan is most famous for being the first to circumnavigate the globe. In 1519, Magellan and co-navigator Rui Faleiro set off on their historic expedition. Magellan was killed in the Philippines, but two of his ships eventually made it back to Europe in 1522, completing the first circumnavigation of the globe.

51. **A.** The Mensheviks and the Bolsheviks were both opposed to the czarist government in Russia but had different views on how a potential workers' revolution should take place. The Bolsheviks, led by Lenin, believed that an immediate revolution of the working-class proletariat against the middle-class bourgeois was necessary. Conversely, the Mensheviks supported the idea of working with the bourgeois to establish a left-wing capitalist regime as a forerunner to a full-blown socialist society.

52. **D.** Throughout much of the nineteenth century, the port of Singapore was controlled by the British, who first established a presence there in 1819. Sir Thomas Stamford Raffles, who worked for the English East India Trading Company, landed at Singapore and purchased the land from a local he had installed to facilitate the transfer over the objections

of the Dutch. Eventually, the Dutch and British came to an agreement, and the Dutch ceded full control of Singapore to England in 1824.

53. **C.** Although the final outcome of the Mexican struggle for independence from Spain was influenced by events unfolding in Europe, its most distinguishing attribute was its origin with the mestizos, who were people of mixed European and Indian descent. Most other struggles in the Americas originated with the Creoles, colonial-born people of European descent.

54. **B.** The Treaty of Tordesillas, which was signed by Spain and Portugal under the authority of Pope Alexander VI, granted Spain exclusive land rights in the New World. Specifically, the treaty created a line of demarcation between Spanish and Portuguese territory. According to the terms of the agreement, all land that was discovered to the west of the line would belong to Spain, and all land to the east would go to the Portuguese. The location of the line was later moved west to allow Portugal to colonize coastal Brazil.

55. **E.** This quotation, taken directly from a translation of the *Dao De Jing*, reflects the traditional Daoist view of government. Adherents of Daoism believe in living a simple life, at harmony with the natural world.

56. **D.** Cuneiform was invented by the people of the Mesopotamian civilization of Sumer. The most widely used form of written language in the ancient Middle East, cuneiform was a pictographic language made by pressing a wedge-shaped stylus into moist clay. The pictographs used in cuneiform represented ideas and, later, sounds.

57. **A.** Ghana fell into decline early in the eleventh century as a result of Muslim invasion. Following the successful conquest of the area by the Almoravid dynasty in 1076, the gold and salt trade was interrupted. This had severe economic consequences from which the Ghanaians could not recover.

58. **B.** In the years leading up to World War II, the fascist dictator Benito Mussolini became interested in expanding his country's colonial holdings

in Africa. After the League of Nations failed to take action against Japan following their military invasion of China, Mussolini invaded Ethiopia.

59. **C.** The Khmer Empire originated in the modern-day region of Cambodia. This dynasty rose to prominence chiefly as the result of its cultivation of rice. Through their ability to grow rice and their strong trading ties with India and China, the Khmer became the dominant dynastic power throughout the entire Southeast Asian mainland. They reached the height of their power in the early thirteenth century.

60. **D.** Russia's departure from World War I was primarily the result of the nation's internal political strife over the monarchical government of Czar Nicholas II. In 1917, Nicholas II was forced to abdicate the throne in response to antigovernment protests over famine and supply shortages brought on by the war. When the new provisional government continued participation in the war, additional political unrest led to the rise of the Communist Party under Lenin.

61. **E.** The traditional Indian concept of the sacred cow developed primarily during the reign of the Mauryan Empire. Though based in part on the revered status that cattle enjoyed during India's Aryan period, the customary belief in the sacredness of cows largely came into practice when the Mauryan ruler Ashoka introduced policies making it illegal to kill cows. Ashoka instated this and similar policies after converting to Buddhism and shifting focus to public works, the promotion of vegetarianism, and the reduction of animal slaughter.

62. **C.** Meroe was one of the major cities of the kingdom of Kush. It rose to power as an important trading hub largely because of its vast supply of iron. Founded in a region rich with natural iron deposits, Meroe quickly became a major entity in the trade of iron as well as weapons and other goods made from iron.

63. **C.** The Roman army was one of the key drivers of the success of Rome and one of its most highly valued assets. The army included a number of legions, each of which had between five thousand and six thousand men.

Legions were supported by cavalry soldiers on horseback. The Roman army was based on conscription, with landowning citizens required to engage in military service and conquered peoples providing troops. Unlike most other military forces, however, the soldiers of the Roman army were required to provide their own weapons and other equipment.

64. **D.** Prussia rose to prominence in the eighteenth century under the leadership of the Hohenzollerns. During their reign over Prussia, the Hohenzollerns created a military state through the formation of an army in which members of the landowning classes, known as the Junkers, served as officers. The Hohenzollerns also decreased the power of territorial assemblies in Prussia.

65. **C.** The evolution and spread of the Bantu culture was due most significantly to their history of migration. Having originated in areas bordering the rainforests in present-day Nigeria, the early Bantu peoples began migrating south and east through Africa around 2000 BCE. Along the way, they assimilated other hunter-gatherer societies and spread their language throughout sub-Saharan African. Eventually, the Bantu language would blend with Arabic to form a new language known as Swahili.

66. **B.** One of the most distinguishing features of the Inca was the system through which they passed wealth from one generation to the next. According to the rules of parallel descent, males inherited strictly from the paternal side of the family, whereas females inherited from the maternal side of the family.

67. **D.** In response to growing concerns about global warming and greenhouse gases, the United Nations produced the Kyoto Protocol in 1997. This international agreement established a basic framework to stabilize the amount of greenhouse gases in the atmosphere and to bring global warming under control. The treaty took effect in 2005.

68. **C.** The greatest similarity between the Korean and Vietnam wars was a desire to prevent the spread of communism. The Korean War was a direct response to the North Korean invasion of South Korea. The

Vietnam War was the result of a communist threat represented by Ho Chi Minh and the Vietcong.

69. **A.** Julius Caesar eventually secured the title of "dictator for life," but he did not declare himself a monarch. Caesar was aware that the Roman upper class was strongly opposed to the idea of a monarchy and was cautious to avoid any suggestion that his rule would be equivalent to that of a monarch.

70. **E.** Overtaking the Inca was a relatively simple task for the Spanish conquistadors. By the time they arrived to seize control in 1532, the once-strong Inca Empire had been severely weakened by civil war. In 1525 the death of Incan ruler Huayna Capac led to a bitter civil war between his sons.

71. **B.** One of the few similarities between Athens and Sparta was that neither city-state allowed women to play any role in politics.

72. **C.** The overthrow of the Qing dynasty in 1912 was primarily the result of rising nationalistic sentiment. Before the displacement of the Qing, the Chinese had endured centuries of foreign control of their land. By the early twentieth century, many Chinese embraced the nationalist movement led by Sun Yixian, who eventually succeeded in his quest to bring the Nationalist Party to power.

73. **E.** After Ferdinand Magellan made first contact with (and was subsequently killed by) the inhabitants of the Philippines in 1521, the Spanish became interested in establishing a permanent presence there. Colonization efforts began in 1565. During the time the Philippines were under Spanish control, the colony served as a conduit for trade between Spain and Mexico.

74. **B.** The fall of the Carolingian dynasty led directly to the introduction of the feudal system in Europe. With the passing of Charlemagne and his son Louis the Pious, the Carolingian dynasty became increasingly fragmented and eventually collapsed. Without the protection of a large government, Europe was forced to endure relentless, vicious attacks by

invaders, particularly the Vikings. The need for a new means of protecting themselves led many Europeans to embrace the feudal system, in which they could secure protection in return for loyalty to a feudal lord.

75. **D.** Perhaps the most significant difference between Lutheranism and Calvinism is the opposing view on the free will of individuals and their ability to determine their own fate. Martin Luther taught the doctrine of justification by faith, which stated that anyone could attain salvation through faith in Christ. John Calvin accepted this idea in part but believed in a doctrine known as election, which stated that fate is predetermined. Only the "elect" can obtain salvation; no human action can significantly alter one's status as elect.

76. **D.** Adherents to the philosophy of cynicism would most likely agree that "life should be lived simply and without material attachments." Simplicity and the rejection of materialism were the central tenets of cynicism. The rival philosophies of stoicism and Epicureanism emphasized brotherhood and pleasure, respectively.

77. **C.** The most significant difference between the League of Nations and United Nations is that the United Nations has an armed military force that is used to enforce its policies when necessary. The inability of the League of Nations to create such a force was one of the primary reasons it was ineffectual in preventing World War II.

78. **A.** The Spanish conquistador Hernán Cortés led the conquest of the Aztec culture. After arriving in Aztec territory in 1519, Cortés and his men were welcomed into Tenochtitlán by the Aztec ruler Montezuma II, who believed that their appearance was an indication of the return of the god of peace. Eventually, Cortés claimed the land for Spain and, with the help of other tribes who had been oppressed by the Aztec, conquered the empire in 1521.

79. **C.** The quote above, attributed to John Locke, is representative of the intellectual movement of deism. Deists believed that while some sort of god might exist, God's only role was to create and maintain the natural laws of the universe.

80. **E.** Japan's primary objective leading up to and during World War II was the Greater East Asia Co-Prosperity Sphere. This program was specifically designed to allow the Japanese to secure an adequate supply of raw materials. Faced with a booming population and tariffs that prevented trade with most Western nations, Japan quickly became unable to support itself. Japan's solution was forceful territorial expansion in order to gain access to the raw materials that the Japanese needed to thrive.

81. **E.** Socrates, one of the first great Greek philosophers, developed a teaching method based on systematic questioning. The Socratic method utilizes questions and answers to encourage students to judge for themselves and learn to rely on reason and rational thought.

82. **D.** Although they made several attempts to establish a presence in Southeast Asia, the Mongols were ultimately unsuccessful at doing so mainly because the regional climate was extremely inhospitable. During their reign in China, the Mongols attempted to extend their empire southward into Cambodia, Vietnam, Burma, Java, and Indonesia. In each instance, however, they could not adapt to the exceptionally warm climate.

83. **A.** The written language of the Mycenaeans, Linear B, was based on the Minoan written language, Linear A. The Mycenaeans were among the most dominant cultures to live on the Greek mainland. It is believed they conquered the Minoans, who lived on Crete, around 1450 BCE. As the Mycenaeans assimilated Minoan culture, they adopted a modified version of their written language.

84. **C.** In general, imperial powers used four methods to exert control over Africa: establishing colonies, founding protectorates, creating spheres of influence, and practicing economic imperialism. While it was similar to a colony, a protectorate was allowed to maintain its own government.

85. **B.** While both the Egyptians and the people of the Indus River valley were invaded and occupied by foreign cultures, the outcomes were different. The Egyptians were invaded by the Hyksos around 1650 and remained under their control before they eventually expelled the foreigners. The

people of the Indus River valley, in contrast, were invaded by the Aryans around 1500 and remained under their control permanently.

86. **D.** An encomienda was a type of land grant that allowed its holder to force the natives under his control to pay monetary tribute and perform labor. In return for this service, the encomienda holder was expected to provide the natives with protection, to pay them for work, and to see to their spiritual needs. Abuse of the system led to its replacement with the repartamiento system.

87. **B.** The most critical point of agreement between Wilson's Fourteen Points and the Treaty of Versailles was the establishment of an international peacekeeping organization. This agreement laid the groundwork for the League of Nations.

88. **E.** The split between Shia and Sunni Muslims, which occurred in the seventh century CE, was primarily the result of disputes over the line of succession after Muhammad's death. In 565, Ali, who was both cousin and son-in-law to Muhammad, became the fourth caliph. When Ali was later assassinated, the Shia Muslims insisted that the caliphate should remain with his descendants, but the Sunni disagreed. This dispute permanently drove the two sects apart.

89. **C.** The most significant factor in the rise of Mussolini and fascism was Italy's frustration with its lack of territorial gains following World War I. Having left the Triple Alliance to join the Allied powers during the war, Italy expected significant territorial gains at the war's end.

90. **C.** The Han dynasty conducted extensive trading via the Silk Roads, introduced the civil service examination, created roads and canals to improve transportation, and levied taxes to fund the bureaucracy and military. It did not, however, begin construction of the Great Wall.

91. **C.** The Concert of Europe was a series of alliances formed during the nineteenth century following the defeat of Napoléon Bonaparte. These alliances required nations to assist one another in the event of civil disturbances or war. The goal of the Concert of Europe was to prevent

further revolutions and ensure the political status quo. Although the Concert of Europe weakened over time, it remained intact until the outbreak of World War I.

92. **B.** Since the chart indicates that Latin influenced 29 percent of the English language, it can be reasonably inferred that the English language was significantly influenced by the Roman occupation of England. When the Romans conquered Britain in 43 CE, they brought Latin with them. The exposure of the English people to the Latin language during the time of Roman occupation likely influenced the development of their own language.

93. **A.** The primary reason for the failure of the South Vietnamese government was the fact that it was corrupt and unpopular. Ngo Dinh Diem, who had been installed as leader, operated as an oppressive dictator.

94. **B.** The common thread between Confucianism and legalism was an emphasis on strong government. Although both philosophies focused on a strong government, Confucianism advocated educated government, whereas legalism emphasized policies of censorship, a prohibition of independent thought, and the control of education.

95. **C.** Humanism was one of the key concepts of the Renaissance. The humanist philosophy emphasized reason, encouraged appreciation for the ancient Roman civilization, and focused on the everyday problems of typical human beings.

Glossary

Age grade: A social group based on age whose members share experiences and carry out various responsibilities deemed appropriate for their age.

Antigone: Greek tragedy written by Sophocles featuring Antigone, the daughter of Oedipus.

Aryans: A nomadic race of people originally from the modern regions of Iran and Afghanistan who invaded the Indus River valley around 1500 BCE.

Augustus: The name the Roman emperor Octavian chose for himself, meaning "exalted one."

Australopithecines: A hominid species that originated in Africa, the earliest example being "Lucy." The first species of hominid to produce and use simple tools made of stone.

Benefice: A special privilege, often a land grant, promised by a feudal lord to his vassals in return for their loyalty and service.

Bishops: Priests in charge of dioceses from whose ranks the pope is chosen.

Blitzkrieg: A type of surprise attack, literally meaning "lightning war," used by the Nazi forces of Adolph Hitler during World War II, particularly against Poland in 1939.

Bourgeoisie: The social middle class, composed of business owners, merchants, and artisans.

Brahmins: Priests who made up the top (Brahman) class of the caste system of the Aryans.

Buddha: The spiritual founder of the religion of Buddhism, originally known as Siddhartha Gautama.

Buddhism: Religion based on the teachings of Buddha and the belief that suffering is a direct result of humankind's desire.

Capitalism: An economic system that favors the use of private ownership and enterprise to generate profit.

Carolingian Gaul: The ancient region of Gaul—which was made up of France, Belgium, Germany, and Italy—during the time it was ruled by the Carolingian line of kings, around the eighth and ninth centuries.

Castes: The distinct levels of the social class system of the Aryans. The Aryans introduced the caste system into the Indus River valley, and it eventually became an important part of Indian culture.

Chinampas: Artificial plots of land created by the Aztec that floated on a lake to increase the amount of territory they had available for agricultural use.

Christianity: Religion based on the teachings of Jesus Christ whose sacred text is the Bible.

Civilization: A complex society in which a large number of people share a broad range of characteristics, including advanced cities and technology, the specialization of labor, and the development of a system of writing or record keeping.

Code of Hammurabi: Code of law based on a system of retaliatory punishment (e.g., an eye for an eye) created by the Babylonian emperor Hammurabi.

Communism: An economic system in which there is no private property and the means of production are shared by all.

The Communist Manifesto: An 1848 booklet written by Karl Marx and Friedrich Engels that promoted a radical form of socialism known as communism.

Confucianism: A Chinese philosophy introduced by Confucius that espoused reverence of elders and ancestors, sound government, and the value of education.

Consuls: The members of the executive branch of the Roman government.

Crusades: A series of wars that took place from about the eleventh century to thirteenth century between Christians and Muslims over control of the Holy Land.

Cuneiform: A system of writing developed by the ancient Sumerians that used pictographs to represent different ideas and sounds.

Daimyo: A Japanese feudal lord who owned an estate and had his own personal army of samurai warriors.

Daoism: Chinese philosophy that was based on following Dao ("the Way") and emphasized living in harmony with nature.

Deism: A religious philosophy that holds that although a god may exist, the deity's only role is to set the natural laws of the universe.

Diocese: A district or region whose churches and parishes are led by a bishop under the authority of the pope.

The Directory: The five-man executive branch of the new government that emerged in France following the French Revolution.

Dorians: A Mediterranean people who came to dominate ancient Greece during its Dark Age, around 1100–800 BCE, during whose reign the polis, or city-state, emerged.

Encomienda: Land grants given to Spanish colonists in the New World that allowed them to exploit Native Americans for labor purposes.

Enlightenment: A seventeenth- and eighteenth-century intellectual movement that emphasized education and reason.

Ephors: Elected officials who ran the Spartan government.

Epic of Gilgamesh: Epic poem that describes the basic religious beliefs of the Sumerians and contains a creation story and a story of the great flood.

Estates: The three classes into which French society was divided between the Middle Ages and the French Revolution.

European Union: An economic and political organization that includes many European nations among its members.

Fief: A land grant that a vassal could receive from a feudal lord as a benefice.

Ghazi: Muslim warriors who fought to conquer non-Muslims in the name of Islam.

Glasnost: Mikhail Gorbachev's 1985 policy designed to encourage openness and the sharing of ideas in the Soviet Union.

Global Warming: An increase in global temperatures as a result of an increase in the amount of carbon dioxide in the atmosphere.

Hellenistic: Relating to the culture that emerged during the time of Alexander the Great and blended the traditions of the East and the West.

Helots: Conquered people who were forced to work as agricultural laborers for the Spartans and accounted for the majority of the Spartan population.

Hieroglyphics: A system of writing developed by the ancient Egyptians that used pictographs to represent different ideas and sounds.

Hinduism: Religion that developed in the Indus River valley civilization after the arrival of the Aryans.

Hominids: Early relatives of modern humans that walked upright.

Homo erectus: Early human species that was the immediate predecessor of Homo sapiens.

Homo habilis: The first hominids (literally meaning "handy man") to be classified in the same species as modern humans.

Homo sapiens: Known as "wise humans," the closest early relatives of modern humans.

Homo sapiens sapiens: The scientific name for modern humans.

House of Commons: A house of the British Parliament that in the past was composed of burgesses and knights and today is a modern law-making body.

House of Lords: A house of the British Parliament that in the past was composed of bishops and nobles and today is a modern law-making body.

Humanism: A Renaissance philosophy that placed emphasis on reason, focused on everyday problems, and viewed Greco-Roman civilization as ideal.

Ice age: A long-term period of reduced global temperatures that results in an increase in glacial activity and size.

Ideograph: A written character that represents an idea.

Iliad: Epic poem written by ancient Greek poet Homer that focuses on the end of the Trojan War and a struggle between King Agamemnon and the hero Achilles.

Imperialism: A practice in which a powerful nation takes over and dominates a weaker country politically, socially, and economically.

Inca: A Mesoamerican civilization that established a large empire in the region of the Andes and along much of the western coast of South America.

Indulgences: Slips of paper that were sold to people under the pretense that their purchase would absolve buyers of their sins.

Industrial Revolution: A period in the eighteenth and nineteenth centuries during which much of the world shifted from agricultural economies to economies based on industry and manufacture.

Iron Curtain: A metaphorical division between Western and Eastern Europe over the issue of communism in the twentieth century.

Irrigation: The application of water to soil by artificial means, usually for agricultural purposes.

Islam: Religion that has faith in one god and originates from the prophet Muhammad.

Isolationism: An approach to foreign policy in which all political and economic entanglements with other countries are avoided.

Judaism: Religion developed among ancient Hebrews whose beliefs center on the existence of a single god who revealed himself to Hebrew prophets.

Justinian Code: A codification of Roman laws, legal treatises, and Byzantine laws created by Justinian, a Byzantine emperor.

Karma: According to Hinduism, the good and evil deeds one does in life.

Khanate: A regional segment of the Mongol Empire controlled by a descendant of Genghis Khan.

Laissez-faire: An economic theory, which holds that governments should never interfere with the natural laws of supply and demand.

Latifundia: Large Roman agricultural estates largely operated by means of slave labor.

Legalism: A Chinese philosophy that advocated strict government and the restriction of personal freedoms.

Legions: Roman military units made up of about five thousand to six thousand soldiers.

Loess: Yellowish silt or loam found in considerable quantities in the Huang He (Yellow River) in China.

***Lysistrata*:** Ancient Greek comedy by Aristophanes that explores the persuasive abilities of women.

Magna Carta: An important English government document signed by King John in 1215 that placed limitations on the power of the king and protected the rights of nobles.

Mahabharata: One of two major Indian epic poems that help to form the sacred texts of Hinduism.

Majordomo: "Mayor of the palace," the highest position of governmental power in Carolingian Gaul.

Mandate of heaven: A concept that the Zhou dynasty claimed gave them divine authority to rule in China.

Medea: A Greek tragedy written by Euripides that follows the murderous exploits of Medea, the wife of the Greek hero Jason.

Model Parliament: The first English Parliament created by King Edward in 1295.

Monotheism: A form of religion based on the worship of a single deity, or god.

Mummification: Funerary practice of the ancient Egyptians designed as a means of preserving a body after death.

Neanderthals: Early species of humans, including *Homo erectus* and *Homo sapiens*.

Ninety-Five Theses: A list of grievances against the Catholic Church that Martin Luther nailed to the door of a cathedral in Wittenberg, Germany, in 1517.

Nomadic: Lifestyle of a social group that moves from place to place to find new sources of food.

Odyssey: Epic poem written by ancient Greek poet Homer that follows the hero Odysseus as he journeys home after the defeat of Troy in the Trojan War.

Oedipus Rex: Greek tragedy written by Sophocles featuring the story of Oedipus, a ruler who inadvertently killed his own father.

Olmec: Earliest known civilization to exist in the Americas.

Oracle: A soothsayer or fortune-teller who is thought to speak for a deity or deities.

Pariahs: Social outcasts of the Aryan caste system, also known as the untouchables.

Patricians: The upper class of Roman society who exercised the most political control.

Pax Romana: A 207-year era of peace in the Roman Empire that began when Augustus assumed total control of Rome in 27 BCE.

Perestroika: Mikhail Gorbachev's 1985 policy that allowed Soviet citizens to own their own small private businesses.

Pharaoh: Ruler of ancient Egypt.

Plebeians: The lower class of Roman society that accounted for the majority of the population.

Polis: Ancient Greek name for the political unit known as a city-state.

Polytheism: A form of religion based on the worship of multiple deities, or gods.

Pope: Chief bishop and highest-ranking leader of the Roman Catholic Church.

Popol Vuh: A sacred text that contains the Mayan version of the creation story.

Predestination: The belief that a person's fate is entirely predetermined by God and cannot be altered.

Prehistory: The period of unrecorded history that spans from the emergence of the earliest humanlike species to the dawn of early civilizations.

Proletariat: A term for the working class that originated in the Roman Empire and that Karl Marx and Friedrich Engels later adopted to fit their communist view of history.

Ramayana: One of two major Indian epic poems that help to form the sacred texts of Hinduism.

Renaissance: Era of European history from about 1300–1600 CE during which human reason and humanity were heavily emphasized.

Rosetta stone: An inscribed Egyptian stone that allowed linguists to decipher the language of hieroglyphics.

Samurai: Male and female soldiers who lived by the code of conduct known as bushido that provided protection to daimyos and their property in feudal Japan.

Scientific Revolution: Period of significant scientific advancement spanning the sixteenth and seventeenth centuries during which scientific knowledge drawn from experiments and research replaced inaccurate traditional beliefs.

Serfdom: The state of being a serf in a feudal manor.

Serfs: European peasants who served a lord and were bound to the land as part of the feudal system.

Settlement: A small community in which people live together with one another.

Shang: A nomadic people who founded the first known dynasty in China around 1600 BCE.

Smelting: The practice of melting down metal ore to produce a purer metal.

Socialism: An economic system in which the factors of production are owned by the public and are used to benefit the common welfare.

Sphinx: A large stone carving created by the Egyptian Pharaoh Khafra, which consisted of his head on the body of a lion.

Swahili: An African language that emerged as a blend of Arabic languages and the language of the Bantu-speaking people.

Tribal Assembly: A Roman lawmaking body composed of members of the plebeian class.

Tribunes: Elected representatives that served as part of the Tribal Assembly.

Triumvirate: A three-man executive council that sometimes held power in Rome in place of a single consul.

Twelve Tables: A written code of laws that established the rights of Roman citizens.

Upanishads: A series of Vedic texts, also called the *Vedanta*, which are the final corpus that make up the sacred scriptures of Hinduism.

Vassals: People who vowed to work for and support a feudal lord in return for protection and some type of benefice.

Vedas: The sacred scriptures of Hinduism, made up of four collections of hymns, chants, prayers, magical and esoteric texts, mantras, and ritual texts.

Vietcong: Communist guerillas that fought against the United States and South Vietnam in the Vietnam War.

Zionism: A movement that began in the 1890s with the goal of establishing a Jewish state in Palestine.

About the Author

Northeast Editing, Inc., is a full-service, concept-to-completion developer of educational material. Since 1992, our staff of writers, editors, and certified teachers has worked closely with leading educational publishers to produce creative, top-notch instructional material, including textbooks, test-preparation guides, and library-reference products for students of all ages. For more information, visit our website at www.northeastediting.com. Northeast Editing, Inc., worked with subject matter expert Brooke Nelson, who has been involved in the writing and editing of history assessment items throughout her career. She has written and edited SAT U.S. History, SAT World History, AP World History, and AP U.S. History practice tests. She is a doctoral student who is interested in teaching and assessment. She earned her bachelor's degree in history and English from the University of California–Riverside, and she earned her master's degree in history at the University of California–Irvine.

Also Available

My Max Score SAT Biology E/M Subject Test
by Maria Malzone • 978-1-4022-7298-1

My Max Score SAT Literature Subject Test
by Steven Fox • 978-1-4022-5613-4

My Max Score SAT Math 1 and 2 Subject Test
by Chris Monahan • 978-1-4022-5601-1

My Max Score SAT U.S. History Subject Test
by Cara Cantarella • 978-1-4022-5604-2

My Max Score SAT ASVAB
by Angie Johnston and Amanda Ross, PhD • 978-1-4022-4492-6

$14.99 U.S./£9.99 UK

Also Available

My Max Score AP Biology
by Dr. Robert S. Stewart Jr. • 978-1-4022-4315-8

My Max Score AP Calculus AB/BC
by Carolyn Wheater • 978-1-4022-4313-4

My Max Score AP English Language and Composition
by Jocelyn Sisson • 978-1-4022-4312-7

My Max Score AP English Literature and Composition
by Tony Armstrong • 978-1-4022-4311-0

My Max Score AP European History
by Ira Shull and Mark Dziak • 978-1-4022-4318-9

My Max Score AP Statistics
by Amanda Ross, PhD, and Anne Collins • 978-1-4022-7286-8

My Max Score AP U.S. Government and Politics
by Del Franz • 978-1-4022-4314-1

My Max Score AP U.S. History
by Michael Romano • 978-1-4022-4310-3

My Max Score AP World History
by Kirby Whitehead • 978-1-4022-4317-2

$14.99 U.S./$17.99 CAN/£9.99 UK

Essentials from
Dr. Gary Gruber
and the creators of My Max Score

"Gruber can ring the bell on any number
of standardized exams."
—*Chicago Tribune*

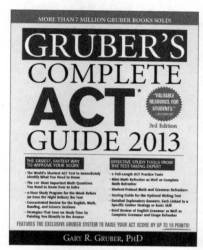

$19.99 U.S./£14.99 UK
978-1-4022-7301-8

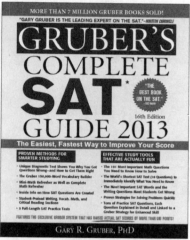

$19.99 U.S./£14.99 UK
978-1-4022-6492-4

$16.99 U.S./$19.99 CAN/£11.99 UK
978-1-4022-4308-0

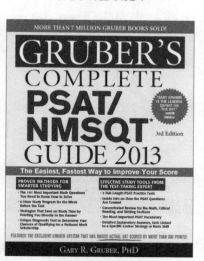

$13.99 U.S./£9.99 UK
978-1-4022-6495-5

"Gruber's methods make the questions
seem amazingly simple to solve."
—*Library Journal*

"Gary Gruber is the leading expert on the SAT."
—*Houston Chronicle*

$16.99 U.S./£11.99 UK
978-1-4022-5337-9

$14.99 U.S./£9.99 UK
978-1-4022-5340-9

$14.99 U.S./£9.99 UK
978-1-4022-5343-0

$12.99 U.S./£8.99 UK
978-1-4022-6072-8